09/06
St. Mary's High School

Comparing Political Regimes

COMPARING
Political
Regimes

A THEMATIC INTRODUCTION TO COMPARATIVE POLITICS

ALAN SIAROFF

broadview press

LIBRARY AND ARCHIVES CANADA CATALOGUING IN PUBLICATION

Siaroff, Alan, 1962-
    Comparing political regimes : a thematic introduction to comparative politics / Alan Siaroff.

Includes bibliographical references and index.
ISBN 1-55111-530-1

    1. Comparative government—Textbooks. I. Title.

JF51.S53 2005   320.3   C2005-902601-4

BROADVIEW PRESS, LTD. is an independent, international publishing house, incorporated in 1985. Broadview believes in shared ownership, both with its employees and with the general public; since the year 2000 Broadview shares have traded publicly on the Toronto Venture Exchange under the symbol BDP.

We welcome comments and suggestions regarding any aspect of our publications—please feel free to contact us at the addresses below or at broadview@broadviewpress.com / www.broadviewpress.com.

Broadview Press gratefully acknowledges the financial support of the Government of Canada through the Book Publishing Industry Development Program for our publishing activities.

North America
Post Office Box 1243,
Peterborough, Ontario, Canada K9J 7H5

Post Office Box 1015,
3576 California Road,
Orchard Park, New York, USA 14127
TEL: (705) 743-8990; FAX: (705) 743-8353

customerservice@broadviewpress.com

UK, Ireland and continental Europe
Plymbridge Distributors Ltd.
Estover Road, Plymouth PL6 7PY, UK
TEL: 44 (0) 1752 202301;
FAX ORDER LINE: 44 (0) 1752 202333;
ORDERS: orders@nbnplymbridge.com
CUST. SERV.: cservs@nbnplymbridge.com

Australia and New Zealand
UNIREPS University of New South Wales
Sydney, NSW 2052 Australia
TEL: 61 2 96640999; FAX: 61 2 96645420
infopress@unsw.edu.au

Edited by Betsy Struthers.
Cover design by Matthew Jubb, Black Eye Design.
Interior by Liz Broes, Black Eye Design.

Printed in Canada

10 9 8 7 6 5 4 3 2 1

Contents

Acknowledgements

I am most grateful to the people at Broadview Press, especially Michael Harrison, Barbara Conolly, and Judith Earnshaw, for their constant support, insider advice, and quick responses. They have been truly a pleasure to work with. I am also grateful to the three anonymous reviewers for Broadview Press for their comments on an earlier draft of the manuscript. Finally, I owe a very big thanks to Betsy Struthers for her thorough editing, which has resulted in countless stylistic improvements.

This book was written with students fully in mind in the hopes that it will answer most or at least many of your questions about comparative politics and perhaps inspire further questions. Professors invariably benefit from getting questions and comments from students about course material, and I personally have always enjoyed getting such questions. Thus, it is to my students—past, present, and future—that I dedicate this book.

Alan Siaroff
The University of Lethbridge

List of Tables and Figures

TABLES

9

FIGURES

CHAPTER ONE

Introduction

IN THIS CHAPTER YOU WILL LEARN

» *why we study comparative politics;*
» *what is a political regime;*
» *what is a sovereign state;*
» *how, where, and why the number of sovereign states has increased over time;*
» *what are (were) the First, Second, and Third Worlds; and*
» *how states are now classified by key international organizations.*

COMPARING POLITICAL REGIMES

This textbook compares and contrasts the political regimes of the countries of the world. It is thus relevant for any core course in comparative politics. That said, the field of comparative politics does have varied foci. Sometimes the term "comparative politics" merely refers to the study of any country outside of Canada such as, for instance, focussing on the government and politics of Germany, Russia, or the United States. However, if only one such country is studied, then any actual cross-country comparisons are usually only implicit. Comparative politics has also involved the study of specific regions or subregions, such as "Politics in Western Europe." Such regional foci may simply be called "area studies," especially if broader theoretical perspectives are lacking. Comparative politics can and should be more than just a description of the government and politics of a country, a few countries, or a region—and in this textbook it is indeed more. First of all, this text analyzes every country now in the world; it is intentionally thorough in this regard. Secondly, it follows a rigorous comparative methodology in outlining the different political regimes that have existed, in placing every country into this typology, and in comparing and contrasting the roles of key political actors (such as national "leaders"), political institutions (such as legislatures and, where these exist, regional governments), political processes (such as elections and democratic transitions), and patterns of political competition (such as the type of party system where there is democratic competition).

Studying comparative politics, and in this case studying all the countries of the world, has at least two main benefits for a student. First of all, it provides the broad context needed for analyzing the political phenomena of whatever country interests you and/or is a matter of "current events." Take, for example, the possibilities of Afghanistan or Iraq becoming—or remaining—democratic. This issue begs certain questions: What do we mean by democracy? How do non-democracies (what we shall call "autocracies") become democracies? What makes for a stable democracy? These are only some of the questions answered in this book. Secondly, studying comparative politics counteracts ethnocentrism, that is, the limited perspective of knowing only one's own country. To this end, your sense of what is unique or supposedly great (or flawed) about Canada politically may well change as you read about other countries.

As for the concept of a "political regime," by this we mean a method or system of government as opposed to the specific individuals in power. This definition is a simplified version of the following more elaborate explanation of a **political regime** as:

> the formal and informal structure of state and governmental roles and processes. The regime includes the method of selection of the government and of representative assemblies (election, coup, decision within the military, [royal prerogative,] etc.), formal and informal mechanisms of representation, and patterns of repression. The regime is typically distinguished from the particular incumbents who occupy

state and governmental roles, the political coalition that supports these incumbents, and the public policies they adopt (except of course policies that define or transpose the regime itself).[1]

SOVEREIGN STATES

Our focus on "countries" means that we are limiting our detailed analysis to sovereign states, excluding for example subnational governments such as Canadian provinces. The concept of a **state**, as you may remember from your introductory politics textbook, involves the combination of a fixed territory, population, and sovereign control (based in a capital), so that the sovereign power effectively rules over the population within this territory. (This notion of "a state" overlaps somewhat with that of "the state," that is, the organizationally differentiated political, bureaucratic, legal, and usually military system of a country, which, as will be shown, can vary in its strength and effectiveness. In the first sense, generally either a state exists or it does not; in the second sense, states can vary along a continuum of capacity.) With fixed territories there are consequent borders between one state and the next, for example the border between Canada and the United States. Population refers to the people who are being governed by the state or, perhaps, those who are citizens of a state with resulting political rights. Sovereignty is the most complex of these three aspects. Generally, it refers to being the highest authority in an area and thus being, as Max Weber stressed, an organization with the monopoly on the legitimate use of force within a territory.[2]

Sovereignty itself is a term with somewhat varying meanings. Krasner notes four of these.[3]

» *Domestic sovereignty* refers to sovereignty *within* a state, wherein the authority structures (or "the state") effectively controls the behaviour of the population, at least in the sense of establishing law(s) and order. The lack of such domestic sovereignty in the context of religious wars was what motivated the writings and philosophies of Bodin and Hobbes.

13

» *Interdependence sovereignty* refers to the right of states to control their borders and to police and, if they wish, limit the movement of people, goods, capital, information, etc. Here is where the issue of globalization is relevant, since aspects of globalization—international air travel, the Internet, capital flows, and so on—clearly seem to impede the ability of states to exercise interdependence sovereignty, while international agreements may even limit their rights in this area. However, one has to remember here that borders were less relevant in nineteenth-century Europe than in the twentieth, and that borders barely existed in pre-colonial Africa but are certainly salient factors there today.[4]

» *Westphalian* or *Vattelian sovereignty* refers to the absence of any external sources of authority over a sovereign state, in which case it would not be sovereign. The term "Westphalian" comes from the Treaty of Westphalia in 1648 which ended the Thirty Years War and from which we assume the notion that states refrain from interfering in the internal affairs of other states. In fact, as Krasner points out, the Treaty of Westphalia was hardly this far-reaching; the broad principle of international non-intervention actually comes a century later in the works of two international legal theorists, Emer de Vattel and Christian Wolff.[5]

» Finally, *international legal sovereignty* involves the notion that any and all states are free and able to enter into international agreements with other states on military, trade, or other matters. Moreover, such agreements are considered binding on the signatories as long as they were not coerced into signing (as per a contract involving individuals).

Although the first two aspects of sovereignty tend to go hand in hand, generally it is possible to have some but not all of these. In particular, a **de facto state**, like the Turkish Republic of Northern Cyprus or even Taiwan, has effective internal and border controls and domestic legitimacy, but lacks international recognition. In contrast, a **de jure state** is recognized as a state by the international community but is so weak and/or illegitimate that it cannot control its own people or its borders.[6]

Part of the rise of sovereignty in European history involved replacing the widespread (but diffuse) control of the Catholic church. The other part involved the centralization of power. Under the system of feudalism which structured mediaeval Europe, power resided at the level of the local lord or noble, of whom there were thousands on the continent. Jurisdictions differed not only in terms of currency (if they used one at all), but also in terms of weights and measures. Trade across even a moderate area was thus very problematic. The sovereign state was, however, not the only system that arose out of the ashes of feudalism. In Italy there were city-states, centred around a dominant city (Florence, Venice, etc.) but including smaller neighbouring cities as well. These city-states at least had fixed borders. There was also the **confederation** (on this concept see Chapter 6) of the Hanseatic League, an alliance of cities around the Baltic Sea, which not only were not contiguous, but which never had a fixed membership; cities simply "joined" and left as they wished.[7] Neither city-states nor confederations had effective, legitimate central control. Consequently, they were not as successful as sovereign states in raising revenue, which was needed to fight wars. Moreover, sovereign states were better in a wide range of areas, such as standardizing weights and measures, introducing a common currency, and establishing centralized justice (including clear property rights and contractual obligations), all of which facilitated trade, economic growth, and, ultimately, tax revenues. Finally, sovereign states could credibly undertake agreements with other sovereign states (but only these) since international legal sovereignty meant that their commitments could be honoured; consequently, this reinforced the international utility of this political structure.[8]

Although the need to fight wars was not new, with the evolution of warfare towards more professional and thus more expensive armies by the sixteenth century, the financing of war became a (if not the) central concern for European political entities. Here the sovereign state showed its superiority in terms of organization and resource extraction. Other political structures, or even sovereign states, that could not "compete" in this regard tended to be conquered by states that were better organized. Thus, war not only arose from greater state capacity but provided a strong incentive to increase this capacity. In Charles Tilly's classic summation, "war made the state, and the state made war."[9] So, by the end of the Napoleonic era there were considerably fewer political entities in Europe, and these surviving states tended to be relatively effective. However, these European patterns should not be generalized globally. Centeno has shown that "[w]ar did not make states in Latin America" since the main Latin American wars of the nineteenth century "occurred under very different historical circumstances than during the European 'military revolution.'"[10] As for Africa and Asia, as we shall see, most of the countries therein achieved independence, and thus sovereignty, after World War II, and have thus existed only in an era when the international order discouraged wars against one's neighbours. Consequently, many of the countries in these areas have survived despite having **weak states** (on this concept see Chapter 2).

GEOGRAPHIC AND HISTORICAL CLASSIFICATIONS OF STATES

Today there are almost 200 sovereign states. Specifically, as of the additions of Timor-Leste (East Timor) and Switzerland in 2002, the United Nations (UN) has 191 members. UN membership is a pretty clear measure of international recognition of a state, although Taiwan merits addition to this list given its broad acknowledgement if not necessarily formal recognition. At one level, a student could be interested in the specifics of any one of these. Consequently, Table 1.1 gives geographical and historical data for all 192 sovereign states. However, in terms of getting a sense of the countries of the world we need more than just an alphabetical list. How are we to group all of these states? One way is by placing them into five broad geographic regions—Africa, the Americas, Asia, Europe, and Oceania—as is done in Table 1.1. These five regions now have respectively 53, 35, 43, 47, and 14 states (although these numbers would change slightly if North Africa and/or the three Transcaucasus states were reclassified).[11] Historically, perhaps the most important factor in contrasting countries is simply their duration, since long-established countries will have had time to consolidate and develop themselves in ways that newly independent states cannot obviously match.[12] Thus, the fact that they joined the UN in the same recent year disguises the reality that Switzerland is one of the world's oldest states whereas Timor-Leste is the newest. (Denmark, France, and Portugal in that order are in fact the three oldest states in the world.)

TABLE 1.1 :: GEOGRAPHIC AND HISTORICAL DATA

COUNTRY	GEOGRAPHIC REGION	GEOGRAPHIC SUBREGION	YEAR OF (MODERN) INDEPENDENCE OR STATE FORMATION	WHERE RELEVANT, INDEPENDENCE WAS ACHEIVED FROM	YEAR OF FIRST CONSTITUTION	YEAR OF CURRENT CONSTITUTION
AFGHANISTAN	Asia	South Asia	1921	(formerly a British protectorate)	1923	1990
ALBANIA	Europe	South-Eastern Europe	1912	Ottoman Empire	1913	1998
ALGERIA	Africa	North Africa	1962	France	1963	1976
ANDORRA	Europe	Western Europe	1993	(formerly a French -Spanish protectorate)	1993	1993
ANGOLA	Africa	Southern Africa	1975	Portugal	1975	1975
ANTIGUA AND BARBUDA	Americas	Caribbean	1981	United Kingdom	1981	1981
ARGENTINA	Americas	South America	1816	Spain	1819	1994
ARMENIA	Europe	Transcaucasus	1991	Soviet Union	1995	1995
AUSTRALIA	Oceania		1901	United Kingdom	1901	1901
AUSTRIA	Europe	Central Europe	1526		1867	1945

*note: the date of state formation for Austria refers to the consolidation of the Hapsburg Empire; the First Republic of Austria was established in 1919

COUNTRY	GEOGRAPHIC REGION	GEOGRAPHIC SUBREGION	YEAR	FROM	FIRST	CURRENT
AZERBAIJAN	Europe	Transcaucasus	1991	Soviet Union	1995	1995
BAHAMAS	Americas	Caribbean	1973	United Kingdom	1973	1973
BAHRAIN	Asia	Middle East	1971	(formerly a British protectorate)	1973	1973
BANGLADESH	Asia	South Asia	1971	Pakistan	1972	1972
BARBADOS	Americas	Caribbean	1966	United Kingdom	1966	1966
BELARUS	Europe	Eastern Europe	1991	Soviet Union	1994	1996
BELGIUM	Europe	Western Europe	1830	Netherlands	1831	1994
BELIZE	Americas	Central America	1981	United Kingdom	1854	1981
BENIN	Africa	West Africa	1960	France	1959	1990
BHUTAN	Asia	South Asia	1949	United Kingdom (as a protectorate)	Unwritten Constitution	
BOLIVIA	Americas (Andean)	South America	1825	Spain	1826	1947
BOSNIA-HERZEGOVINA	Europe	South-Eastern Europe	1992	Yugoslavia	1995	1995

*note: under Ottoman rule for centuries, then occupied by the Austro-Hungarian Empire in 1878, then awarded to the Kingdom of Serbs, Croats, and Slovenes (later Yugoslavia) in 1919

COUNTRY						
BOTSWANA	Africa	Southern Africa	1966	(formerly a British protectorate)	1960	1966
BRAZIL	Americas	South America	1822	Portugal	1824	1988

continues…

COUNTRY	GEOGRAPHIC REGION	GEOGRAPHIC SUBREGION	YEAR OF (MODERN) INDEPENDENCE OR STATE FORMATION	WHERE RELEVANT, INDEPENDENCE WAS ACHIEVED FROM	YEAR OF FIRST CONSTITUTION	YEAR OF CURRENT CONSTITUTION
BRUNEI	Asia	South East Asia	1984	(formerly a British protectorate)	1959	1984
BULGARIA	Europe	South-Eastern Europe	1908	Ottoman Empire	1879	1991
BURKINA FASO	Africa	West Africa	1960	France	1960	1991
BURMA/ MYANMAR	Asia	South East Asia	1948	United Kingdom	1947	1974
BURUNDI	Africa	Central Africa	1962	Belgium	1961	1998
CAMBODIA	Asia	South East Asia	1953	France	1947	1993
CAMEROON	Africa	Central Africa	1961	(divided between France and United Kingdom)	1961	1972
CANADA	Americas	North America	1867	United Kingdom	1791	1982
CAPE VERDE	Africa	West Africa	1975	Portugal	1975	1992
CENTRAL AFRICAN REPUBLIC	Africa	Central Africa	1960	France	1962	1995
CHAD	Africa	Central Africa	1960	France	1959	1996
CHILE	Americas	South America	1818	Spain	1818	1981
CHINA	Asia	East Asia	1368		1954	1982
COLOMBIA	Americas (Andean)	South America	1819	Spain	1811	1991
COMOROS	Africa	Southern Africa	1975	France	1961	1999
CONGO, DR (Kinshasa)	Africa	Central Africa	1960	Belgium	1960	1997
CONGO, R (Brazzaville)	Africa	Central Africa	1960	France	1963	2002
COSTA RICA	Americas	Central America	1821/1838	Spain	1844	1949
*note: part of the United Provinces of Central America from 1823 to 1838						
CROATIA	Europe	South-Eastern Europe	1991	Yugoslavia	1990	1990
*note: under Hungarian rule prior to the creation of the Kingdom of Serbs, Croats, and Slovenes (later Yugoslavia) in 1919						
CUBA	Americas	Caribbean	1902	Spain	1901	1976
*note: a de facto protectorate of the United States until 1933						
CYPRUS (Greek)	Europe	South-Eastern Europe	1960	United Kingdom	1960	1960
CZECH REPUBLIC	Europe	Central Europe	1992	(dissolution of Czechoslovakia in 1992)	1920/1993	1993
*note: under Austrian rule prior to the creation of Czechoslovakia in 1918						
DENMARK	Europe	Northern Europe	899		1849	1953
DJIBOUTI	Africa	East Africa	1977	France	1981	1992
DOMINICA	Americas	Caribbean	1978	United Kingdom	1978	1978
DOMINICAN REPUBLIC	Americas	Caribbean	1844	first Spain (1821) then Haiti	1844	1966

COUNTRY	GEOGRAPHIC REGION	GEOGRAPHIC SUBREGION	YEAR OF (MODERN) INDEPENDENCE OR STATE FORMATION	WHERE RELEVANT, INDEPENDENCE WAS ACHEIVED FROM	YEAR OF FIRST CONSTITUTION	YEAR OF CURRENT CONSTITUTION
ECUADOR	Americas	South America (Andean)	1830	Spain	1830	1998
EGYPT	Africa	North Africa	1922	United Kingdom	1923	1971
EL SALVADOR	Americas	Central America	1821/1838	Spain	1841	1983
*note: part of the United Provinces of Central America from 1823 to 1838						
EQUATORIAL GUINEA	Africa	Central Africa	1968	Spain	1968	1991
ERITREA	Africa	East Africa	1993	Ethiopia	1997	1997
*note: an Italian colony until World War II						
ESTONIA	Europe	Northern Europe	1991	Soviet Union	1918/1992	1992
*note: independent in the interwar period						
ETHIOPIA	Africa	East Africa	1682		1931	1995
FIJI	Oceania	Melanesia	1970	United Kingdom	1966	1998
FINLAND	Europe	Northern Europe	1918	Russia	1906	2000
*note: Swedish until 1809, then Russian						
FRANCE	Europe	Western Europe	987		1791	1958
GABON	Africa	Central Africa	1960	France	1967	1991
GAMBIA	Africa	West Africa	1965	United Kingdom	1970	1997
GEORGIA	Europe	Transcaucasus	1991	Soviet Union	1921/1995	1995
GERMANY	Europe	Western Europe	1871		1871	1949
GHANA	Africa	West Africa	1957	United Kingdom	1925	1992
GREECE	Europe	South-Eastern Europe	1832	Ottoman Empire	1844	2001
GRENADA	Americas	Caribbean	1973	United Kingdom	1974	1974
GUATEMALA	Americas	Central America	1821/1839	Spain	1851	1985
*note: part of the United Provinces of Central America from 1823 to 1838						
GUINEA	Africa	West Africa	1958	France	1958	1991
GUINEA-BISSAU	Africa	West Africa	1973	Portugal	1973	1984
GUYANA	Americas	South America	1966	United Kingdom	1792	1980
HAITI	Americas	Caribbean	1804	France	1801	1987
HONDURAS	Americas	Central America	1821/1838	Spain	1839	1982
*note: part of the United Provinces of Central America from 1823 to 1838						
HUNGARY	Europe	Central Europe	1867	(as a union with Austria)	1848	1989
*note: the union (Dual Monarchy) with Austria ends in 1918, and a separate Hungarian state is established by 1920						
ICELAND	Europe	Northern Europe	1918	Denmark	1874	1944
INDIA	Asia	South Asia	1947	United Kingdom	1950	1950
INDONESIA	Asia	South East Asia	1945	Netherlands	1945	1945
IRAN	Asia	Middle East	1501		1906	1979
IRAQ	Asia	Middle East	1932	(formerly a British protectorate)	1925	1968

continues...

COUNTRY	GEOGRAPHIC REGION	GEOGRAPHIC SUBREGION	YEAR OF (MODERN) INDEPENDENCE OR STATE FORMATION	WHERE RELEVANT, INDEPENDENCE WAS ACHEIVED FROM	YEAR OF FIRST CONSTITUTION	YEAR OF CURRENT CONSTITUTION
IRELAND	Europe	Western Europe	1921	United Kingdom	1919	1937
ISRAEL	Asia	Middle East	1948	(formerly part of a British protectorate)	Unwritten Constitution	
ITALY	Europe	Western Europe	1860		1861	1948
IVORY COAST	Africa	West Africa	1960	France	1959	2000
JAMAICA	Americas	Caribbean	1962	United Kingdom	1944	1962
JAPAN	Asia	East Asia	1609		1889	1947
JORDAN	Asia	Middle East	1946	United Kingdom	1928	1952
KAZAKHSTAN	Asia	Central Asia	1991	Soviet Union	1993	1995
KENYA	Africa	East Africa	1963	United Kingdom	1954	1963
KIRIBATI	Oceania	Micronesia	1979	United Kingdom	1979	1979
KOREA, NORTH	Asia	East Asia	1948	Japan	1948	1972
KOREA, SOUTH	Asia	East Asia	1948	Japan	1948	1987

*note: under United States military government from 1945 to 1948

COUNTRY	GEOGRAPHIC REGION	GEOGRAPHIC SUBREGION	YEAR OF (MODERN) INDEPENDENCE OR STATE FORMATION	WHERE RELEVANT, INDEPENDENCE WAS ACHEIVED FROM	YEAR OF FIRST CONSTITUTION	YEAR OF CURRENT CONSTITUTION
KUWAIT	Asia	Middle East	1961	(formerly a British protectorate)	1938	1962
KYRGYZSTAN	Asia	Central Asia	1991	Soviet Union	1993	1993
LAOS	Asia	South East Asia	1953	(formerly a French protectorate)	1947	1991
LATVIA	Europe	Northern Europe	1991	Soviet Union	1922/1991	1993

*note: independent in the interwar period

COUNTRY	GEOGRAPHIC REGION	GEOGRAPHIC SUBREGION	YEAR OF (MODERN) INDEPENDENCE OR STATE FORMATION	WHERE RELEVANT, INDEPENDENCE WAS ACHEIVED FROM	YEAR OF FIRST CONSTITUTION	YEAR OF CURRENT CONSTITUTION
LEBANON	Asia	Middle East	1946	France	1926	1926
LESOTHO	Africa	Southern Africa	1966	(formerly a British protectorate)	1966	1993
LIBERIA	Africa	West Africa	1847		1839	1986
LIBYA	Africa	North Africa	1951	Italy	1951	1977

*note: under Anglo-French administration after World War II

COUNTRY	GEOGRAPHIC REGION	GEOGRAPHIC SUBREGION	YEAR OF (MODERN) INDEPENDENCE OR STATE FORMATION	WHERE RELEVANT, INDEPENDENCE WAS ACHEIVED FROM	YEAR OF FIRST CONSTITUTION	YEAR OF CURRENT CONSTITUTION
LIECHTENSTEIN	Europe	Western Europe	1719		1818	1921
LITHUANIA	Europe	Northern Europe	1991	Soviet Union	1922/1990	1992

*note: independent in the interwar period

COUNTRY	GEOGRAPHIC REGION	GEOGRAPHIC SUBREGION	YEAR OF (MODERN) INDEPENDENCE OR STATE FORMATION	WHERE RELEVANT, INDEPENDENCE WAS ACHEIVED FROM	YEAR OF FIRST CONSTITUTION	YEAR OF CURRENT CONSTITUTION
LUXEMBOURG	Europe	Western Europe	1867		1868	1919
MACEDONIA	Europe	South-Eastern Europe	1991	Yugoslavia	1991	1991

*note: under Ottoman rule for centuries until conquered by Serbia in 1912-1913

COUNTRY	GEOGRAPHIC REGION	GEOGRAPHIC SUBREGION	YEAR OF (MODERN) INDEPENDENCE OR STATE FORMATION	WHERE RELEVANT, INDEPENDENCE WAS ACHEIVED FROM	YEAR OF FIRST CONSTITUTION	YEAR OF CURRENT CONSTITUTION
MADAGASCAR	Africa	Southern Africa	1960	France	1959	1992
MALAWI	Africa	Southern Africa	1963	United Kingdom	1966	1995
MALAYSIA	Asia	South East Asia	1963	United Kingdom	1957	1957
MALDIVES	Asia	South Asia	1965	United Kingdom	1968	1998
MALI	Africa	West Africa	1960	France	1960	1992
MALTA	Europe	Western Europe	1964	United Kingdom	1964	1974

COUNTRY	GEOGRAPHIC REGION	GEOGRAPHIC SUBREGION	YEAR OF (MODERN) INDEPENDENCE OR STATE FORMATION	WHERE RELEVANT, INDEPENDENCE WAS ACHIEVED FROM	YEAR OF FIRST CONSTITUTION	YEAR OF CURRENT CONSTITUTION
MARSHALL ISLANDS	Oceania	Micronesia	1986	(formerly a United States protectorate)	1979	1979
MAURITANIA	Africa	West Africa	1960	France	1959	1991
MAURITIUS	Africa	Southern Africa	1968	United Kingdom	1968	1968
MEXICO	Americas	North America	1810	Spain	1814	1917
MICRONESIA	Oceania	Micronesia	1986	(formerly a United States protectorate)	1979	1979
MOLDOVA *note: most of Moldova was part of Romania until World War II	Europe	Eastern Europe	1991	Soviet Union	1994	1994
MONACO	Europe	Western Europe	1861	France	1911	1962
MONGOLIA	Asia	East Asia	1912	China	1924	1992
MOROCCO	Africa	North Africa	1956	France	1962	1992
MOZAMBIQUE	Africa	Southern Africa	1975	Portugal	1975	1990
NAMIBIA	Africa	Southern Africa	1990	(formerly a South African protectorate)	1990	1990
NAURU	Oceania	Micronesia	1968	(formerly an Australian protectorate)	1968	1968
NEPAL	Asia	South Asia	1769		1959	1990
NETHERLANDS	Europe	Western Europe	1581		1815	1983
NEW ZEALAND	Oceania		1852	United Kingdom	Unwritten Constitution	
NICARAGUA *note: part of the United Provinces of Central America from 1823 to 1838	Americas	Central America	1821/1838	Spain	1838	1987
NIGER	Africa	West Africa	1960	France	1960	1999
NIGERIA	Africa	West Africa	1960	United Kingdom	1922	1999
NORWAY *note: the royal union with Sweden ends in 1905	Europe	Northern Europe	1814	Denmark (as a union with Sweden)	1814	1814
OMAN	Asia	Middle East	1971	(formerly a British protectorate)	1996	1996
PAKISTAN	Asia	South Asia	1947	United Kingdom	1973	1973
PALAU	Oceania	Micronesia	1994	(formerly a United States protectorate)	1981	1981
PANAMA *note: a de facto protectorate of the United States until 1936	Americas	Central America	1903	Colombia	1904	1994
PAPUA NEW GUINEA	Oceania	Melanesia	1975	Australia	1975	1975
PARAGUAY	Americas	South America	1811	Spain	1813	1992

continues...

COUNTRY	GEOGRAPHIC REGION	GEOGRAPHIC SUBREGION	YEAR OF (MODERN) INDEPENDENCE OR STATE FORMATION	WHERE RELEVANT, INDEPENDENCE WAS ACHEIEVED FROM	YEAR OF FIRST CONSTITUTION	YEAR OF CURRENT CONSTITUTION
PERU	Americas	South America (Andean)	1821	Spain	1823	1993
PHILIPPINES	Asia	South East Asia	1946	United States	1902	1987
POLAND	Europe	Central Europe	1919	(divided among Austria, Germany, and Russia)	1815	1997
PORTUGAL	Europe	Western Europe	1143		1822	1976
QATAR	Asia	Middle East	1971	(formerly a British protectorate)	1970	2003
ROMANIA	Europe	South-Eastern Europe	1878	Ottoman Empire	1861	1991
RUSSIA	Europe	Eastern Europe	1480		1905	1993
RWANDA	Africa	Central Africa	1962	Belgium	1962	1995
SAINT KITTS AND NEVIS	Americas	Caribbean	1983	United Kingdom	1976	1983
SAINT LUCIA	Americas	Caribbean	1979	United Kingdom	1979	1979
SAINT VINCENT AND THE GRENADINES	Americas	Caribbean	1979	United Kingdom	1979	1979
SAMOA (Western)	Oceania	Polynesia	1962	(formerly a New Zealand protectorate)	1962	1962
SAN MARINO	Europe	Western Europe	1631		1600	1600
SÃO TOMÉ AND PRÍNCIPE	Africa	Central Africa	1975	Portugal	1975	1990
SAUDI ARABIA	Asia	Middle East	1932		1992	1992
SENEGAL	Africa	West Africa	1960	France	1958	2001
SERBIA AND MONTENEGRO	Europe	South-Eastern Europe	1878	Ottoman Empire	1835	2003

*notes: Serbia autonomous from 1815; the Kingdom of Serbs, Croats, and Slovenes formed in 1918, renamed Yugoslavia in 1929; the remaining two parts formed a confederation in 2003

COUNTRY	GEOGRAPHIC REGION	GEOGRAPHIC SUBREGION	YEAR OF (MODERN) INDEPENDENCE OR STATE FORMATION	WHERE RELEVANT, INDEPENDENCE WAS ACHEIEVED FROM	YEAR OF FIRST CONSTITUTION	YEAR OF CURRENT CONSTITUTION
SEYCHELLES	Africa	Southern Africa	1976	France	1976	1993
SIERRA LEONE	Africa	West Africa	1961	United Kingdom	1961	1991
SINGAPORE	Asia	South East Asia	1965	United Kingdom	1959	1959

*note: part of Malaysian Federation from 1963 to 1965

| SLOVAKIA | Europe | Central Europe | 1992 | (dissolution of Czechoslovakia in 1992) | 1993 | 1993 |

*note: under Hungarian rule prior to the creation of Czechoslovakia in 1918

| SLOVENIA | Europe | Central Europe | 1992 | Yugoslavia | 1991 | 1991 |

*note: under Austrian (Hapsburg) rule prior to the creation of the Kingdom of Serbs, Croats, and Slovenes (later Yugoslavia) in 1919

| SOLOMON ISLANDS | Oceania | Melanesia | 1978 | United Kingdom | 1978 | 1978 |

COUNTRY	GEOGRAPHIC REGION	GEOGRAPHIC SUBREGION	YEAR OF (MODERN) INDEPENDENCE OR STATE FORMATION	WHERE RELEVANT, INDEPENDENCE WAS ACHEIEVED FROM	YEAR OF FIRST CONSTITUTION	YEAR OF CURRENT CONSTITUTION
SOMALIA	Africa	East Africa	1960	(divided between United Kingdom and Italy)	1960	2000
SOUTH AFRICA	Africa	Southern Africa	1910	United Kingdom	1909	1997
SPAIN	Europe	Western Europe	1479		1808	1978
SRI LANKA	Asia	South Asia	1948	United Kingdom	1947	1978
SUDAN	Africa	East Africa	1956	United Kingdom	1952	1998
SURINAME	Americas	South America	1975	Netherlands	1975	1987
SWAZILAND	Africa	Southern Africa	1968	(formerly a British protectorate)	1968	1978
SWEDEN	Europe	Northern Europe	1388		1809	1975
SWITZERLAND	Europe	Western Europe	1291		1848	2000
*note: Swiss independence not formally recognized until 1648						
SYRIA	Asia	Middle East	1944	France (previously Ottoman)	1930	1973
TAIWAN	Asia	East Asia	1947		1947	1947
*note: still officially a province of China						
TAJIKISTAN	Asia	Central Asia	1991	Soviet Union	1994	1994
TANZANIA	Africa	East Africa	1961	United Kingdom	1961	1977
THAILAND	Asia	South East Asia	1782		1932	1997
TIMOR-LESTE (East Timor)	Asia	South East Asia	2002	first Portugal (1975) then Indonesia	2001	2001
TOGO	Africa	West Africa	1960	France	1963	1992
TONGA	Oceania	Polynesia	1970	(formerly a British protectorate)	1875	1875
TRINIDAD AND TOBAGO	Americas	Caribbean	1962	United Kingdom	1949	1976
TUNISIA	Africa	North Africa	1956	France	1861	1959
TURKEY	Europe	South-Eastern Europe	1473		1876	1982
*note: the date for Turkey refers to the creation of a centralized Ottoman Empire based in Istanbul (Constantinople); the modern Turkish Republic was founded in 1923						
TURKMENISTAN	Asia	Central Asia	1991	Soviet Union	1992	1992
TUVALU	Oceania	Polynesia	1978	United Kingdom	1978	1986
UGANDA	Africa	East Africa	1962	United Kingdom	1962	1995
UKRAINE	Europe	Eastern Europe	1991	Soviet Union	1978/1991	1996
UNITED ARAB EMIRATES	Asia	Middle East	1971	(formerly a British protectorate)	1971	1971
UNITED KINGDOM	Europe	Western Europe	1707		Unwritten Constitution	

continues…

COUNTRY	GEOGRAPHIC REGION	GEOGRAPHIC SUBREGION	YEAR OF (MODERN) INDEPENDENCE OR STATE FORMATION	WHERE RELEVANT, INDEPENDENCE WAS ACHEIVED FROM	YEAR OF FIRST CONSTITUTION	YEAR OF CURRENT CONSTITUTION
UNITED STATES	Americas	North America	1776	United Kingdom	1781	1788
URUGUAY	Americas	South America	1830	Spain	1830	1966
UZBEKISTAN	Asia	Central Asia	1991	Soviet Union	1992	1992
VANUATU	Oceania	Melanesia	1980	(formerly under Anglo-French joint rule)	1980	1980
VENEZUELA	Americas	South America (Andean)	1830	Colombia (Spanish until 1821)	1811/1830	1999
VIETNAM	Asia	South East Asia	1954	France	1959	1992
YEMEN	Asia	Middle East	1962	United Kingdom (South Yemen)	1964	1991

*note: North Yemen becomes independent in 1918 after the collapse of Ottoman rule

| ZAMBIA | Africa | Southern Africa | 1964 | United Kingdom | 1964 | 1996 |
| ZIMBABWE | Africa | Southern Africa | 1980 | United Kingdom | 1979 | 1979 |

*note: a unilateral declaration of independence was made by the white minority of then-Rhodesia in 1965

Note: Some countries were divided after independence and later reunified (Germany, Vietnam, Yemen).

The following historical patterns come from examining the years of independence or state formation of the states that exist today and from looking only at continuous independence through today. First, only 20 states date back to before 1800. These states are mostly European, although the United States also became independent in this era. The United States is thus the contemporary world's nineteenth oldest state. Then in the first half of the nineteenth century, or more precisely from 1804 to 1847, 22 more states, overwhelmingly in Latin America, were formed or became independent.[13] However, in the *second* half of the nineteenth century, or more precisely from 1852 to 1878, only nine new and still ongoing states came into existence, and these few new states were overwhelmingly in Europe. Indeed, after the Treaty of Berlin in 1878, which recognized the independence of Romania, Serbia, and Montenegro,[14] there was over a 20-year break until the formation of Australia in 1901. That said, the latter half of the nineteenth century did see the creation of Canada, which is (tied for) forty-sixth in terms of longevity. Then from 1901 (Australia) through 1944 (Syria) another 16 new states were added. These were scattered over various regions, but arose ultimately in the Middle East at the end of this period. The real explosion of the number of states comes after World War II, starting with Indonesia in 1945.[15] Indeed, from 1945 (Indonesia) to 1990 (Namibia) no less than 101 of today's states were formed or became independent—over half of the total extant today. These states arose first throughout Africa and Asia, and later on (from 1962 onwards) also in the Caribbean and Oceania. This explosion largely reflected the processes of decolonization in these regions. Finally, the period from 1991 to the present has seen a relatively high number of new states, 24, overwhelmingly in Europe but also in Central Asia due to the break-ups of the Soviet Union, Yugoslavia, and Czechoslovakia.

POLITICAL AND ECONOMIC CLASSIFICATIONS OF STATES

In terms of political and economic differences among states, throughout much of the postwar period the most common distinction was a threefold grouping into the First World, the Second World, and the Third World. The First World comprised the developed capitalist economies of the United States, Canada, Western Europe, Japan, Australia, and New Zealand, which are often simply referred to as the "West."[16] The Second World comprised the Soviet Union and Eastern Europe (broadly defined), that is, countries that were seen as developed but which followed a communist economic and political system. Thus, the distinction between the First World and the Second World was primarily a political one. Finally, the Third World included everywhere else: African, Asian, Latin American, and Caribbean countries that were generally non-aligned but more crucially were seen as less developed. As Spero pointed out, the Western system of First World countries has involved many dense patterns of *interdependence*, with reasonable symmetry among the countries concerned. In contrast, the North-South system between the First and Third Worlds also involved much interaction, but this was between unequal actors with the Third World in a situation of *dependence*; that is, Third World countries were dependent on those of the First World for market access, investment, and finance (with the reverse not being true). Finally, the Second World economies were closely tied to each other in terms of economic planning and trade, but as a group they interacted little with the rest of the world. So, Spero characterized the East-West system as one of *independence*.[17] That said, for the purposes of comparative politics and economics, almost every country fell into one of these three groupings. (Countries such as Israel, South Africa, and China were in various ways borderline cases.)

With the ending of communism the Second World no longer exists as such, but it would be a leap to put many Eastern European and especially Soviet successor states into the First World. Furthermore, if there is no longer a grouping called the Second World, then it obviously does not make much sense to still use the term *Third* World. Consequently, two alternatives are common these days. The first is to call African, Asian, Caribbean, Latin American, and Middle Eastern countries "developing states" or "less developed states" in contrast to the developed states of the First World. The second, more geographic, approach is to refer to the "South" versus the "North," since Third World countries generally are to the south of the First World (Australia and New Zealand excepted, of course). Table 1.2 thus lists countries according to this North/South distinction. However, the increasing heterogeneity of the "developing world," with countries at varying levels of development, makes one question whether *any* single category can cover all of the "South," that is, all of Africa, Asia, the Caribbean, Latin America, and the Middle East.

Consequently, the World Bank puts countries into four groupings based on per capita income: "low," "lower middle," "upper middle," and "high." The United Nations goes further in its broadly based **Human Development Index (HDI)**. The HDI combines three factors: (1) per capita income, which is corrected for variations in purchasing power and is adjusted by being logged;[18] (2) life expectancy; and (3) a combination of literacy rates and school enrollments. These combined factors lead to a standardized score in which higher values indicate higher levels of development. Based on the HDI, the UN then groups countries into "low," "medium," and "high" human development. Table 1.2 thus includes both the World Bank and the UN HDI categories for all countries, where possible. (Later on in Chapter 5 we shall analyze some of the component factors of these measures, in particular per capita income and

TABLE 1.2 :: ALTERNATE CLASSIFICATIONS OF DEVELOPMENT

COUNTRY	NORTH/SOUTH CATEGORY 1990	WORLD BANK (PER CAPITA) INCOME GROUP CATEGORY 2002	UNITED NATIONS HUMAN DEVELOPMENT INDEX CATEGORY 2002	LEVEL OF MASS CONSUMPTION (BASED ON PERSONAL AUTOMOBILES) 2001
AFGHANISTAN	South	low	–	low
ALBANIA	North	lower middle	medium	low
ALGERIA	South	lower middle	medium	medium
ANDORRA	North	high	–	–
ANGOLA	South	low	low	low
ANTIGUA AND BARBUDA	South	high	high	very high
ARGENTINA	South	upper middle	high	medium
ARMENIA	(North)	lower middle	medium	low
AUSTRALIA	North	high	high	very high
AUSTRIA	North	high	high	very high
AZERBAIJAN	(North)	low	medium	low
BAHAMAS	South	high	high	very high
BAHRAIN	South	high	high	high
BANGLADESH	South	low	medium	low
BARBADOS	South	high	high	medium
BELARUS	(North)	lower middle	medium	high
BELGIUM	North	high	high	very high
BELIZE	South	upper middle	medium	medium
BENIN	South	low	low	low
BHUTAN	South	low	medium	–
BOLIVIA	South	lower middle	medium	low
BOSNIA-HERZEGOVINA	North	lower middle	medium	low
BOTSWANA	South	upper middle	medium	low
BRAZIL	South	lower middle	medium	medium
BRUNEI	South	high	high	very high
BULGARIA	North	lower middle	medium	very high
BURKINA FASO	South	low	low	low
BURMA/MYANMAR	South	low	medium	low
BURUNDI	South	low	low	low
CAMBODIA	South	low	medium	low
CAMEROON	South	low	medium	low
CANADA	North	high	high	very high
CAPE VERDE	South	lower middle	medium	low

continues...

COUNTRY	NORTH/SOUTH CATEGORY 1990	WORLD BANK (PER CAPITA) INCOME GROUP CATEGORY 2002	UNITED NATIONS HUMAN DEVELOPMENT INDEX CATEGORY 2002	LEVEL OF MASS CONSUMPTION (BASED ON PERSONAL AUTOMOBILES) 2001
CENTRAL AFRICAN REPUBLIC	South	low	low	low
CHAD	South	low	low	low
CHILE	South	upper middle	high	medium
CHINA	South	lower middle	medium	low
COLOMBIA	South	lower middle	medium	low
COMOROS	South	low	medium	low
CONGO, DR (Kinshasha)	South	low	low	low
CONGO, R (Brazzaville)	South	low	low	low
COSTA RICA	South	upper middle	high	medium
IVORY COAST (Côte d'Ivoire)	South	low	low	low
CROATIA	North	upper middle	high	very high
CUBA	South	lower middle	high	low
CYPRUS (Greek)	South	high	high	very high
CZECH REPUBLIC	North	upper middle	high	very high
DENMARK	North	high	high	very high
DJIBOUTI	South	lower middle	low	low
DOMINICA	South	upper middle	medium	medium
DOMINICAN REPUBLIC	South	lower middle	medium	low
ECUADOR	South	lower middle	medium	low
EGYPT	South	lower middle	medium	low
EL SALVADOR	South	lower middle	medium	low
EQUATORIAL GUINEA	South	low	medium	low
ERITREA	South	low	low	low
ESTONIA	(North)	upper middle	high	very high
ETHIOPIA	South	low	low	low
FIJI	South	lower middle	medium	medium
FINLAND	North	high	high	very high
FRANCE	North	high	high	very high
GABON	South	upper middle	medium	low
GAMBIA	South	low	low	low
GEORGIA	(North)	low	medium	medium
GERMANY	North	high	high	very high
GHANA	South	low	medium	low
GREECE	North	high	high	high
GRENADA	South	upper middle	medium	—
GUATEMALA	South	lower middle	medium	medium
GUINEA	South	low	low	low

COUNTRY	NORTH/SOUTH CATEGORY 1990	WORLD BANK (PER CAPITA) INCOME GROUP CATEGORY 2002	UNITED NATIONS HUMAN DEVELOPMENT INDEX CATEGORY 2002	LEVEL OF MASS CONSUMPTION (BASED ON PERSONAL AUTOMOBILES) 2001
GUINEA-BISSAU	South	low	low	low
GUYANA	South	lower middle	medium	low
HAITI	South	low	low	low
HONDURAS	South	lower middle	medium	low
HUNGARY	North	upper middle	high	high
ICELAND	North	high	high	very high
INDIA	South	low	medium	low
INDONESIA	South	low	medium	low
IRAN	South	lower middle	medium	low
IRAQ	South	lower middle	—	low
IRELAND	North	high	high	very high
ISRAEL	South	high	high	high
ITALY	North	high	high	very high
JAMAICA	South	lower middle	medium	medium
JAPAN	North	high	high	very high
JORDAN	South	lower middle	medium	low
KAZAKHSTAN	(North)	lower middle	medium	medium
KENYA	South	low	low	low
KIRIBATI	South	lower middle	—	—
KOREA, NORTH	South	low	—	—
KOREA, SOUTH	South	high	high	high
KUWAIT	South	high	high	very high
KYRGYZSTAN	(North)	low	medium	low
LAOS	South	low	medium	low
LATVIA	(North)	upper middle	high	very high
LEBANON	South	upper middle	medium	very high
LESOTHO	South	low	low	low
LIBERIA	South	low	—	low
LIBYA	South	upper middle	medium	medium
LIECHTENSTEIN	North	high	—	very high
LITHUANIA	(North)	upper middle	high	very high
LUXEMBOURG	North	high	high	very high
MACEDONIA	North	lower middle	medium	medium
MADAGASCAR	South	low	low	low
MALAWI	South	low	low	low

continues...

COUNTRY	NORTH/SOUTH CATEGORY 1990	WORLD BANK (per capita) INCOME GROUP CATEGORY 2002	UNITED NATIONS HUMAN DEVELOPMENT INDEX CATEGORY 2002	LEVEL OF MASS CONSUMPTION (based on personal automobiles) 2001
MALAYSIA	South	upper middle	medium	high
MALDIVES	South	lower middle	medium	low
MALI	South	low	low	low
MALTA	North	high	high	very high
MARSHALL ISLANDS	—	lower middle	—	—
MAURITANIA	South	low	low	low
MAURITIUS	South	upper middle	medium	low
MEXICO	South	upper middle	high	medium
MICRONESIA	South	lower middle	—	—
MOLDOVA	(North)	low	medium	medium
MONACO	North	high	—	very high
MONGOLIA	South	low	medium	low
MOROCCO	South	lower middle	medium	low
MOZAMBIQUE	South	low	low	low
NAMIBIA	South	lower middle	medium	low
NAURU	—	—	—	—
NEPAL	South	low	medium	—
NETHERLANDS	North	high	high	very high
NEW ZEALAND	North	high	high	very high
NICARAGUA	South	low	medium	low
NIGER	South	low	low	low
NIGERIA	South	low	low	low
NORWAY	North	high	high	very high
OMAN	South	upper middle	medium	medium
PAKISTAN	South	low	low	low
PALAU	—	upper middle	—	—
PANAMA	South	upper middle	medium	medium
PAPAU NEW GUINEA	South	low	medium	low
PARAGUAY	South	lower middle	medium	low
PERU	South	lower middle	medium	low
PHILIPPINES	South	lower middle	medium	low
POLAND	North	upper middle	high	very high
PORTUGAL	North	high	high	very high
QATAR	South	high	high	high
ROMANIA	North	lower middle	medium	medium
RUSSIA	North	lower middle	medium	medium
RWANDA	South	low	low	low

COUNTRY	NORTH/SOUTH CATEGORY 1990	WORLD BANK (per capita) INCOME GROUP CATEGORY 2002	UNITED NATIONS HUMAN DEVELOPMENT INDEX CATEGORY 2002	LEVEL OF MASS CONSUMPTION (based on personal automobiles) 2001
SAINT KITTS AND NEVIS	South	upper middle	high	high
SAINT LUCIA	South	upper middle	medium	medium
SAINT VINCENT AND THE GRENADINES	South	lower middle	medium	medium
SAMOA (Western)	—	lower middle	medium	low
SAN MARINO	North	high	—	—
SÃO TOMÉ AND PRÍNCIPE	South	low	medium	low
SAUDI ARABIA	South	upper middle	medium	medium
SENEGAL	South	low	low	low
SERBIA AND MONTENEGRO	North	lower middle	—	—
SEYCHELLES	South	upper middle	high	medium
SIERRA LEONE	South	low	low	low
SINGAPORE	South	high	high	medium
SLOVAKIA	North	upper middle	high	high
SLOVENIA	North	high	high	very high
SOLOMON ISLANDS	—	low	medium	—
SOMALIA	South	low	—	low
SOUTH AFRICA	South	lower middle	medium	medium
SPAIN	North	high	high	very high
SRI LANKA	South	lower middle	medium	low
SUDAN	South	low	medium	low
SURINAME	South	lower middle	medium	medium
SWAZILAND	South	lower middle	medium	low
SWEDEN	North	high	high	very high
SWITZERLAND	North	high	high	very high
SYRIA	South	lower middle	medium	low
TAIWAN	South	high	—	high
TAJIKISTAN	(North)	low	medium	low
TANZANIA	South	low	low	low
THAILAND	South	lower middle	medium	low
TIMOR-LESTE (East Timor)	South	low	low	—
TOGO	South	low	low	low
TONGA	—	lower middle	medium	medium
TRINIDAD AND TOBAGO	South	upper middle	high	medium
TUNISIA	South	lower middle	medium	low

continues...

COUNTRY	NORTH/SOUTH CATEGORY 1990	WORLD BANK (per capita) INCOME GROUP CATEGORY 2002	UNITED NATIONS HUMAN DEVELOPMENT INDEX CATEGORY 2002	LEVEL OF MASS CONSUMPTION (based on personal automobiles) 2001
TURKEY	South	lower middle	medium	medium
TURKMENISTAN	(North)	lower middle	medium	medium
TUVALU	—	—	—	—
UGANDA	South	low	low	low
UKRAINE	North	lower middle	medium	medium
UNITED ARAB EMIRATES	South	high	high	medium
UNITED KINGDOM	North	high	high	very high
UNITED STATES	North	high	high	very high
URUGUAY	South	upper middle	high	high
UZBEKISTAN	(North)	low	medium	—
VANUATU	—	lower middle	medium	low
VENEZUELA	South	upper middle	medium	medium
VIETNAM	South	low	medium	low
YEMEN	South	low	low	low
ZAMBIA	South	low	low	low
ZIMBABWE	South	low	low	low

Sources

Column 2: Andrew Webster, *Introduction to the Sociology of Development*, 2nd ed. (Basingstoke: Macmillan, 1990) 5, Map 1.1.

Column 3: World Bank, World Development Report 2003

Column 4: United Nations, Human Development Report 2003

Column 5: Calculated from Euromonitor International, *International Marketing Data and Statistics 2003, European Marketing Data and Statistics 2003*.

adult literacy values, since these are argued to be of particular significance for democratic development.)

Finally, Table 1.2 also gives an alternative sense of development, that of mass consumption of goods (as opposed to these only being accessible to and/or consumed by an elite). Following the classic work of W.W. Rostow, the diffusion of private automobiles is used as an indicator of the extent to which a country has reached what Rostow calls the "mass consumption phase."[19] Here we shall divide countries into the following four categories: low mass consumption (fewer than 50 private automobiles per 1000 people), medium mass consumption (from 50 to 149 private automobiles per 1000 people), high mass consumption (from 150 to 249 private automobiles per 1000 people), and very high mass consumption (250 or more private automobiles per 1000 people). For historical context, one can note that the United States—the first mass consumer society—reached the level of high mass consumption in 1925 and the level of very high mass consumption in 1950.[20]

ANALYZING POLITICAL REGIMES

Yet all of these measures, even the HDI, are essentially measures of economic and social development. These are important factors as they relate to political development, but the latter must be the ultimate point of analysis for comparing political regimes. This textbook thus takes the following approaches and sequence. First, the next chapter discusses what is meant by development across a wide range of aspects, and how these ideally should occur. Then we shall outline in detail what is meant by democracy, which will involve five components. All of the countries of the world today can and will be put into one of four categories: liberal democracies, electoral democracies, semi-liberal autocracies, and closed autocracies. These categories will be defined and contrasted. We then look specifically at the (potentially undemocratic) role of the military in politics. After this, explanations and statistical analyses will be made of the factors conducive to *individual* countries being more or less democratic. Next we shall group together the liberal and electoral democracies and go into more detail on their political institutions and party politics. We shall then examine the autocracies (non-democracies), which can be totalitarian, sultanistic, or authoritarian, although in fact these divide further into eight different subtypes of autocracies. We shall then look at transitions to democracy, including both the notion of global democratic "waves" (and "reverse waves") and an assessment of the prospects for new democracies to become "consolidated." Conversely, we shall see why and how democracies "break down." Finally, we shall assess the potential for specific countries, and thus the world as a whole, to become both more democratic and less democratic in the future.

A NOTE ON MATHEMATICAL FORMULA

Political science students are rarely fans of mathematics, and in this book mathematical calculations are kept to a minimum. However, you will need to note a few of these. The first such calculation is the *t-test*, which is used to assess differences among (the means of) two groups of data. A higher (absolute) number indicates a greater difference. That said, as is the nature of statistical calculations, what really matters is whether the *t* score is statistically significant, by which we mean whether its level of significance is .05 or *less*. Consequently, ever lower values—down to .000—would indicate ever higher significance. Second, there is the *Pearson chi-square test*, used where data is grouped into a "N by N" (at least, and usually, a "2 by 2") table. A higher number here indicates the tendency of one specific category of a given variable to be associated with one specific category of the/an other variable. Again, what is key here is the significance level. Third, there is *multiple regression*. This assesses the combined explanatory nature of several independent variables on one dependent variable (in what is called a "model"). A variable that may "explain" (relate to) some other variable on its own may in fact lose this causal relationship when other, stronger, variables are included. A multiple regression will thus establish what, collectively, are the most useful explanatory variables for the dependent variable in question. A multiple regression will still provide *t* scores and significance levels for each independent variable in the model, as well as for a constant. Additionally, the overall relationship is given in the form of an adjusted r^2, which ranges from 0 (absolutely no relationship with the dependent variable) to 1 (a full explanation of absolutely all the variation in the dependent variable, which is, of course, "too much to expect"). An adjusted r^2 of 0.500 or higher is generally seen as indicating a strong explanatory relationship.

A separate relevant calculation is that of the "effective number" of something, for our purposes such things as ethnic groups and seats won by political parties. If we count something by integers (1, 2, 3, 4, etc.), then we are counting each with the same value of 1. This is fine if we want to treat everything the same, but problematic if the "things" are of greatly different size. Thus, the effective number of something, indicated by N, is a calculation that weights each item by size (as a percentage of the overall total). Where everything is of the same size, then the effective number is the same as the actual integer number; otherwise, though, it is different. Some examples of this are as follows:

WITH TWO THINGS:

A has 50%	A has 66.7%	A has 90%
B has 50%	B has 33.3%	B has 10%
N = 2.00	N = 1.80	N = 1.22

WITH THREE THINGS:

A has 33.3%	A has 44%	A has 70%	A has 90%
B has 33.3%	B has 44%	B has 20%	B has 5%
C has 33.3%	C has 12%	C has 10%	C has 5%
N = 3.00	N = 2.49	N = 1.85	N = 1.23

WITH FOUR THINGS:

A has 25%	A has 40%	A has 44%	A has 70%
B has 25%	B has 30%	B has 44%	B has 10%
C has 25%	C has 20%	C has 8%	C has 10%
D has 25%	D has 10%	D has 4%	D has 10%
N = 4.00	N = 3.33	N = 2.53	N = 1.92

Note that N can never be less than 1.00, which occurs when there is only one thing, that is, A has 100%.

NOTES

1   Ruth Collier and David Collier, *Shaping the Political Arena: Critical Junctures, the Labor Movement, and Regime Dynamics in Latin America* (Princeton, NJ: Princeton University Press, 1991) 789.

2   Max Weber, *Max Weber: The Theory of Social and Economic Organization*, trans. A.M. Henderson and Talcott Parsons, ed. Talcott Parsons (New York, NY: The Free Press, 1964) 156.

3 Stephen D. Krasner, "Abiding Sovereignty," *International Political Science Review* 22:3 (2001): 229–51, especially 231–33.

4 On Africa, see Jeffrey Herbst, *States and Power in Africa: Comparative Lessons in Authority and Control* (Princeton, NJ: Princeton University Press, 2000) 252.

5 Krasner 232.

6 Robert H. Jackson calls these entities "quasi-states." See his *Quasi-States: Sovereignty, International Relations and the Third World* (Cambridge, UK: Cambridge University Press, 1990).

7 This lasted until 1667.

8 This paragraph is drawn from Hendrik Spruyt, *The Sovereign State and Its Competitors: An Analysis of Systems Change* (Princeton, NJ: Princeton University Press, 1994).

9 Charles Tilly, "Reflections on the History of European State-Making," *The Formation of Nation-States in Western Europe*, ed. Charles Tilly (Princeton, NJ: Princeton University Press, 1975), quote on p. 42.

10 Miguel Angel Centeno, "Blood and Debt: War and Taxation in Nineteenth-Century Latin America," *American Journal of Sociology* 102:6 (May 1997): 1565–1605; quotes from abstract on p. 1565.

11 North African states are often grouped with the Middle Eastern states of Asia for historical (Ottoman control) and religious reasons. The three Transcaucasus states (Armenia, Azerbaijan, and Georgia) are on the border between Europe and Asia, as is Turkey.

12 This distinction obviously leaves aside all of those historical states that no longer exist today, at least not independently.

13 Although the term "Latin America" is commonly used in analysis, one should note that this is not a geographically based subregion of the Americas, but rather a cultural subregion grouping together countries whose inhabitants speak primarily a Romance language—Spanish, Portuguese, or French (in that order of frequency)—and are predominantly Catholic. Consequently, "Latin America" normally refers to (only) 20 of the 35 states of the Americas, as follows: Argentina, Bolivia, Brazil, Chile, Colombia, Costa Rica, Cuba, the Dominican Republic, Ecuador, El Salvador, Guatemala, Haiti, Honduras, Mexico, Nicaragua, Panama, Paraguay, Peru, Uruguay, and Venezuela.

14 Serbia and Montenegro in fact acquired their initial sovereignty as separate independent states (and were recognized as such by the Treaty of Berlin).

15 Technically speaking, World War II was not quite over in Asia when Indonesia proclaimed its independence in August 1945.

16 Membership in the Organisation for Economic Co-operation and Development (OECD) was a good indicator of "First World status" up through the 1980s.

17 Joan Edelman Spero, *The Politics of International Economic Relations*, 4th ed. (New York, NY: St. Martin's Press, 1990) 11–15.

18 That is, the HDI compresses the effects of increased per capita income by logging this, since it is felt that "achieving a respectable level of human development does not require unlimited income." *United Nations Human Development Report 2003*: 341.

19 W.W. Rostow, *The Stages of Economic Growth: A Non-Communist Manifesto*, 3rd ed. (New York, NY: Cambridge University Press, 1990) 76–77 and 82–85.

20 An alternative to Rostow's liberal and consumption-oriented focus is the Marxist concept of "world systems theory," which is essentially production-oriented. "World systems theory" refers to the North, or much of it, as the highly skilled and industrialized "core" of the world economy, which is financially and technologically dominant and which structures the patterns of global production. Other countries are either "peripheral" if they are agricultural or "semi-peripheral" if they have experienced some industrialization.

CHAPTER TWO

Development and Political Development

IN THIS CHAPTER YOU WILL LEARN:

» *how development (or modernization) has both economic and political aspects;*

» *what is meant by political development and the central role of institutionalization in this;*

» *how and why scholars feel political development should be sequenced;*

» *which countries have exemplified this ideal sequence of political development;*

» *what are the different types of states (in terms of state effectiveness and penetration);*

» *what is meant by building state capacity, and the challenges in doing this; and*

» *what factors facilitate national identity.*

THE GOALS OF DEVELOPMENT

There is reasonable scholarly debate about what is meant by development. In part, this is because some scholars argue for (or are criticized for having) a sense of development which is very much focussed on emulating Western countries. For example, Huntington has noted that:

By the mid-1970s, substantial bodies of literature thus existed elaborating the importance of growth, equity, democracy, stability, and autonomy for developing societies and analyzing the ways in which those societies might best make progress toward those goals. Implicit in the widespread acceptance of these goals was also the acceptance of an image of the Good Society: wealthy, just, democratic, orderly, and in full control of its own affairs, a society, in short, very much like those found in Western Europe and North America. A backward society was poor, inequitable, repressive, violent, and dependent. Development was the process of moving from the latter to the former.[1]

This "modernization school" argument tended to produce three different debates, the first two within the school and the last one between the school and its critics. The first debate was whether all these goals were equally desirable. The second was whether all these goals were equally compatible or whether some had to be sacrificed (at least for a time) to achieve others. Thus, it was (and is) argued that democracy will impede economic development. The third debate was whether all these goals were still possible. This was the critique of the "dependency school," who argued that the "core" nations of the North Atlantic had so structured the international economic and political order that it was next to impossible for "peripheral" nations to develop since these were permanently stuck in a dependent situation. At a minimum, this critique implied that without autonomy the other goals of development would be difficult if not impossible to achieve.

Of these goals, the notions of wealth and egalitarianism are more socio-economic. To these could be added other economic and social aspects of modernity or modernization: high(er) levels of education and literacy, a shift from agriculture to industry and services, urbanization, long(er) life expectancy, low(er) infant mortality, etc. Certainly, these features are part of a(ny) broader notion of development; as was noted in the introduction, wealth, life expectancy, and education are combined in the UN's Human Development Index (HDI). Yet none of these are explicitly political. What, then, is left for (and meant by) **political development**? Huntington's list includes democracy, order, and autonomy, to which can be added the notion of institutionalization. Elsewhere Huntington defines institutionalization generally as "the process by which organizations and procedures acquire value and stability" and thus become complex (with formal internal structures and hierarchies), adaptable, coherent, and autonomous from other institutions.[2] In terms of specifically political organizations one means, of course, standard political institutions such as executives, legislatures, and judiciaries which collectively both make and implement national laws and policies, as well as arms-length organizations such as electoral bodies. Above and beyond these, Huntington lays particular stress on the role of political parties in structuring political demands or "inputs" in modern societies with their consequent mass participation in politics.[3]

Regarding the notion of order, this may sound somewhat "fascist," but what Huntington means here is political stability and the ability of governments to govern, which in turn he relates back to their level of **political institutionalization**. His classic work in this regard, *Political Order in Changing Societies*, is blunt in setting out the "problem" here; although this was written in the 1960s (and, obviously, although the Soviet Union no longer exists), it is still worth quoting today for distinguishing between countries not according to their form of government (their regime type) but instead their degree of (legitimate) government:

> The United States, Great Britain, and the Soviet Union have strong, adaptable, coherent political institutions: effective bureaucracies, well-organized political parties, a high degree of popular participation in public affairs, working systems of civilian control over the military, extensive activity by the government in the economy, and reasonably effective procedures for regulating succession and controlling political conflict. [They] command the loyalties of their citizens and thus have the capacity to tax resources, to conscript manpower, and to innovate and to execute policy. If the [Soviet] Politburo, the [British] Cabinet, or the [United States] President makes a decision, the probability is high that it will be implemented through the government machinery.

> [The situation is quite different] in many, if not most, of the mod-
> ernizing countries of Asia, Africa, and Latin America. These coun-
> tries ... suffer real shortages of food, literacy, education, wealth,
> income, health, and productivity ... however, there is a greater
> shortage: a shortage of political community and of effective, author-
> itative, legitimate government ... in many cases, governments simply
> do not govern....
>
> In many modernizing countries governments are still unable to
> [control the governed], much less [control themselves]. The pri-
> mary problem is not liberty but the creation of a legitimate public
> order.... Authority has to exist before it can be limited, and it is
> authority which is in scarce supply.[4]

Obviously, Huntington is assuming here that government is a good in
itself, a point rejected by anarchists. Yet, it is hard to see any goal of development being achieved in a state of anarchy. What is then, perhaps, actually
controversial among the list of political goals above is democracy. Many
would argue that it is naïve to assume that everyone and every society wants
to be democratic, much less will be. Writing in the 1960s, Rustow and Ward
clearly stressed the "non-linkage" between democracy and modernization, even
if they do note the linkage between egalitarianism and modernization:

> In the political sphere, it is advisable not to link the broad histor-
> ical concept of modernization with any particular regime or ideol-
> ogy. ... Democracy and representative government are not implied
> in our definition of modernization. Czar Peter of Russia [Peter the
> Great], Sultan Mahmud of Turkey, and Emperor Meiji of Japan
> were modernizers, but decidedly not democrats or conscious fore-
> runners of democracy. Germany was more modern in the 1930s
> than in the 1880s, though its government was less representative
> and less liberal. ...
>
> There are nonetheless certain definite political characteristics
> that modernizing societies share. Commonly modernization ... pro-
> ceeds toward some form of mass society—democratic or authori-

tarian. Under whatever regime, the hallmarks of the modern state are a vastly expanded set of functions and demands. Public services come to include education, social security, and public works while civic duties involve new forms of loyalty, tax payment and, in a world of warring states, military service. The very concepts of public service and civic duty, indeed, are among the vital prerequisites of modern politics.

The tendency, moreover, is for services and obligations to become universal: schooling for all children, a road into every village, conscription for all men, and a tax out of every pay envelope. Hence political modernization clearly has egalitarian tendencies. The performance of all the new or expanded services usually means a vast increase in public employment, just as the more intensive interaction among citizens is accompanied by a vast expansion in the network of communications.[5]

If not democracy, then development and modernization do seem to imply increased state capacity. This in turn requires a change in bureaucratic structures. As Max Weber pointed out, in medieval Europe there was a "patrimonial" system of government in which not only was the ruler an all-powerful autocrat, but he (or rarely she) personally and arbitrarily appointed, and promoted, individuals to administrative positions based entirely on the ruler's personal judgements. Likewise, the ruler arbitrarily modified these positions or responsibilities, which were thus fluid and without fixed limits or clear relations of authority (except to the ruler). The officials concerned often came from the personal household of the ruler and in any case had no particular technical qualifications. Finally, as an extension of the ruler, these officials may or may not have deigned to serve the public; usually a payment of tribute was required to get something done. In the modern (Western) state, these administrative patterns have been replaced by a permanent **bureaucracy**, which is based on a rational hierarchy of authority and which employs full-time civil servants who are hired by formal contracts and promoted based on training and experience, who have defined rights and duties and fixed salaries, and who serve the public neutrally and without (using their position for) direct personal gain.[6]

TRADITIONAL VERSUS MODERN SOCIETIES

These changes, as perhaps are obvious, parallel Weber's broader distinction of a shift from *traditional authority* based on the personal authority of the chief (or hereditary monarch), down through those whose authority was an extension of that of the chief or monarch, to *(rational) legal authority* based on legal rules and the authority to determine these set by the occupants of hierarchical political and bureaucratic offices (not personally by the specific individuals who happen to occupy them). Weber also noted a third type of authority, *charismatic authority*, based on the unique or indeed superhuman personal qualities of an individual who is seen to have divine inspiration. Charismatic authority can occasionally be the basis for political organization, but this rarely outlasts the individual.[7] Moreover, as Weber noted, over time there is a "routinization of charisma" inasmuch as "in its pure form charismatic authority may be said to exist only in the process of originating. It cannot remain stable, but becomes either traditionalized or rationalized, or a combination of both."[8] Thus, ultimately, we are left with traditional versus legal-rational authority.

More broadly, in traditional society, or what Weber called "status societies," one's birth determines one's social position, not just for monarchs but for everyone. In such societies, kinship is paramount. People are also more oriented to the past and tend to be fatalistic, if not superstitious. In contrast, in modern society, or what Weber called "class societies," one's social position is determined, and thus can be raised (or lowered), by hard work and achievement (or the lack of these). In theory, all are equal before the law. Individualism is important; family ties are less central. People tend to be forward-oriented and rational, generally rejecting tradition as a valid reason in itself. Individuals and society as a whole believe in progress (both personally and collectively), leading to emphases on entrepreneurialism and science. Interpersonal behaviour is likewise generally based on the impersonal rationality of contracts and assessments of other's qualifications, rather than on family or personal ties.[9]

In summary, then, modern political societies will differ from traditional ones in terms of what is considered a legitimate decision—one based on legal-rational procedures and not on traditional authority. This can be seen as a difference in **political culture**, that is, the attitudes, values, and beliefs that individuals have with respect to their political regime/system and the way(s) it allocates power and resolves political conflicts. We shall see in Chapter 4 that the extent to which political culture is developed will affect the likelihood of military intervention.

SEQUENCING POLITICAL DEVELOPMENT

Ironically, even if there is some debate about whether to consider democracy the ultimate goal of political development, there has been for a long time a fair consensus among scholars regarding the ideal sequence by which political development should occur if one wishes to produce a stable, democratic state. This sequence goes as follows:[10]

» First, there should be a national identity producing national unity. In Nordlinger's analysis, "a national identity may be said to exist when the great majority of the politically relevant actors accord the nation's central symbols and its political elite(s) greater loyalty than that which they maintain toward subnational units, such as tribes, castes, and classes, and toward political elite(s) residing outside the system's territory."[11] The resulting national unity is thus where people "have no doubt or mental reservations as to which political community they belong to."[12]

» Second, there follows the establishment and institutionalization over time of state structures which are legitimate and effective. These institutions are usually ultimately codified in a constitution.[13]

» Third, the various elite groups then engage in competition with each other, usually by forming rudimentary political parties. Even if these parties have small memberships and minimal organization, they can still become institutionalized over time. The "prize" for which they are competing may not be total power if there is still a relevant monarch. Nevertheless, if successful, this stage of elite competition will produce alternations back and forth in power, leading to toleration on the part of elites and their commitment to the protodemocratic procedure of regular elections. Rustow calls this the "habituation phase," where these new habits lead to the internalization of democratic norms.[14]

» Fourth, if not already existing (as in republics), there is the establishment of responsible government, by which monarchs and nobles give up their political power to elected governments.

» Fifth and finally, there is a slow expansion of voting rights until there is universal suffrage.[15]

There are several reasons for this sequence. Without a national identity, any government institution will have great difficulty in getting its wishes followed—unless of course it uses coercion, but this obviously will not increase the legitimacy of the state. State-building should be a slow process, since whenever there is a large expansion of organizational structures individuals tend to be more concerned with the competition for promotion than with the overall performance of the organization.[16] Moreover, any state structure which is new or rapidly expanding will be less coherent than an already institutionalized one; too many such expanding structures will be problematic. Political competition even among elites will need time for the more conservative to trust the more liberal ones (that is, to trust that they will not go too far). Robert Dahl summarized the historical solution in successful societies:

> the rules, the practices, and the culture of competitive politics developed first among a small elite, and the critical transition from non-party politics to party competition also occurred initially within the restricted group. Although ... party conflict was often harsh and bitter, the severity of conflict was restrained by ties of friendship, family [and] class ... that pervaded the restricted group of notables who dominated the political life of the country.[17]

A slow expansion of the franchise incorporates and socializes new groups bit by bit into an already existing political culture of tolerance and modera-

TABLE 2.1 :: THE SEQUENCING OF POLITICAL DEVELOPMENT IN THE ADVANCED INDUSTRIAL STATES

COUNTRY	DECADE OF PARTY SYSTEM INSTITUTION-ALIZATION	YEAR OF RESPONSIBLE GOVERNMENT	YEAR OF UNIVERSAL MALE SUFFRAGE
AUSTRALIA	1900s	1901*	1903***
AUSTRIA	1890s	1918	1907
BELGIUM	1880s	1831	1919
CANADA	1860s	1867**	1920
DENMARK	1870s	1901	1915
FINLAND	1860s	1917	1906
FRANCE	1900s	1875	1848
GERMANY	1860s	1918	1869****
GREECE	1910s	1875	1844/1864
ICELAND	(1910s)	1915	1920
IRELAND	1920s	1921	1923
ITALY	1910s	1861	1912/1919
JAPAN	1890s	1947	1925
LUXEMBOURG	1900s	1919	1918
NETHERLANDS	1880s	1848	1917
NEW ZEALAND	1890s	1854	1879
NORWAY	1880s	1884	1898
PORTUGAL	1910s	1911	1918
SPAIN	1930s	1869	1869
SWEDEN	1880s	1917	1921
SWITZERLAND	1890s	1848	1848
UNITED KINGDOM	1860s	1832	1918
UNITED STATES	1820s	1789	1870

   * 1856 in each colony   ** 1854 in the province of Canada
*** before federation in each of the colonies   **** 1849 in Prussia
Note: Dates in brackets are pre-independence.

tion. On the other hand, if there is no expansion to include new groups, the society is likely to become radicalized. Last but not least, if universal suffrage comes "too soon" in the absence of established political parties and other strong institutions, this will likely either overwhelm the system or lead to a conservative reaction and ultimately to repression, as in Southern Europe. Table 2.1 gives the dates of party system institutionalization (defined here as stable competition between two or more parties, each with a clear voting

47

base), responsible government, and universal male suffrage for the advanced industrial countries. Looking at the dates, one sees that where universal male suffrage came last (with or without universal female suffrage at the same time), countries overwhelmingly underwent a stable and successful pattern of political development. Where universal male suffrage came earlier or at the same time as the other factors, political development was unstable, with breakdowns and/or shifts to non-democratic rule.[18] Where universal suffrage came before responsible government, this led to the creation of mass "irresponsible" parties, since these could not aspire to government, as was the case in Imperial Germany. Finally, where responsible government came first, or at least before institutionalized parties, the result was either governmental instability for a time as governments collapsed quickly (Belgium, France, New Zealand, United Kingdom, and for that matter some Canadian provinces) or heavy **clientelism** as governments "bought" legislative support or even rigged elections (Italy, Spain).

Although the United Kingdom is usually given as a country with stable political development, it did experience the violent breakaway of most of Ireland in 1916-22. If one wants to note ideal patterns of political development, it is really the three Scandinavian countries of Denmark, Norway, and Sweden that stand out. Norway in particular experienced a political development characterized by a cohesive national identity beginning in the ninth century and growing under the external control of first Denmark and then Sweden, very little violence (and none in achieving independence from Sweden in 1905), ever-increasing democracy, and a "remarkably stable and effective" democratic system[19] in a country with strong regional, cultural, and class divisions (or as we shall call these later, "cleavages").[20]

Denmark, Norway, Sweden, and the United Kingdom all share the trait of being (constitutional) monarchies. As Lipset notes, most of the (historically) stable Western democracies are monarchies.[21] Monarchies seem most relevant in the fourth and fifth aspects of political development, since their support or at least acceptance of these changes goes a long way to reassuring both traditional elites and the groups pressing for change. That is, "[t]he preservation of the monarchy has apparently retained for these [Western] nations the loyalty of the aristocratic, traditionalist, and clerical sectors of the population which resented increased democratization and equalitarianism. And by accepting the lower strata and not resisting to the point where revolution might be necessary, the conservative orders won or retained the loyalty of the new 'citizens.'"[22] Such behaviour can be contrasted with that of monarchs in Imperial Russia or the Mideast. Of course, even though the general point about monarchies aiding political development still applies today in a theoretical sense, this is not much help if a country does not have a (legitimate) monarchy.

At the opposite extreme from a country like Norway, then, are many countries in Africa and Asia which at the time of independence had no national identity or viable political institutions nor (as noted above) did much to improve state capacity, but nevertheless in the spirit of the times introduced elections with universal suffrage. It is no great surprise that democracy did not take root in these countries and that political instability and/or non-democratic rule have been quite common. Is this the fault of colonialism? Certainly the map of Africa in particular was drawn with little concern for traditional tribal identities. Yet perhaps the bigger issue is the nature of colonial rule. In countries that were British colonies, stable political institutions and competitive elections often predated independence. For example, Trinidad and Tobago had its first elections in 1925 (with a limited franchise and for only some of the seats on the Legislative Council), decades before its independence in 1962. In India as well there were elections before independence (although no completely free national ones), and the All-India Congress Party dated back to 1885 and was highly organized. This institution is invariably argued to be one of the factors central to India's (initial) political and democratic stability, the other being the competent Indian Civil Service, dating back to the early 1800s.[23] In contrast, other colonial powers, such as the Belgians or French, generally left their ex-colonies with little in the way of institutions or stable political patterns at the time of independence. Likewise, most of the new countries of Eastern and Central Europe that appeared as a result of the collapse of empires due to World War I lacked any institutionalized administrative structures, in large part because non-ethnic majority bureaucrats left instead of staying around to work for the new state.[24]

STATES AS INSTITUTIONS

There are three different types of states, that is, the bureaucratic structures of a regime. In the "default" type, which we shall call an **effective state**, the state controls the national territory and the borders and has sufficient domestic penetration to ensure that national laws and policies are in effect throughout the country. To this end, there is a stable judicial system, the bureaucracy is based on the aforementioned Weberian principles, and there is sufficient state capacity to raise tax revenues and (in the contemporary world) to provide at least primary education for the vast majority of children. Such an effective state is certainly not all-powerful, but it is legitimate both throughout the country and across the various social classes.[25] Canada and the United States, for example, both possess effective states.

In contrast, a **weak state** lacks one or more of these points and is thus ineffective in one or more ways. There are many weak states, as listed in Table 2.2. A weak state may not be able to impose national policies throughout the country; indeed, its effect may be limited to the capital. Elsewhere it lacks a presence, or what presence it has is seen as illegitimate and ignored.[26] Within a weak state, individual state actors may well arbitrarily act to enrich themselves personally rather than follow any legal obligations. It is for this reason that Evans prefers the term "predatory state" to "weak state," at least for countries like Zaire.[27] In any case, a weak state will generally be inadequate for economic and social development.

As noted, a weak state will be in control of the national capital at least and able to impose most of its policies there. However, at the extreme a state may simply cease to function. This is a **collapsed state**, in which there is truly no state authority, but rather anarchy or civil war.[28] Lebanon, Somalia, Sierra Leone, and Zaire, for example, have all seen their states collapse in recent times. Of course, since "politics, like nature, abhors a vacuum," one may wonder why a neighbouring country does not take over a country whose state has collapsed or at least grab some choice territory. Historically, this was certainly the pattern in Europe and also that of Japan *vis-à-vis* the collapse of the Chinese state in the 1930s. However, as was noted in the introduction, the postwar world has laid great stress on the inviolability of national borders. The

TABLE 2.2 :: WEAK STATES IN THE WORLD TODAY

Afghanistan	Congo, R (Brazzaville)	Lebanon	Senegal
Albania	Djibouti	Liberia	Serbia and Montenegro
Algeria	Ecuador	Macedonia	Sierra Leone
Angola	El Salvador	Madagascar	Solomon Islands
Argentina	Eritrea	Maldives	Somalia
Armenia	Ethiopia	Mali	Sri Lanka
Bangladesh	Gabon	Mauritania	Sudan
Benin	Gambia	Moldova	Tajikistan
Bolivia	Georgia	Mozambique	Tanzania
Burkina Faso	Ghana	Nepal	Togo
Burma/Myanmar	Guatemala	Nicaragua	Turkmenistan
Burundi	Guinea	Niger	Uganda
Cameroon	Guinea-Bissau	Nigeria	Uzbekistan
Central African Republic	Haiti	Pakistan	Venezuela
Chad	Iraq	Papua New Guinea	Yemen
Colombia	Ivory Coast	Peru	Zambia
Comoros	Kazakhstan	Philippines	
Congo, DR (Kinshasa)	Kyrgyzstan	Rwanda	

international community thus tries to re-establish collapsed states and has never officially declared a state to have failed for good.

Lastly, opposite a weak state one might expect "strong states," and Migdal has certainly used this term.[29] At first glance Communist states might appear to be strong. Yet by state strength, as opposed to mere adequacy, we mean a situation in which the state (bureaucracy) is highly autonomous from political actors and social interests. Thus, Communist states are "merely" effective to their ends. The real world example of a strong state—or "super-effective" state—is the one that has promoted capitalist development successfully and is thus called a *(capitalist) developmental state*. This term refers in particular to the East Asian cases of Japan, South Korea, and Taiwan, but it has also been used for France, all of which are countries where industrial development and planning have been central in the postwar era (earlier as well in Japan).[30] Besides autonomy, the bureaucracy in the key economic ministries of developmental states is known for being highly meritocratic and highly respected, what Johnson summarizes as being "a powerful, talented, and prestige-laden economic bureaucracy" in Japan.[31] These bureaucracies attract, and select, the

51

top students from the most elite universities and schools, such as the Tokyo University Law School and the *École nationale d'administration* in France. Such developmental states can only occur where the civil service has enormous prestige (not so the case in North America), where the state is very centralized (not so the case in federalism), where the bureaucracy is in fact small and skilled, and where economic development is the overriding national goal (even at the expense of consumers and/or the environment).

STATE-BUILDING

Consequently, we are unlikely to see many more developmental states. We may, however, see some weak states become effective. Shifting "upwards" in this regard—for example, from a weak state to an effective one or even establishing a weak state where no state existed—can be seen as the phenomenon of *building state capacity* or, in Mann's phrasing, developing the *infrastructural power* of the state.[32] As outlined earlier, creating or increasing such state capacity would seem both to be a part of political development and to aid socio-economic development. So why do more states not do this? The answer relates in part to national attitudes to bureaucracy, as noted. However, it is also the case that if a bureaucracy is autonomous, with its own recruitment procedures and qualifications, then it cannot be used for political patronage. As Geddes notes, the bureaucracy (and appointments to it) can be used to provide benefits to constituents, or to provide benefits to other politicians whose support one needs, or to provide benefits to members of a supportive political party, or to develop and implement policies in the broad national interest—but these are alternatives, not a package of choices.[33] For politicians who are primarily focussed on their own short-term interests, the establishment of an autonomous, merit-based bureaucracy is hardly something to be supported. That said, public pressure and modernization may well lead to more bureaucratic autonomy, such as happened with the creation in 1908 of Canada's Civil Service Commission (now Public Service Commission) based on the merit principle.

However, the building of state capacity does not occur in a vacuum. It is easier, or harder, depending on aspects of political geography, which facilitates control or penetration, and national identity, which facilitates legitimacy. In terms of political geography, Whittlesey argues that the ideal shape of the state is "chunky rather than elongate," with population density strongest in the centre and diminishing towards the borders, and with these borders involving where possible geographic barriers such as oceans, mountains, deserts, jungles, etc.[34] There are obviously some trade-offs involved here. For example, Chile is bordered by the Pacific Ocean on the West, the Andes mountains in the East, and the Atacama desert in the North (which is good), but all this comes at the "price" of being very elongate. Poland (in its various incarnations) has always had a desirably chunky shape but with few natural barriers, with the unfortunate result that it is has been invaded often throughout its history. Small island states tend not to have such trade-offs. Of the larger states, Japan and Spain are good examples of countries with all of these various features, although they have been challenged by internal mountain ranges.

In contrast to shape, Whittlesey does not feel that there is an ideal size for a state. Bigger is better in the sense of (likely) providing more, and more varied, natural resources. However, bigger states are more likely to have multiple centres of population density and greater challenges in terms of communications. One knows the importance of railways, and later air travel, for integrating each of Canada and the United States. Prior to the introduction of these technologies, roads and rivers were the sole methods of non-ocean transport, but only roads could go most anywhere. Where the road network was (is) dense and of good quality, then state capacity was (is) facilitated; think of the Roman Empire ("all roads lead to Rome"). As Whittlesey summarizes, "Efficient transportation consolidates political areas, whether the Roman Empire or the United States of America. The lack of ready means of circulation is a source of political weakness whatever the density of population, as the plight of [pre-Communist modern] China proves."[35]

Thus, although the size of state may well affect the challenge of establishing communications, *all* states except the tiniest are faced with the challenge of ensuring effective communications, especially roads, so as to facilitate the penetration of state authority. This point can be related to the weakness of many states in contemporary Africa. Herbst's recent comprehensive study points out that numerous sub-Saharan African states have an unfavourable or

53

neutral geography in regard to population distribution, and moreover that few such states have been willing or able to increase their road densities greatly. Indeed, in a couple of African countries there are fewer kilometres of roads today than there was at independence![36]

NATION-BUILDING

The size of a country also leads to the issue of national identity—the first factor in the ideal sequence of political development. As Whittlesey notes, "a large state may be weaker than a less well-endowed smaller state because the material conditions of political unity function only in the presence of the emotion of nationality."[37] In other words, state-building is easier when there is a clear national identity involved and perhaps easiest where there is complete ethnic homogeneity. However, states with what amount to ethnically homogeneous populations are very few in the world: Iceland, Japan, and North and South Korea stand out here, although the Scandinavian countries were also this way until postwar immigration. That said, immigration if accompanied by some level of assimilation will not lessen national identity provided this existed beforehand. So, perhaps a better way to phrase the issue is to assess the level of ethnic homogeneity at independence. Relating ethnicity to size, it is certainly the case that the homogeneous nations mentioned are not huge, yet there are also many small countries with multiple ethnic groups—for example, Belgium, Bhutan, Bosnia-Herzegovina, Cameroon, Ghana, Moldova, Sierra Leone, Trinidad and Tobago, and the United Arab Emirates.

In any case, even if there is ethnic diversity, national identity is facilitated if there is a dominant ethnic core (provided it is tolerant of minorities). Thus, the national histories of much of Western Europe started with a core ethnic nation (such as the English) or territory (such as the Île de France or the allied German-speaking cantons of Uri, Schwyz, and Unterwalden). Over the course of many centuries, other territories were added to these (sometimes willingly, sometimes not) until there was created, respectively, today's United Kingdom, France, and Switzerland. This long time-span meant that an initial state expanded into new territories which sooner or later usually considered it legitimate—a much easier situation than that of much of Africa and Asia, where independence put multiple ethnic groups into new countries, few of whom could claim any historical dominance.[38] One exception, as Smith notes, is India, where national identity is centred around the Hindi-speaking Hindus of northern and central India.[39] As for Canada, we cannot forgot our initial British majority. On the one hand, this majority accommodated the French minority through federalism and assimilated many subsequent waves of immigrants. On the other hand, for generations this dominant ethnic group saw itself as "British"; *Canadian* identity would develop slowly.

Countries that do not have a strong sense of national identity (even for the dominant group) at independence have to establish this identity if they wish to facilitate the legitimacy of the state. This requires a conscious process of "nation-building," some of which comes through state-building, especially the creation of standardized mass education. However, nation-building also involves the creation (or strengthening) of an intangible national identity. As Smith stresses, "[t]he 'nation' is not, as we see, built up only through the provision of 'infrastructures' and 'institutions,' as 'nation-building' theories assumed; but from the central fund of culture and symbolism and mythology provided by shared historical experiences."[40] "Shared historical experiences" is a broad category, but moreover a vague one. The reality is that creation of national identity involves differentiating one's nation from some *other* nation(s), and thus the role of the *other* is crucial. Such differentiation, moreover, has come most strongly through war, at least in Western Europe where war not only "made the state," as noted earlier, it made or at least reinforced the nation. As Howard's study of Europe notes, "Self-identification as a Nation implies almost by definition alienation from other communities, and the most memorable incidents in the group-memory consisted in conflict with and triumph over other communities."[41]

A similar argument could be made for the United States, starting with its War of Independence, especially since those still loyal to Britain fled to Canada. But what if independence involves no struggle? In Africa, for example, only a few states (Angola, Guinea-Bissau, Mozambique, Namibia, and Zimbabwe) had to fight a war to gain independence.[42] Most Latin American countries technically fought wars, but these were so brief (Colombia excepted) as to have little effect in terms of establishing a national identity. Consequently, Latin American countries overwhelmingly suffered from political instability and weak or even failed states during their first decades of independence. Exceptions were Brazil, which retained a monarchy until 1889, and Chile due to its military successes. As Valenzuela writes,

> It is doubtful that Chileans considered themselves a nation before independence.... However, the clear-cut [1839] military victory in the war against the Peru-Bolivia Confederation, a victory without parallel in Latin America, gave the small, divided nation a powerful new sense of confidence and purpose, creating tangible symbols of patriotism and nationality. These feelings were [later] reinforced with the [1883] victory of Chilean forces in the War of the Pacific, which led to the incorporation of large portions of Peruvian and Bolivian territory.[43]

Needless to say, it is not so much the fighting of a war but the actual winning of one which builds national identity. This point applies as well to more peaceful international events, such as participation in the Olympics.

NOTES

1 Samuel P. Huntington, "The Goals of Development," *Understanding Political Development*, ed. Myron Weiner and Samuel P. Huntington (Glenview, IL: Scott, Foresman/Little, Brown, 1987) 6.

2 Samuel P. Huntington, *Political Order in Changing Societies* (New Haven, CT: Yale University Press, 1968) 12.

3 Huntington, *Political Order in Changing Societies* 89.

4 Huntington, *Political Order in Changing Societies* 1-8 *passim*.

5 Dankwart A. Rustow and Robert E. Ward, "Introduction," *Political Modernization in Japan and Turkey*, ed. Robert E. Ward and Dankwart A. Rustow (Princeton, NJ: Princeton University Press, 1964) 4–5.

6   Max Weber, "The Theory of Social and Economic Organization," *From Max Weber: Essays in Sociology*, ed. H.G. Gerth and C.W. Mills (New York, NY: Oxford University Press, 1946) 342–45.

7   Weber, "The Theory of Social and Economic Organization" 328ff.

8   Weber, "The Theory of Social and Economic Organization" 363–64.

9   Max Weber, *Economy and Society*, Vol. 2, ed. Günther Roth and Claus Wittich (New York, NY: Bedminster Press, 1968) 928.

10 The following draws from Eric A. Nordlinger, "Political Development: Time Sequences and Rates of Change," *World Politics* 20:3 (April 1968): 494–520; Dankwart A. Rustow, "Transitions to Democracy: Toward a Dynamic Model," *Comparative Politics* 3 (April 1970): 337–64; and Larry Diamond, Jonathan Hartlyn, and Juan J. Linz, "Introduction: Politics, Society, and Democracy in Latin America," *Democracy in Developing Countries: Latin America*, 2nd ed., ed. Larry Diamond *et al.* (Boulder, CO: Lynne Rienner, 1999) 13–15.

11 Nordlinger, "Political Development" 498.

12 Rustow 350.

13 Table 1.1 gives the years of every contemporary state's first and current constitutions for reference.

14 Rustow 360.

15 An alternative way that was traditionally used in analyzing political development was to view this as a series of crises or challenges that all nations must meet to achieve democratic stability—these being crises of identity, authority/legitimacy, penetration, participation, and distribution. See Leonard Binder *et al.*, *Crises and Sequences in Political Development* (Princeton, NJ: Princeton University Press, 1971).

16 Nordlinger, "Political Development" 513.

17 Robert A. Dahl, *Polyarchy: Participation and Opposition* (New Haven, CT: Yale University Press, 1971) 36.

18 It was certainly the case in Latin America that universal (male) suffrage came well after the creation of elected responsible governments. However, as we shall see, most of these systems lacked national unity and an effective state.

19 Harry Eckstein, *Division and Cohesion in Democracy: A Study of Norway* (Princeton, NJ: Princeton University Press, 1966) 11.

20 Nordlinger, "Political Development" 512; Eckstein, Chapter II and 119–20.

21 Seymour Martin Lipset, *Political Man: The Social Bases of Politics*, expanded ed. (Baltimore, MD: Johns Hopkins University Press, 1981) 65–66.

22 Lipset 66.

23 Huntington, *Political Order in Changing Societies* 84.

24 The two exceptions here were Czechoslovakia and Finland. These countries also had decades of competitive elections before independence. Not coincidentally, they were the only two newly independent countries in the region whose democracies survived the interwar period.

25 The notion of including a stable judicial system as one of the components of a state is that of J.G. Merquior, "Patterns of State-Building in Argentina and Brazil," *States in History*, ed. John A. Hall (Oxford, UK: Basil Blackwell, 1986) 276.

26 In some weak states, the state presence may not just be ignored but indeed be physically opposed. Rotberg thus uses the term "failed state" to refer to those states experiencing civil war or insurrections combined with—or indeed resulting from—the failure of the state to deliver socio-economic "goods" (security, public services, economic growth) in the areas it does control. He lists Afghanistan, Angola, Burundi, the Democratic Republic of the Congo, Liberia, Sierra Leone, and Sudan as the failed states of this decade, with Somalia as a collapsed state (below). Robert I. Rotberg, "The New Nature of Nation-State Failure," *The Washington Quarterly* 25:3 (Summer 2002): 85–96.

27 Peter Evans, *Embedded Autonomy: States and Industrial Transformation* (Princeton, NJ: Princeton University Press, 1995) 44–45.

28 I. William Zartman, ed., *Collapsed States: The Disintegration and Restoration of Legitimate Authority* (Boulder, CO: Lynne Rienner, 1995).

29 Joel S. Migdal, *Strong Societies and Weak States: State-Society Relations and State Capabilities in the Third World* (Princeton, NJ: Princeton University Press, 1988).

30 See Chalmers Johnson, *MITI and the Japanese Miracle: The Growth of Industrial Policy, 1925-1975* (Stanford, CA: Stanford University Press, 1982); Robert Wade, *Governing the Market: Economic Theory and the Role of Government in East Asian Industrialization* (Princeton, NJ: Princeton University Press, 1990); and more generally Meredith Woo-Cumings, ed., *The Developmental State* (Ithaca, NY: Cornell University Press, 1999).

31 Johnson 21.

32 Michael Mann, "The Autonomous Power of the State: Its Origins, Mechanisms and Results," *States in History*, Ed. John A. Hall (Oxford, UK: Basil Blackwell, 1986) 113.

33 Barbara Geddes, *Politician's Dilemma: Building State Capacity in Latin America* (Berkeley and Los Angeles, CA: University of California Press, 1994) 134–39.

34 Derwent Whittlesey, *The Earth and the State: A Study of Political Geography* (New York, NY: Henry Holt and Company, 1944) 23.

35 Whittlesey 11.

36 Herbst, Chapter Five on "National Design and the Broadcasting of Power."

37 Whittlesey 23.

38 Anthony D. Smith, "State-Making and Nation-Building," *States in History*, ed. John A. Hall (Oxford, UK: Basil Blackwell, 1986) 245–57 *passim*.

39 Smith 255.

40 Smith 258.

41 Michael Howard, *War and the Nation State* (Oxford, UK: Clarendon Press, 1978) 9.

42 Herbst 128.

43 Arturo Valenzuela, "Chile: Origins and Consolidation of a Latin American Democracy," *Democracy in Developing Countries: Latin America*, 2nd ed., ed Larry Diamond *et al.* (Boulder, CO: Lynne Rienner, 1999) 212–13.

CHAPTER THREE

Electoral Democracies, Liberal Democracies, and Autocracies

IN THIS CHAPTER YOU WILL LEARN:

» *what are the minimal factors needed for an electoral democracy;*

» *what is the "fallacy of electoralism";*

» *what are the five specific aspects of liberal democracy, and how these developed historically;*

» *what is a semi-liberal autocracy;*

» *what is a closed autocracy;*

» *what are the differences between liberal democracy, electoral democracy, semi-liberal autocracy, and closed autocracy;*

» *where each country in the world fits into this typology; and*

» *what critiques have been made of and improvements suggested for liberal democracies.*

DEMOCRACY AND THE DEMOS

Democracy is a difficult concept to define, or at least one that is hard to define succinctly. The word has its root in the Greek term *demos*, meaning "the people," combined with the suffix "-cracy" from the Greek *kratos*, meaning "power" or "strength." Thus, the people are clearly part of a democracy. But in what way or ways? In his Gettysburg Address of 1863, Abraham Lincoln eloquently spoke of "government of the people, by the people, and for the people." Yet each of these aspects is problematic at some level. If one speaks of government "of the people," this refers to the actual decision-makers. But nowhere in the world does a national legislature, for example, exactly mirror its society in terms of age (parliamentarians are on average older than their national means), gender (every national parliament has a male majority, although the extent of this varies greatly), education (parliamentarians tend to be better educated than the average citizen, and many would defend this), or occupational background (politicians, at least in North America, overwhelmingly come from legal backgrounds). The issue here may be simply the possibility of an "average person" holding office, however average may be defined.

In terms of government "by the people," this implies that the people are somehow participating in the process. This could be by voting, speaking out publicly on an issue, and/or contacting a government official. Yet outside of Switzerland, where it is the constitutional and political reality that most issues will be dealt with ultimately through public initiatives or referenda, rarely is it the case that the people anywhere actually take decisions on policies. (An *initiative* is a citizen-sponsored or "bottom-up" proposal for a policy change, whereas a *referendum* is a vote whereby the population has the final say on proposed government legislation or constitutional changes.[1]) Democracies are essentially delegative rather than direct, although political analysts like Robert A. Dahl (see below) argue that they should be (more) direct to be truly democratic. Certainly in Canada it has been a political convention since the Charlottetown Accord (although not a formal constitutional requirement) that major constitutional changes will require approval in a national referendum.

Finally, in terms of government "for the people," this could mean government in the public interest, or more simply "good government." But this could be delivered by a benevolent dictator, and certainly many dictators claim to be acting in the national interest. The issue is who decides whether the government, or a specific policy, is a good one. Rousseau wrote of the "general will," but this does not seem to exist naturally. There must be some *political* process for determining what the people want. This will lead us shortly into the realm of elections. It is worth noting here that (some) people may not understand a proposed policy, or even if they understand it, they may not have a strong opinion on it as long as it is still theoretical. Consequently, people tend to have clearer opinions on *actual* policies and *actual* governments. Since people are thus generally able to decide whether what they have had for, say, the last four years has been "good government," they are able to decide whether they want "more of the same."

ELECTIONS AND ACCOUNTABILITY

And if the people do not like what they have had? Presumably, then, the people would remove the current government at the next election. Indeed, one rare succinct definition of democracy is that of Przeworski: "Democracy is a system in which parties lose elections."[2] In fact, this simple statement carries some important assumptions: first, there is someone else to vote for; second, the governing party (or president) will actually hand over power; and third, elections are not just a way, but the only acceptable way, to remove governments. Each of these points is understood to be part of democracy. Moreover, as Przeworski notes further, elections occur under set rules (an institutional framework) that structure the competition.[3] In a sense, then, the role of the people in a democracy, at a minimum, involves choosing between the electoral alternatives on offer. Mirroring this point, it is in being chosen by the voters that one acquires a democratic right to govern. This essentially is the definition of democracy offered several decades ago by Schumpeter: "the democratic method is that institutional arrangement for arriving at political decisions in which individuals acquire the power to decide by means of a competitive struggle for the people's vote."[4] Thus, democracy involves *competition*; if there is only one party (or choice on the ballot), there cannot be democracy. Competition and elections also provide for vertical *accountability*, that is, accountability of the government party or parties to the voters. Even if this accountability is admittedly after-the-fact, the desire to be re-elected should produce "good government," or at least better government, than if there is no accountability at all.

Conversely, if a political system has no competition and no (true) accountability, then those in power will presumably stay there indefinitely, regardless of the wishes of the people. Such a political system we call an **autocracy**. The Greek root *auto* means "self," and thus an autocracy is literally the (absolute) rule by one individual (the autocrat). However, for our purposes, autocracy also applies to rule by a group as long as they are unaccountable to the *demos* as a whole. Autocracies do have great variations within them, but for now the key point is that an autocracy is the opposite of a democracy.

ELECTORAL DEMOCRACY VERSUS LIBERAL DEMOCRACY

Schumpeter's definition of democracy can certainly be called minimalist. He does not even assume that political competition will be perfectly fair; instead, he draws a parallel with business competition in the marketplace, which he notes is hardly ever perfect.[5] Business competition can involve fraud, false advertising, and the general attempt of bigger firms to squeeze out smaller ones. Sometimes, established firms can collude to keep control over a market. Ideally, though, procedures are in place to prevent such restraints on business competition. It is the same for political competition: this involves not just two or more parties (candidates) competing, but procedures to ensure the fairness of the competition, such as laws against bribery or coercion. In political competition the key test is usually whether an opposition party (or candidate) has a reasonable opportunity to defeat the incumbent party (candidate), and where failure to do so is because the voters in fact prefer "more of the same" to the alternative(s) rather than because of fraud or coercion. For the population to assess opposition proposals fairly, they must have access to them and (relatively) unbiased commentary on them. Although Schumpeter does not equate democracy with freedom per se, he does note that a situation in which everyone is free to run for office (though few may have the resources to do so) is likely to lead to "a considerable amount of freedom of discussion *for all*" and likewise "a considerable amount of freedom of the press."[6] In summary, then, Schumpeter sees democracy as involving sufficient (if imperfect) competition for political office in the context of some amount of civil liberties. At the time he wrote, this seemed an acceptable definition of democracy, inasmuch as the countries which had competitive elections were rarely "flawed" on other matters. However, nowadays most political systems have elections with at least some degree of competition, if only because of international pressure to hold elections. Furthermore, it is inevitably the case that elections are relatively rare events (usually every four or five years),[7] whereas democracy is ideally an ongoing process.

Consequently, to equate elections with democracy is to commit what Terry Lynn Karl and others call the "fallacy of electoralism," the assumption that an election, if simply held, will produce representative yet competitive parties (or candidates), effective and accepted political institutions, and a legitimate government which is then able to govern. As Karl notes, electoralism as an ideology "elevates elections over all other dimensions of democracy."[8] Certainly, having an elected and thus downwardly accountable government is a key difference from an autocracy, but full democracy needs more than this. Indeed, a non-competitive, non-democratic election (of which many have occurred) may produce citizens who are cynical of elections even if these do become, or have earlier been, (somewhat) free and fair. Russians under Putin appear to fit this description.

Even if an election is basically free and fair, it is nevertheless crucial to distinguish between the minimal nature of an **electoral democracy** and a full-fledged **liberal democracy**. The recent work of Larry Diamond is very clear on this regard:

> *Electoral* democracy is a civilian, constitutional system in which the legislative and chief executive offices are filled through regular, competitive, multiparty elections with universal suffrage [thus producing the vertical accountability of responsible government].
>
> ... In addition to the elements of electoral democracy, [*liberal* democracy] requires, first, the absence of reserved domains of power for the military or other actors not accountable to the electorate, directly or indirectly. Second, in addition to the vertical accountability of rulers to the ruled (secured mainly through elections), it requires the horizontal accountability of officeholders to one another; this constrains executive power and so helps protect constitutionalism, legality, and the deliberative process. Third, it encompasses extensive provisions for political and civil pluralism as well as for individual and group freedoms, so that contending interests and

values may be expressed and compete through ongoing processes of articulation and representation, beyond periodic elections.

Freedom and pluralism, in turn, can be secured only through a "rule of law," in which legal rules are applied fairly, consistently, and predictably across equivalent cases, irrespective of the class, status, or power of those subject to the rules.[9]

Consequently, one should note that whereas an electoral democracy is not a liberal democracy, a liberal democracy is an electoral democracy and then some. In other words, one can group together liberal democracies and electoral democracies into a complete list of electoral democracies, if that is one's only concern or threshold. For example, the Freedom House organization, which divides the world into often-cited "free," "partly free," and "not free" countries and territories (with somewhat different breakpoints than are used for the four categories below), also now makes a separate list of electoral democracies which includes all of its "free" countries but not all of its "partly free" ones.

THE FIVE ELEMENTS OF LIBERAL DEMOCRACY

For our purposes, liberal democracy involves no less than five separate elements, as outlined in Table 3.1. First there is **responsible government**, a concept with which many students of political science have some trouble. Responsible government does not mean only that the government is responsible to the people, in the sense of accountability "downwards," but that the government is *only* responsible to the people and not to any other political actor who may be "pulling the strings," perhaps behind the scenes. The two potential other political actors worth stressing here are (1) a monarch and (2) the military. At one extreme, one could argue that a monarch is by definition an affront to democracy, since a monarch is neither elected nor accountable. A more moderate distinction, though, and the one we shall use, is to ask whether the monarch exercises any real political power or is merely a symbolic figurehead. Only in the former case does a monarch violate the principle of responsible government. This pattern—most common in the Middle East—will be returned

TABLE 3.1 :: DEFINITIONAL FEATURES OF LIBERAL DEMOCRACY (five-factor)

1. RESPONSIBLE GOVERNMENT

 » Political decisions are taken in a reasonably transparent way by elected officials (or those under their authority) who are thus directly or ultimately accountable to the electorate, and not to a tutelary monarch or military.
 » Governments are thus never overthrown nor forced out of office by such tutelary actors.
 » Non-accountable head of state (such as a monarch) has at most a minimal political role and no power over policy.
 » There is full civilian executive control over the military.

2. FREE AND FAIR COMPETITION FOR POLITICAL OFFICE

 » Elected officials are chosen and peacefully removed in free, fair, and relatively frequent elections with minimal or ideally no coercion of the voters.
 » Political parties can freely form and compete in elections (note that in some countries anti-democratic parties are banned).

3. FULL AND EQUAL RIGHTS OF POLITICAL PARTICIPATION

 » Practically all adults have the right to vote.
 » There is only one vote per person.
 » Likewise, most adults have the right to run for office.

4. FULL CIVIL LIBERTIES

 » There is freedom of expression, including the right to criticize public officials and governmental policies.
 » There is freedom of the press, with various alternative, non-governmental sources of information.
 » There is freedom of organization (into autonomous groups).
 » There is freedom of religion.

5. A WELL-FUNCTIONING STATE, WITH EFFECTIVE AND FAIR GOVERNANCE

 » The state, that is, the political-bureaucratic system, penetrates effectively and more or less evenly throughout the country.
 » The rule of law clearly exists and is upheld by an independent, unbiased judiciary.
 » Political and bureaucratic corruption is minimal or ideally non-existent.

to in Chapter 8 in the discussion of authoritarianism. As for the military, it must be under civilian control for there to be a liberal democracy. Conversely, if the military controls the civilian government, then the accountability is going in an undemocratic way. Military intervention in recent decades has been most common in Latin America and Africa, but has occurred also in parts of Asia and even (Southern) Europe. It is an important enough topic to be dealt with in depth in the next chapter.

The struggle for responsible government was and is central to the struggle for democracy. Power being finite, the issue is whether it is concentrated in the hands of democratically chosen politicians or non-democratic actors. It is not enough to have an elected "government" if it is not the *real* government: responsible government includes the "explicit criterion that the elected government must to a reasonable degree have effective power to rule."[10] In this vein, J. Samuel Valenzuela has emphasized the problematic factor of "non-democratically generated *tutelary powers*," which

> attempt to exercise broad oversight of the government and its policy decisions while claiming to represent vaguely formulated fundamental and enduring interests of the nation-state. A regime cannot be considered a consolidated democracy if those who win government-forming elections are placed in state power and policy-making positions that are subordinate in this manner to those of nonelected elites. ... Part of the process of building European democracies in the nineteenth and early twentieth centuries was to eliminate the tutelary power held by monarchs, making cabinets and prime ministers accountable only to elected parliaments, and armies subordinate to decisions taken by the government rather than the crown. In recent transition settings, the military have often sought to place themselves in such a tutelary role.[11]

In fact, such a tutelary role has a long tradition in most Latin American militaries.

The second element of liberal democracy is that of *free and fair competition* or, alternatively, the holding of free and fair elections. The terms "free" and "fair" have some overlap, but the basic distinction is as follows: "free" refers to the opportunities and rights of individuals not just to run for office (or to form political parties and run for office as party candidates) but also to be able to campaign publicly and access the media. Freedom in this context is thus the ability to participate. "Fair" refers to the electoral process, which must be unbiased with regards to the various candidates and parties and transparent in its procedures. Harassment of opposition candidates, bribery or alternatively coercion of voters, stuffing of individual ballot boxes, "pre-marking" of ballots, and manipulation of the vote totals are all examples of unfair or biased electoral practices. In a liberal democracy, elections are normally unaffected by such flaws, being carried out in a highly professional if not indeed "squeaky clean" manner in terms of the actual voting on election day and the subsequent official vote tabulations, which are transparent and thus can be monitored by the competing candidates/parties. In contrast, in electoral democracies there may well be localized voting irregularities. However, these irregularities do not affect who is the overall winner and thus do not thwart the voters' wishes in contrast to autocracies which can and do engage in widespread and systematic election fraud and/or exhibit (prior to this) widespread and systematic pro-regime bias in the election campaign.

A necessary (but not sufficient) component of a fair election is a secret ballot,[12] whose introduction represents a key historical step in election fairness. The use of a secret ballot began in Australia, or more specifically South Australia, in 1856 and then spread out to other countries. (Indeed, for a time in the United States the secret ballot was known simply as the "Australian ballot.") In Canada, the central role of ensuring the fairness of federal elections is played by the Chief Electoral Officer (who personally cannot vote) and the Chief Electoral Office, which dates back to 1920. The number of analogous offices worldwide has expanded greatly in the past two decades as a means of removing the administration of elections from the government of the day.[13] One key country, however, which lacks such an office is the United States, and this has led to such problems and controversy as occurred in its 2000 presidential elections. Finally, it must be stressed that without responsible government, elections may (rarely) still be free and fair, but they will not be "relevant" in the sense of determining the government. The 2002 parliamentary elections in Morocco were a recent example of this phenomenon. So too have been all elections in Monaco.

The third element of a liberal democracy is that of *full and equal rights of political participation.* (Of course, it is unlikely that absolutely everyone will use such rights, but that is the nature of rights.) "Full" here refers to having universal adult suffrage, as opposed to excluding women, the poor, the illiterate, aboriginals, and so on, all of whom have been excluded at times historically throughout the world. After World War I, universal (white) male suffrage was common, and in almost all Protestant nations universal (white) female suffrage was also granted. In nations of other religions, universal female suffrage was generally not granted until after World War II. Yet even this did not necessarily bring full suffrage, as literacy requirements continued in many nations, especially in Latin America. Indeed, voting rights for illiterates were not granted until the late 1970s in Ecuador and Peru, and not until 1988 in Brazil. It should also be stressed that nowadays "adulthood" for voting purposes is set at 18 years in the vast majority of countries,[14] but this still ranges from 16 in Brazil and now 15 in Iran to 20 or 21 in some East/Southeast Asian countries. A cut-off of 21 (which, in fact, was the Western norm until the 1970s) is still a clear drop from nineteenth-century Europe, when and where the minimum age for suffrage was as high as 30 years (Denmark) and often 25. Moreover, those higher age thresholds in the nineteenth century occurred in the context of much shorter lives: in 1900 the average life expectancy in Western Europe was 46 and only 35 in Spain![15] And since countries were at a lower level of socio-economic development, there was much greater variations of life expectancy across social classes. Consequently, high minimum ages for suffrage produced an indirect (but probably intentional) class bias in the electorate independent of any wealth requirements. The same point can be made for literacy tests, although these were often directed more at aboriginals (in South America) or blacks in the United States South.[16]

"Equal" political participation in this context refers to each voter having but one vote or, more generally, the same number of votes, since some electoral systems (Germany, New Zealand, etc.) give everyone two votes (see Chapter 7 below). Historically, however, countries such as Belgium, Prussia (Germany), and the United Kingdom not only restricted who could vote but effectively or in fact gave extra or additional votes to certain voters based on a *régime censitaire*, that is, based on property or income (tax payments) or business ownership; a *principe capacitaire*, that is, education level; and/or even male head of household status. "One person one vote"—and no more—was not fully established in the United Kingdom until 1948, for example.[17]

The fourth element of a liberal democracy is that of *full civil liberties*. Civil liberties are often constitutionally enumerated and entrenched, such as in the Canadian Charter of Rights and Freedoms. One can note that the Schumpeterian definition of democracy does not assume full civil liberties.

However, two decades after Schumpeter's book, the political scientist Robert A. Dahl argued that civil liberties are part of the necessary institutional guarantees (or requirements) for proper political competition and participation.[18] Since that time, civil liberties have been seen as central to democracy—at times perhaps a bit too central, since some politicians, especially in the United States, seem to equate democracy with freedom. In fact, one can have a reasonable amount of civil liberties without responsible government or even elections, if, for example, one lives under an autocratic but tolerant monarch. One of the virtues of the annual surveys of freedom by the New York-based Freedom House organization is that it gives separate scores for political rights and for civil liberties, allowing one to see where these diverge.

The fifth and final element of a liberal democracy is the need for a *legally based, limited, but well-functioning state*. Civil liberties cannot truly exist in the absence of a general rule of law (as Diamond notes), and the rule of law requires an independent and unbiased judiciary as a separate component of the state. The rule of law must apply to everyone, including members of the state itself. This point goes back to the traditional German notion of a **Rechtsstaat**, that is, a "state subject to law." The law protects the citizens against the power of the state, specifically the abuse (arbitrary use) of this power. More precisely, in the classical analysis of Carl Schmitt:

> A state may be termed a *Rechtsstaat* only when all administrative authority—especially that of the police—is subject to the conditions and procedure of law, and when intervention into the sphere of individual freedom is permissible solely on the basis of a law. Its identifying characteristic is the lawlike nature of the administration. The guarantee of its citizens' freedom lies in the law.[19]

Indeed, citizens in a *Rechtsstaat* not only have legally based civil liberties and freedoms, but they can use the courts—and now in most liberal democracies an ombudsman or equivalent—to seek restitution from any abuse, neglect, or unfairness by state officials. It is worth stressing that the creation of a *Rechtsstaat* was an achievement of nineteenth-century liberals (especially but not exclusively in Europe), parallelling their initiation of responsible government. Yet, since universal suffrage (or even universal male suffrage) came often much later, one can note that the emergence of a *Rechtsstaat* in the West came long before full democratization.[20]

A country cannot be considered a liberal democracy if it lacks a *Rechtsstaat*. Nor can the state be weak in the sense of Chapter 2, since in those (geographic) areas outside of its effective control the rule of law and, indeed, all democratic rules are not properly enforceable. Colombia today is a paradigmatic example of this problem. Finally, it is not just elections that must be fair but the whole determination and implementation of government policies. A liberal democracy cannot be said to exist if politicians and/or bureaucrats exhibit endemic corruption. Political corruption has received increasing analysis over the past decade or so, in particular with the Berlin-based Transparency International organization producing annual rankings of countries in terms of their (lack of) corruption.[21] As is the case with full civil liberties, the notion of a well-functioning state was not dealt with (or perhaps it was just assumed) by political analysts several decades ago, but it (or analogous terms) are now part and parcel of many international comparisons of democracy.

Finally, let us stress again that of the five elements of liberal democracy, the first three—responsible government, free and fair competition, and full and equal rights of political participation—are what are needed nowadays to be an electoral democracy (as opposed to an autocracy). One of the main international texts laying out these factors is the 1990 Copenhagen Document of the then-Conference on Security and Co-operation in Europe. The Appendix to this chapter gives in full the key article here as a detailed "check list" of the components of electoral democracy. That said, if one goes back (far enough) into history, all electoral democracies in terms of the first two elements would have lacked the third element of "one (adult) person one vote." Consequently, in Chapter 9 we shall introduce the qualified notion of a "moderately inclusive electoral democracy."

POLITICAL REGIMES IN THE WORLD TODAY (END 2004)

Even if there is a tendency for most, if not all, of the five elements of liberal democracy to go together, they are conceptually and empirically separate. In particular, we have noted that civil liberties can exist under autocracy. Thus, just as we can distinguish liberal democracies from electoral democracies, we can distinguish what we shall call *semi-liberal autocracies*, with some civil liberties from *closed autocracies*, which have none or next to none. The term "semi-liberal" as opposed to simply "liberal" is used to connote the fact that in semi-liberal autocracies we are talking about fewer civil liberties than in a liberal democracy or, indeed, in most electoral democracies.

Table 3.2 outlines four regime types in decreasing levels of democracy from left to right. Consequently, a liberal democracy is the most democratic regime type, whereas a closed autocracy is the least; indeed, a closed autocracy is the antithesis of democracy. Electoral democracies and semi-liberal autocracies fall between these two extremes, having some to most civil liberties but lacking the full civil liberties and, in particular, the strong rule of law found in liberal democracies. Again, though, the key distinction between an electoral democracy and a semi-liberal autocracy is that in the former the government can be voted out and thereby replaced whereas in the latter it effectively cannot. The concept of a semi-liberal autocracy is in effect what Ottaway refers to as "semi-authoritarianism." As she notes:

> The most important characteristic of semi-authoritarian regimes is the existence and persistence of mechanisms that effectively prevent the transfer of power through elections from the hands of the incumbent leaders or party to a new political elite or organization. It is the existence of such mechanisms that makes the term *semi-authoritarian* more appropriate than any that contains the word *democracy*—if power cannot be transferred by elections, there is little point in describing a country as democratic, even with qualifiers. These mechanisms for blocking power transfers function despite the existence of formally democratic institutions and the degree of political freedom granted to the citizens of the country. Semi-authoritarian states [semi-liberal autocracies] may have a rea-

TABLE 3.2 :: DEMOCRACIES AND AUTOCRACIES AS REGIME TYPES

	LIBERAL DEMOCRACY	ELECTORAL DEMOCRACY
POLITICAL PARTIES AND ELECTIONS AND OVERALL POLITICAL OPPOSITION	Free and fair competition involving two or more parties; citizens can change their government through elections; an open and usually strong political opposition.	Two or more parties exist; open political opposition; citizens can change their government through elections, but elections are sometimes not completely free and fair.
SOCIO-ECONOMIC PLURALISM	Many autonomous actors in economy and broader society (of course not all have equal political influence).	Often quite extensive social and economic pluralism.
CIVIL LIBERTIES	Full civil liberties.	Civil liberties are usually incomplete if not indeed limited.
IDEOLOGY	Emphasis on rule of law, individualism, and minority rights.	Usually no formal guiding ideology.
MOBILIZATION	Participation largely generated autonomously by civil society and by competing parties.	Participation largely generated autonomously by civil society and by competing parties.
LEGITIMACY OF AUTHORITY	Legitimacy comes from legal-rational authority, even if some leaders may be aided by their personal charisma.	Legitimacy usually comes from legal-rational authority, although the processes are imperfect.
CONSTRAINTS ON AUTHORITY	Clearly constrained by the constitution, the courts and the rule of law, a professional bureaucracy, and socio-political pluralism.	Clearly constrained by the constitution; only somewhat constrained by the courts and the rule of law, the bureaucracy, and socio-political pluralism.
POLITICAL ACCOUNTABIL-ITY TO POPULATION	Definite political accountability to the voters at elections and to society in a ongoing sense.	General political accountability to the voters at elections and to society in a ongoing sense.
LEADERSHIP DURATION	Leaders must subject themselves to periodic free and fair elections; transitions are legitimate and smooth.	Certain political leaders must subject themselves to periodic elections; tutelary actors shielded from this.
TRANSITION TO (LIBERAL) DEMOCRACY		Usually a gradual removal of selected remaining barriers.

Source: Based in part on Juan J. Linz and Alfred Stepan, *Problems of Democratic Transition and Consolidation: Southern Europe, South America, and Post-Communist Europe* (Baltimore, MD: The Johns Hopkins University Press, 1996) Table 3.1 and 4.2, with modifications.

SEMI-LIBERAL AUTOCRACY	CLOSED AUTOCRACY
Usually more than one party; limited political pluralism and consequent political opposition; however, national elections are not free and fair enough to actually change the government (or do not determine the government).	Either one official party or all parties are forbidden, although political independents can sometimes be elected if not openly anti-regime.
Some social and economic pluralism, perhaps predating the autocratic regime.	No significant social pluralism; usually some economic and religious pluralism.
Civil liberties are limited or at best incomplete.	No or next to no civil liberties.
No formal guiding ideology; at best distinctive tendencies.	No formal guiding ideology; at best distinctive tendencies; usually nationalistic.
Participation largely generated autonomously by civil society, but with some restrictions.	Emphasis on demobilization, except at some historical points.
Wide range of legitimizing factors, including the illusion of legal-rational authority.	Legitimacy comes from tradition and/or claims of acting in the national interest.
Constrained only somewhat (if at all) by the constitution, courts, the rule of law, and/or the bureaucracy; constrained more by socio-political pluralism, especially the independent media.	A leader or perhaps a small group enjoys legally undefined limits but in fact is (are) somewhat constrained by the bureaucracy, the military, and/or economic actors.
No true political accountability.	No political accountability.
Individual leaders may well be of limited duration; often elections to "confirm" new leader however produced.	Leadership usually for life unless overthrown.
A variety of scenarios; however, a stable negotiated transition can occur in competitive autocratic regimes with developed civil societies.	Needs to go first through a semi-liberal autocratic phase with some socio-political pluralism, unless defeat in war and resulting occupation by foreign power(s) willing to democratize.

sonably free press. The regime may leave space for autonomous organizations of civil society to operate, for private businesses to grow and thus for new economic elites to arise. The regime may hold fairly open elections for local or regional governments or even allow backbenchers from the government party to be defeated in elections. ... [However,] there is no way to challenge [successfully] the power of the incumbents. At the center, competition is a fiction; even if elections are held, outsiders are not allowed to truly challenge the power of the incumbents. Elections are not the source of the government's power [even if so claimed for the purposes of legitimization], and thus voters cannot transfer power to a new leadership.[22]

Table 3.3 classifies all of the countries of the world into the four regime types listed in Table 3.2 as of the end of 2004. First, there are now 65 cases of liberal democracy, making this the largest of the four groups. Within this group is a subset of countries in which political and bureaucratic corruption is clearly minimal and conversely where there is a very high integrity of state personnel. This subset is based on largely impressionistic distinctions, however, and is thus for interest rather than a definition distinction. Next, there are 51 countries which are electoral democracies without being liberal democracies.[23] Elections are still central for determining who has the power, but the countries lack full civil liberties and/or a clear rule of law. A few of these electoral democracies (for example, Guatemala, Peru, and Turkey) also have incomplete civilian control over their militaries. Liechtenstein is classified here due to the continuing real political power of its Grand Duke, a fact recently made explicit in its constitutional revision of 2003. Next are 42 semi-liberal autocracies. These include Singapore, which will be discussed in Chapter 8. Singapore is known for an efficient, uncorrupt bureaucracy, but the country remains dominated by a People's Action Party (PAP) that maintains power in part by harassing and intimidating what limited political opposition exists. Another semi-liberal autocracy, Monaco (where the government—led by a French national civil servant—is accountable to the Prince but not to the freely and fairly elected legislature) is worth noting for its "liberal" amount of civil liberties, which is certainly higher than (almost) all electoral democracies. A similar point can be made for Tonga.

TABLE 3.3 :: DEMOCRACIES AND AUTOCRACIES AS OF THE END OF 2004
(total of 192 regimes)

LIBERAL DEMOCRACIES (N = 65) with very high integrity of state personnel where a "+"

Andorra	Estonia	Lithuania	Samoa
Australia +	Finland +	Luxembourg +	San Marino
Austria +	France +	Malta	Slovakia
Bahamas +	Germany +	Marshall Islands	Slovenia
Barbados +	Ghana	Mauritius	South Africa
Belgium +	Greece	Micronesia	Spain +
Belize	Grenada	Nauru	Suriname
Benin	Guyana	Netherlands +	Sweden +
Botswana	Hungary	New Zealand +	Switzerland +
Canada +	Iceland +	Norway +	Taiwan
Cape Verde	Ireland +	Palau	Tuvalu
Chile +	Israel	Poland	United Kingdom +
Costa Rica	Italy	Portugal	United States +
Cyprus	Japan	Saint Kitts and Nevis	Uruguay
Czech Republic	Kiribati	Saint Lucia	Vanuatu
Denmark +	Korea, South	Saint Vincent & the	
Dominica	Latvia	Grenadines	

ELECTORAL DEMOCRACIES (N = 51)

Albania	Guatemala	Moldova	São Tomé and Príncipe
Antigua and Barbuda	Honduras	Mongolia	Senegal
Argentina	India	Mozambique	Serbia and Montenegro
Bangladesh	Indonesia	Namibia	Seychelles
Bolivia	Jamaica	Nicaragua	Sierra Leone
Brazil	Kenya	Niger	Solomon Islands
Bulgaria	Lesotho	Nigeria	Sri Lanka
Colombia	Liechtenstein	Panama	Thailand
Croatia	Macedonia	Papua New Guinea	Timor-Leste (East Timor)
Dominican Republic	Madagascar	Paraguay	Trinidad and Tobago
Ecuador	Malawi	Peru	Turkey
El Salvador	Mali	Philippines	Venezuela
Georgia	Mexico	Romania	

SEMI-LIBERAL AUTOCRACIES (N = 42) with very high integrity of state personnel where a "+"

Afghanistan	Chad	Ivory Coast	Qatar
Algeria	Comoros	Jordan	Russia
Angola	Congo, R (Brazzaville)	Kuwait	Singapore +
Armenia	Djibouti	Lebanon	Tanzania
Bahrain	Ethiopia	Malaysia	Tonga
Bhutan	Fiji	Maldives	Uganda
Bosnia-Herzegovina	Gabon	Mauritania	Ukraine
Burkina Faso	Gambia	Monaco	Yemen
Cambodia	Guinea-Bissau	Morocco	Zambia
Cameroon	Iran	Nepal	
Central African Republic	Iraq	Pakistan	

continues...

CLOSED AUTOCRACIES (N = 34)

Azerbaijan	Equatorial Guinea	Libya	Togo
Belarus	Eritrea	Oman	Tunisia
Brunei	Guinea	Rwanda	Turkmenistan
Burma/Myanmar	Haiti	Saudi Arabia	United Arab Emirates
Burundi	Kazakhstan	Somalia	Uzbekistan
China	Korea, North	Sudan	Vietnam
Congo, DR (Kinshasa)	Kyrgyzstan	Swaziland	Zimbabwe
Cuba	Laos	Syria	
Egypt	Liberia	Tajikistan	

Finally, there are 34 cases of closed autocracies, the smallest numerically of the four categories. Overall, the first two categories combined give us 116 of the world's 192 regimes, or 60 per cent. This is certainly an encouraging breadth of democratization. On the other hand, only about a third of the world's regimes are liberal democracies, and there does not seem to be the prospect of a vast increase in their number. (Chapter 10 will analyze the prospects for more, or fewer, democracies in the world.)

To repeat, this list is the way the countries line up as of the end of 2004. Obviously, if one goes back a period of time, such a list will be somewhat different. For example, South Africa was a semi-liberal, racially based autocracy before 1994 and its transition to democracy. Mexico was also a semi-liberal autocracy through the early 1990s, inasmuch as national elections were clearly not free and fair. They got "better" starting in the 1970s, but even as late as 1988 there was a presidential election in which most independent observers assume that the votes and vote totals were doctored to produce a win for Carlos Salinas, the candidate of the ruling Institutional Revolutionary Party (PRI). However, by the 1990s—in part due to an independent electoral commission established by constitutional reform in 1990 and made fully autonomous from the executive in 1996—Mexican elections were increasingly free and fair, culminating in the victory of Vincente Fox of the opposition PAN in the 2000 presidential election. On the other hand, both Egypt and Zimbabwe were semi-liberal autocracies in the late 1990s, but in both the regime has cut back on political openness and eliminated civil liberties, making both closed autocracies as of the early 2000s.

BEYOND LIBERAL DEMOCRACY?

Despite the fact that only a minority of regimes worldwide are liberal democracies, one can argue (especially if one lives in such a system) that political systems can still do better in some way(s). We have already noted that democracies function indirectly, in that elected representatives make the decisions. So one way in which a system could go beyond liberal democracy is to have (more) *direct democracy*, in which the population as a whole makes the decision on specific issues. This, in fact, is done for most controversial issues in Switzerland. It is also done at the state level in parts of the United States, especially its Western states (most notably Oregon and California). However, since direct democracy is rarely combined with compulsory voting, the "population as a whole" in fact boils down to whoever shows up to vote, and in Switzerland this is normally less than 50 per cent, meaning basically the better-off and more educated voters. Moreover, referenda on policy issues often involve large sums of money being spent to sway the voters, and it is no surprise that most of the time the side with more money is the victorious one.

A more substantive (but still hardly universal) critique of liberal democracy is that it is focussed on political *procedures* and not *policy outcomes*; in other words, it may involve accountable, competitive, and procedurally fair government, but there is no guarantee that the policies produced by such a government are substantively equal to everybody, for example, in providing equal access to health care and education.[24] In this vein, Huber, Rueschemeyer, and Stephens distinguish between formal and social democracy, the latter involving high levels of political participation across all social categories (what they call separately participatory democracy) and "increasing equality in social and economic outcomes." For them, the key factors leading from formal democracy to social democracy are working-class organization in terms of political parties, trade unions, and peasant leagues, as well as an effective state which is autonomous from the dominant socio-economic interests. These combine to produce the welfare state policies which are central to social democracy.[25] Of course, a list of such social democracies would be rather brief and largely drawn from Northern Europe—in short, a tiny subset of all democracies or even of all liberal democracies.

THE COPENHAGEN DOCUMENT

The Organization for Security and Co-operation in Europe (OSCE), previously the Conference on Security and Co-operation in Europe (CSCE), groups together the countries of Europe, (post-Soviet) Central Asia, and Canada and the United States. On 29 June 1990 the member states adopted the Document of the Copenhagen Meeting of the Conference on the Human Dimension of the CSCE, more commonly known simply as the Copenhagen Document. Within this document are wide-ranging commitments to democratic practices, including the holding of genuinely free and fair elections, and the willingness to invite CSCE (now OSCE) observers to observe one's own elections so as to enhance democratic electoral processes. Although not phrased as such, this document speaks thoroughly to the concept and various aspects of electoral democracy[26] at the start of Article 6 and especially in Article 7, as follows:

6. The participating States declare that the will of the people, freely and fairly expressed through periodic and genuine elections, is the basis of the authority and legitimacy of all government. ...

7. To ensure that the will of the people serves as the basis of the authority of government, [the] participating States will
    7.1: hold free elections at reasonable intervals, as established by law;
    7.2: permit all seats in at least one chamber of the national legislature to be freely contested in a popular vote;
    7.3: guarantee universal and equal suffrage to all citizens;
    7.4: ensure that votes are cast by secret ballot or by equivalent free voting procedure and that they are counted and reported honestly with the official results made public;
    7.5: respect the rights of citizens to seek political or public office, individually or as representatives of political parties and organizations, without discrimination;
    7.6: respect the rights of citizens and groups to establish, in full freedom, their own political parties or other political organizations and provide such parties and organizations with the necessary legal guarantees to

enable them to compete with each other on a basis of equal treatment before the law and by the authorities;

7.7: ensure that law and public policy work to permit political campaigning to be conducted in a fair and free atmosphere in which neither administrative action, violence nor intimidation bars the parties and the candidates from freely presenting their views and qualifications, or prevents the voters from learning and discussing them or from casting their vote free of fear of retribution;

7.8: provide that no legal or administrative obstacle stands in the way of unimpeded access to the media on a non-discriminatory basis for all political groupings and individuals wishing to participate in the electoral process;

7.9: ensure that candidates who obtain the necessary number of votes required by law are duly installed in office and are permitted to remain in office until their term expires or is otherwise brought to an end in a manner that is regulated by law in conformity with democratic parliamentary and constitutional procedures.

NOTES

1 On direct democracy in Switzerland see Wolf Linder, *Swiss Democracy: Possible Solutions to Conflict in Multicultural Societies*, 2nd ed. (Basingstoke, UK: Macmillan, 1998) Chapter 3. More generally, see David Butler and Austin Ranney, *Referendums around the World: The Growing Use of Direct Democracy* (Washington, DC: American Enterprise Institute, 1994).

2 Adam Przeworski, *Democracy and the Market: Political and Economic Reforms in Eastern Europe and Latin America* (New York, NY: Cambridge University Press, 1991) 10.

3 Przeworski 10.

4 Joseph A. Schumpeter, *Capitalism, Socialism, and Democracy*, 3rd ed. (New York, NY: Harper and Brothers, 1950) 269.

5 Schumpeter 271.

6 Schumpeter 271–72.

7 There are some exceptions here. The United States House of Representatives is elected every two years, and national elections in Australia and New Zealand must be held at least every three years. On the other hand, some Latin American presidents are, or have been, elected for six-year terms.

8 Terry Lynn Karl, "Electoralism," *International Encyclopedia of Elections*, ed. Richard Rose (Washington, DC: CQ Press, 2000) 95. See also Philippe C. Schmitter and Terry Lynn Karl, "What Democracy Is ... and Is Not," *Journal of Democracy* 2:3 (1991): 78; Terry Lynn Karl, "The Hybrid Regimes of Central America," *Journal of Democracy* 6:3 (1995): 72–86.

9 Larry Diamond, *Developing Democracy: Toward Consolidation* (Baltimore, MD: Johns Hopkins University Press, 1999) 10–11.

10 David Collier and Steven Levitsky, "Democracy With Adjectives: Conceptual Innovation in Comparative Research," *World Politics* 49:3 (April 1997): 443.

11 J. Samuel Valenzuela, "Democratic Consolidation in Post-Transitional Settings: Notion, Process, and Facilitating Conditions," *Issues in Democratic Consolidation: The New South American Democracies in Comparative Perspective*, ed. Scott Mainwaring, Guillermo O'Donnell, and J. Samuel Valenzuela (Notre Dame, IN: University of Notre Dame Press, 1992) 62-63.

12 Jørgen Elklit and Palle Svensson, "What Makes Elections Free and Fair?," *Journal of Democracy* 8:3 (July 1997): 35–37.

13 Rafael López-Pintor, *Electoral Management Bodies as Institutions of Governance* (New York, NY: Bureau for Development Policy, United Nations Development Program, 2000).

14 André Blais, Louis Massicotte, and Antoine Yoshinaka, "Deciding Who has the Right to Vote: A Comparative Analysis of Election Laws," *Electoral Studies* 20:1 (2001): 43–51.

15 Angus Maddison, *The World Economy: A Millennial Perspective* (Paris, FR: OECD, 2001) 30.

16 Richard S. Katz, *Democracy and Elections* (New York, NY: Oxford University Press, 1997) 231.

17 Stein Rokkan, *Citizens, Elections, Parties: Approaches to the Comparative Study of the Processes of Development* (New York, NY: David McKay and Oslo: Universitetsforlaget, 1970) 148–49.

18 Dahl, *Polyarchy* 2–4.

19 Carl Schmitt, *Verfassungslehre* (1928; Berlin: Duncker and Humblot, 1970) 130, as translated by and quoted in Rune Slagstad, "Liberal Constitutionalism and its Critics: Carl Schmitt and Max Weber," *Constitutionalism and Democracy*, ed. Jon Elster and Rune Slagstad (Cambridge, UK: Cambridge University Press and Oslo: Norwegian University Press, 1988) 106.

20 Juan J. Linz and Alfred Stepan, "Toward Consolidated Democracies," *Journal of Democracy* 7:2 (April 1996): 19.

21 To be more precise, Transparency International ranks countries in terms of *perceived* levels of corruption.

22 Marina Ottaway, *Democracy Challenged: The Rise of Semi-Authoritarianism* (Washington, DC: Carnegie Endowment for International Peace, 2003) 15; italics in original.

23 In early 2005, subsequent to this classification, Ukraine also became (again) an electoral democracy.

24 Howard Handelman, *The Challenge of Third World Development*, 3rd ed. (Upper Saddle River, NJ: Prentice Hall, 2003) 28.

25 Evelyne Huber, Dietrich Rueschemeyer, and John D. Stephens, "The Paradoxes of Contemporary Democracy: Formal, Participatory, and Social Dimensions," *Comparative Politics* 29:3 (April 1997): 324.

26 The main aspect of electoral democracy not explicitly mentioned in this list is the elimination or prevention of tutelary powers exercised by a monarch or the military. Of course, such tutelary powers are not really an issue in contemporary Europe or Central Asia.

CHAPTER FOUR

The Military in Politics

IN THIS CHAPTER YOU WILL LEARN:

» *why the role of the military is a particular challenge for modern states;*
» *that civilian control over the military has been a challenge in most every region of the world;*
» *why national militaries intervene into politics;*
» *how the level of national political culture relates to the (il)legitimacy and thus the likelihood of military intervention;*
» *how countries can increase their civilian control over the military; and*
» *how civil-military relations vary on a continuum, and how this contiuum relates to (liberal) democracy.*

THE BASIC PROBLEM

As noted, both monarchies and the military are actors that can potentially invalidate responsible government. However, whereas there is no absolute "need" to be a monarchy as opposed to a republic, most countries feel that they require some sort of military force for national protection. The resulting trade-off has been made clear by Muthiah Alagappa, who comments that "the central paradox of the modern state is how to create a military strong enough to protect the nation-state from external and internal threats but at the same time prevent it from dominating the state or becoming an instrument for internal repression."[1] Richard H. Kohn seconds this view, noting that "the purpose of the military is to defend society, not define it."[2]

In a modern democracy, not only should there be institutional separation between the military and other parts of government, but the military must be subordinate to the state and civil authorities must have legitimate control over the means of forcible coercion; in other words, there must be civilian control over the military. By civilians we mean all organizations and individuals that are not attached to the military, including the majority of the state administrative structure and civil society. Civilian control is thus generally defined as governments and their agencies having the authority to determine the organization, resources, and purpose of the armed forces without threat of military interference.[3] Civilian control and military influence are consequently two sides of the same issue and are often measured by plotting their relationship with each other along the spectrum of a continuum, as we shall do in the final section of this chapter, "Measuring Civil-Military Relations."

Felipe Agüero, however, downplays the term "civilian control," suggesting that it indicates some potential for "antagonistic relations" between the two actors.[4] The armed forces, presumably, have behaved in some fashion that not only requires checks and balances to be imposed by the civilian regime but also requires constant civilian intervention in military affairs to ensure harmonious relations between the two actors. Instead of the term civilian control, Agüero recommends that social scientists use the term "civilian supremacy" in their analyses; in fact, we shall use both (with supremacy the stronger category) in our continuum below. Specifically, Agüero defines **civilian supremacy** as the "ability of a civilian, democratically elected, government to conduct general policy without interference from the military, to define the goals and general organization of national defense, to formulate and conduct defense policy, and to monitor the implementation of military policy."[5]

Ideally, the civilian supremacy model requires non-military decision-makers to determine such things as the military's function or purpose, its extent and composition, its allocation of resources, and its involvement in domestic politics and foreign affairs (including war and defence). While the military may retain jurisdiction in determining its own professional functions, it must necessarily be under the policy control of civilian authorities and remain subordinate to the rule of law. The military must be subordinate not only to executive politicians like the president or prime minister but to the entire structure of government.[6]

Lyle N. McAlister points out that all armed forces (even those traditionally controlled by civilians) are political to some degree. Consequently, he defines military intervention as "the armed forces or parts thereof deliberately participating in governmental processes for purposes transcending legitimate service interests."[7] Military intervention ranges from brief and limited military incursions into civilian affairs to complete military control of the state. As we shall see, states themselves vary from democracies with long histories of civilian supremacy to others where the military has customarily dominated society and those that have yet to develop any institutional apparatus for restraining the armed forces from political activities.

EXPLANATIONS FOR MILITARY INTERVENTION

There are a number of factors that can be used to explain military intervention. Welch and Smith divide such explanations into internal factors (such as the political awareness of the armed forces, its mission, and its organizational characteristics stemming from its structural differentiation, functional specialization, autonomy, cohesion, and professionalism) and external or environmental factors (such as those arising from social, economic, and/or political variables).[8] Similarly, Jack Child distinguishes between "push" and "pull" factors leading to military intervention. Push factors come from within, inciting the military to greater political activism. These factors include basic needs for expanding the institution, feelings of responsibility for maintaining order and teaching social and moral values to civilians, cleavages within the military that spill over into domestic politics, and personal ambitions by individuals or small groups within the military. Pull factors come from without, and include such things as invitation (where civilian authorities invite the military in as a means of balancing or maintaining power), threats by external and internal enemies (subversion), interference (on the part of civilians involving themselves in military affairs), and self-protection (if the military feels that its institutional values are under attack).[9]

That said, however, we can and shall analyze the main reasons for military intervention into (civil) governance in terms of six main areas: (1) the degree of the military's professionalism; (2) the historical character and related ideology of the military's missions and roles; (3) the strength—or weakness—of national political institutions; (4) the military's position relative to those political institutions in terms of protecting its corporate interests; (5) general government performance; and last but not least (6) the overall political culture of the society. Some of these points will be reiterated later on in Chapter 9 with regards to democratic breakdowns.

First of all, the degree of military professionalism is one of the earliest theories explaining military intervention, going back to Huntington's work in the 1950s.[10] Professionalism assumes that the armed forces have developed some expertise in the form of specialized training, a hierarchical system of command and advancement, their own norms of behaviour, and an ethical code that promotes political and social responsibility.[11] Herbert M. Howe stresses that professional militaries respect state institutions; that is, they remain subject to civil authority and the rule of law, tolerate ethnic and ideological diversity, accept human rights, and are apolitical, refraining from intervening in politics.[12]

In contrast, Howe reports on the lack of professionalism in many African armies, noting they are composed of the "unemployed and unemployable [and] poorly educated young men [who] join for the opportunity to 'eat, drink, [and take a] look.'"[13] He warns that the unprofessional nature of African militaries—specifically, their lack of technical expertise and lack of responsibility to the state—may contribute to the instability of the regime.[14] He adds that the lack of discipline, compounded by the irregularity of pay, often leads to corruption and low morale. This corruption usually takes the form of appropriating defence funds for personal gains, making patronage purchases in return for personal rewards (such as financial kickbacks or outright selling of military hardware purchased with public funds to the highest private bidder), making patronage appointments to prominent positions, and/or overlooking human rights abuses by people under their command.

88

That said, the predominance of personal rule—what we shall later call **sultanistic regimes**—in Africa but also elsewhere is central to the existence of unprofessional militaries, since such regimes are shaped by the ruler's personal preferences rather than by any codified system of laws or principles of professional hierarchies. Yet we should not generalize about all of Africa. For example, the Nigerian military is based on the British military tradition, with key leadership positions held historically by Africans with extensive training in the former mother country. Of course, Nigeria has never been sultanistic. However, in noting the professionalism of the Nigerian armed forces, Auma-Osolo explicitly rejects Huntington's thesis, pointing to the numerous coups and coup attempts in that country.[15]

Professionalism, in fact, is just as likely to result in military intervention as to prevent it.[16] Soldiers often see themselves as "highly competent, dedicated professionals whose superior training and technical skills ... make them far more competent governors than the incumbents."[17] Professionally competent militaries can see fit to intervene in civilian regimes, with goals ranging from maintaining security (such as eliminating subversion), promoting development (via economic growth and nation-building), or simply maintaining stability (by purging corruption and incompetence). The military in this manner sees itself as apolitical: existing above the political process, acting as guardians of the state.[18] In cases where the armed forces have "stepped in" to regulate the state, Auma-Osolo notes that they may delay returning the reins to civilians under the pretext that civilians are "corrupt, inconsiderate to the rest of the citizenry and therefore incompetent to rule."[19]

A second and more decisive reason for military intervention is its historical missions and roles and resulting ideology. Military institutions have their own pasts, meaning that their "central characteristics [are] shaped in response to longer term influences and past events."[20] There is a wide spectrum here, from countries that "have virtually no indigenous military traditions" to those that "have grand military traditions going back more than a thousand years."[21] Brian Loveman points out that a "tutelary-guardianship" role for the military can originate from its "historical mission" to ensure that progress and the rule of law are maintained.[22] Michael C. Desch adds that military missions shape the pattern of civil-military relations based on the definition of the military's key tasks.[23] These tasks may be conflict-oriented, such as fighting external wars or suppressing internal subversion, or they may be non-military roles such as (internal or external) nation-building, providing social welfare and humanitarian relief (these have essentially become the tasks of the Canadian military, for example) which are presumably less likely to lead to an interventionist mentality.

Traditionally, the colonial military mission in South America included internal order as well as external defence, and historically it was used to suppress indigenous resistance to colonization and disperse demonstrations. The "burden" of internal security increased the scope of the military's professional action, changing the relationship between the state and the military by challenging the legitimacy of civilian government. It represented a permanently politicized military that manipulated the state to control civil society, ensuring national security and national well-being.[24] Similarly, African politicians have traditionally relied on their armed forces to maintain order and stability, often licensing them to apply coercion and violence as necessary. Civilian governments in Africa routinely employ military force to suppress political opponents, put down student demonstrations, or disrupt labour strikes.[25]

The military's perceived role as "guardians of the state" may have evolved into a guiding ideology at some point in its history. The doctrine of "Atatürkism" in Turkey, for example, has underpinned the Turkish military's politicized history and its longstanding ideological belief that it retains the authority to check civilian leadership. Military ideology need not be right-wing overall; for example, Peru was governed by a leftist military after 1968. Such relative ideologies may be a function of the level of national development. As Huntington points out, "the more backward a society is, the more progressive the role of its military; the more advanced a society becomes, the more conservative and reactionary becomes the role of its military."[26]

The armed forces may also justify their actions by citing links between themselves and authorities "higher" than the government, such as the constitution or a monarchical head of state.[27] In many Latin American nations, the military "duty" to maintain (domestic) order was and often still is entrenched in the constitution.[28] Even when not specifically empowered by the constitution, a national military may perceive itself as the interpreter of the constitution and reproach—or remove—governments that it perceives to be in violation of said constitution. For example, based on its reading of Brazil's 1946 constitution, the Brazilian military felt that it was to obey the president only when he was acting "within limits of the law."[29] With regards to "higher" links to a monarch, a good example is the Thai military, which historically acted as a defender of the monarchy and subsequently developed a code of ethics that restrained it from accepting full civilian supremacy. In more modern times, Thailand's armed forces have also been "mission orientated" towards promoting democracy (in their sense) and modernization, as well as defending against Communism and other potential enemies of the state.[30]

Institutional factors—that is, the strength of institutions—are a third reason for military intervention into civilian affairs. In his study of Thailand's modernization, Fred Riggs noted that military intervention is a function of unbalanced institutional development.[31] When the institutions for bureaucratic and military action are more developed than those for (mass) participation and governance—or particularly when the latter political institutions fail—the military and bureaucracy are "compelled" to intervene. Military control is a likely occurrence following the build-up of its power relative to other state institutions and society. Once in power, the military can maintain its power by "curtailing, destroying or mobilizing alternative centers of power and embarking on a state-building role with the intent of penetrating, controlling, and directing all other state agencies."[32] For their part, civilian institutions can undermine themselves by enlisting the aid of the military to (help) maintain public order and even promote national development, presumably when and where the civilian institutions are inadequate to these ends. When armed forces have autonomous jurisdiction over important aspects of state activity (such as internal security, economic policy, and revenue collection), this prevents full democracy.

A fourth reason for military intervention can be seen in the military's protection of its own institutional position. Alagappa suggests that the military's degrees of corporate structure and bureaucratic development are strong determinants of its propensity to intervene in civilian affairs.[33] The corporate interests of the armed forces include control over organization, internal security, intelligence gathering, recruitment, doctrine, training, promotions, salaries, and procurement of arms—many of the traits characterized by Huntington's conceptualization of professionalism. More generally, institutions will characteristically act in self-preservation: defending their interests; promoting their right to autonomy, adequate funding, and responsibility; and acting to safeguard the continuity of the institution itself. The military is no different in this regard. While it is generally accepted that, by nature of its specialization, the military has expertise and autonomy in certain areas, Pion-Berlin identifies "overlapping decision sites" between civil authorities and the military, and warns that corporate autonomy and military submission may be inversely proportional.[34] The greater the autonomy of the armed forces, the more likely that it will defend its interests from civilian interference. Likewise, the lower a military's level of autonomy, the greater its submission to civilian authority. In this regard, an autonomous military may have—and fight to preserve—military-controlled economic resources, such as raw materials or at least the revenue from these, manufacturing plants, and even (in Burma/Myanmar) department stores!

Weak civilian governments may attempt to prevent potential coups by appeasing the military, allowing them significant autonomy. In other words, in exchange for basic (conditional) political subordination, civil authorities will refrain from attempting to impose further reform in a compromise. Stronger civilian leaders, however, often seek to strengthen their position by influencing or controlling outright the promotions and appointments of politically loyal or neutral officers to senior military positions. As a consequence, the military may assert itself to protect its corporate interests, defying civilian and constitutional supremacy.[35] Latin America has provided numerous cases where the military has acted to resist restructuring and protect senior officers from being persecuted for human rights abuses. More generally, a "veto coup" occurs when the military intervenes to prevent changes that it perceives as detrimental to its interests.[36] For a recent example, after several instances of interference in the operational and policy-making affairs of the Pakistani national army (specifically the attempts to replace its leading General Musharraf), the civilian authorities were overthrown in 1999 under the pretext of "corruption and incompetence."[37]

Performance failures of civilian governments are often cited as one of the main justifications for military intervention; as noted, they are our fifth factor.[38] Nordlinger lists such failures as bureaucratic corruption, unconstitutional and illegal behaviour (such as arbitrarily altering or ignoring laws and wielding excessive power), inability to deal with faltering economies, apparent helplessness in handling political opposition (which often results in public disorder), or even relying upon coercive measures to maintain power.[39] The 1991 coup in Thailand, for example, was justified as the only means to "clean up the political system, remove corrupt politicians, and return to purified democracy."[40] More in keeping with defence matters strictly speaking, military interventions have frequently been justified by the government's powerlessness to resolve internal and/or international security problems.

Conversely, where civilian governments are associated not with performance failures but performance successes, the military is likely to lack objective reasons for intervention. In a broader sense, coups and coup attempts have been less likely in countries with higher economic development. This may be simply because economic development tends to produce social mobilization that checks and/or reduces the military's political role (see below). However, economic development is not an empirically *sufficient* condition for civilian control—Argentina presents, perhaps, the classic case of the occurrence of military coups in a socially and economically developed society. This paradox leads us to our sixth and final factor, the issue of a country's political culture.

POLITICAL CULTURE AND MILITARY INTERVENTION

Alagappa suggests that countries with high levels of political culture are less prone to military intervention.[41] In Chapter 2 we noted how countries vary in terms of their political cultures, specifically as to what is considered legitimate decision-making behaviour. In this vein, would a military coup ever be considered legitimate? Not according to either traditional or legal-rational authority, but perhaps according to charismatic authority if the coup leader possessed this. Usually, though, military coups are staged by rather "faceless" generals. The issue becomes the inverse, that is, whether a military coup would be seen as particularly *illegitimate*. To this end, Finer argues that national political cultures can be assessed and ranked in levels, according to the following three criteria:

» Does there exist a wide public approval of the procedures for transferring [political] power, and a corresponding belief that no exercise of power in breach of these procedures is legitimate?

» Does there exist a wide public recognition as to who or what constitutes the sovereign authority, and a corresponding belief that no other persons or centre of power is legitimate or duty-worthy?

» Is the public proportionality large and well-mobilized into private associations? Do we find cohesive churches, industrial associations and firms, labour unions, and political parties [that are capable of acting independently of the state]?[42]

The higher a nation ranks on the first two criteria, the more likely it is that a military coup (or any other seizure of power) would be seen as illegitimate. The higher a nation ranks on the third criteria—essentially what can be called the level of civil society—the more society can mobilize itself in defence of the legitimate holders of power. Consequently, the strength of social mobilization (civil support) for civilian structures, leaders, and policies acts as a deterrent to military action by increasing the costs of intervention and reducing the military's bargaining power. Short of a fully revolutionary situation, military interventions would be limited somewhat by the prospect of large-scale civil-military conflict. Thus, the massive mobilization of opposition would undermine or ideally prevent military intervention.[43]

Finer goes further and outlines four categories of national political culture: mature, developed, low, and minimal.[44] (Note that "developed" is not the highest term here.) In countries with a *mature political culture*, such as Canada, the United States, or Northwest Europe, a military coup is simply unthinkable, even by the military itself. If one were actually tried, it would have no legitimacy. In countries with a *developed political culture*, although there is an established civil society, there is also some question or dispute as to how power should be transferred and who or what should be the legitimate sovereign authority. In cases of a developed political culture, such as Weimar Germany or the French Fourth Republic, a military coup is in fact thinkable but would be broadly resisted by well-mobilized associations (although presumably not so broadly as in a mature political culture). Thus, with a developed political culture a military coup certainly may be tried or threatened, but it would be most unlikely to succeed (fully). For example, the Kapp *putsch* of March 1920 in Germany failed—although it did cause the government to flee Berlin—and was ultimately abandoned in the face of widespread strikes in support of the Republic. In Spain in February 1981, only a few years after democratization and in the midst of political instability, rebel civil guards seized the *Cortes* (parliament), holding the deputies at gunpoint for 36 hours. The rebels hoped others on the far right would rally to their cause of reversing democracy. Instead, there was widespread public revulsion and an effective condemnation of the uprising by King Juan Carlos. The uprising was quickly thwarted. In August 1991 in the Soviet Union, selected hard-line Communists and generals staged a coup to overthrow Mikhail Gorbachev. Gorbachev was placed under house arrest for a couple of days, but there were public demonstrations against the coup (led by Russian President Boris Yeltsin, who escaped capture), and most of the military did not support it. The "August putsch," as it was known, fizzled out after three days. Of course, it probably did not help the coup leaders that they were drunk when they addressed the country on television!

In countries with a *low political culture*, such as in much of Latin America during the twentieth century and still today in places like Pakistan, no governing system is seen as unquestioningly legitimate; that is, there is an ongoing dispute regarding political institutions and procedures. The level of civic mobilization is moderate to low. In such countries, coups have not only been frequent but usually successful—provided that there are issues, even short-term ones, which produce dissatisfaction with the civilian government (as discussed above). In countries with a *minimal political culture*, such as in much of Latin America during the nineteenth century or places in Central Africa, political structures lack such institutionalization, and society is so localized and unorganized that legitimacy is not really a relevant concept. Coups occur without any broader justification or resistance. Finally, Finer notes that kinship societies with *traditional monarchies* constitute a largely historical fifth class, one in which the monarchical structure has legitimacy but there is no civic organization. Presumably, any military forces would act in the name of the ruling dynasty.

Finer's categories are generally comprehensive, but to them we could add cases of, let us say, a *polarized* (intermediate) *political culture*, which has high political mobilization as in the first two categories but which combines this with a *major* dispute about the legitimacy of the regime (or alternate regimes). Such political polarization may well lead to a successful military coup (in the sense of the military seizing power), but to maintain power the military in such mobilized societies will have to repress—to a greater or lesser extent violently—a well-organized and hitherto influential labour movement and/or political left. This was the pattern in the "bureaucratic authoritarian" regimes of the 1960s to the 1980s that occurred mainly in Latin America. Specifically, Munck lists six such regimes that fit this pattern: Argentina from 1966 to 1973 and again from 1976 to 1983, Brazil from 1964 to 1985, Chile from 1973 to 1990, Greece from 1967 to 1974, and Uruguay from 1973 to 1985.[45] Indeed, it was no coincidence that, of these regimes, the two that were less modern in a socio-economic sense—Brazil and Greece—were clearly less repressive than the other cases, where sustained repression, including political "disappearances," were needed to break the left.

In summary, then, the military has difficulty exerting influence when there is high political culture; the government is seen as having a legitimate and moral right to govern; there is high public involvement with high attachments to civil institutions; and there is widespread public approval, legitimacy, and a procedure for transferring power.[46] Kohn offers a warning here, however:

> even in democracies with rich traditions of unbroken civilian dominance, war and security can (and have) become so important in national life and so central to the definition of the state that the military, particularly during or after [said] crisis or war, can use

its expertise or public standing to limit civilian influence into military affairs.[47]

INCREASING CIVILIAN CONTROL OF THE MILITARY

If a country has little effective civilian control over the military, what can it do? We shall divide civilian attempts to increase—or for that matter retain—control over the military into (1) institutional/legal and (2) socialization/reorientation processes. The first strategy for attaining control over a politicized military is through institutional means, such as by making changes to the constitution (explicitly outlining the role of the armed forces *vis-à-vis* the civilian authorities) and establishing institutional balances against the military. Although the military holds a monopoly on armed force, it is assumed (or perhaps hoped) that the rule of law will be respected in light of popular legitimacy. Once democratic rule is gained (or restored) and sufficiently consolidated, the state's constitution and institutional framework can be redefined to limit or eliminate the political role of the military.[48] Portugal, for example, established a legal framework for promoting civilian supremacy by passing the Armed Forces and National Defence Law in 1982, eight years after the start of its democratization.[49]

Another way to establish (and consolidate) civilian control is to create institutions and organizations that will oversee military activities and declare that they defer to the rule of law.[50] Howe notes that independent expertise is important in providing oversight committees with the specialized knowledge necessary to understand the military and facilitate greater dialogue between the armed forces and the civil bureaucracy.[51] Patricio Aylwin, the President of Chile between 1990 and 1994, created the Truth Commission as an agency to improve military accountability.[52] The organization conducted investigations into the various human rights transgressions conducted over the previous two decades under former General Augusto Pinochet. Likewise, the Spanish government established the Joint Chiefs of Staff to improve communications between the civilian government and the military (with hopes that it would be easier to control a single defence ministry rather than separate ones attached to each division of the armed forces).[53] This is a risky tactic, however, as a country's Joint Chiefs have the potential to form a unified force that would not only see itself with new organizational power and a single voice, but also would no longer be under the control of civilians.

Another means of establishing and consolidating civilian supremacy over the military is through a process of socialization and reorientation. This includes modernizing the armed forces (providing it with meaningful pursuits, redefining its mission and roles, and reducing its size) and introducing civilian elements to its command structure. Agüero defines military modernization as the process of moving the military out of a "state of backwardness [and] turning it into an efficient fighting force."[54] The updating of equipment and training protocols alone offers little opportunities for civilians to attain supremacy over the military. Modern equipment amplifies the amount of force that can be brought to bear by the armed forces and does not guarantee subordination. The modernization process also involves shifting missions more specifically to an external defence role, reducing the size of the armed forces, and limiting its resources and influence in the process.

Theoretically, the simplest means of consolidating civilian supremacy is to reduce the size of the armed forces. Kohn notes that, generally, "standing forces should also be kept as small as security permits ... so that the populace will consent to provide the resources, the military will be devoted solely to external defense, and civil-military friction will be reduced."[55] Ways of shrinking the total size of the armed forces include the implementation of ceilings on staffing levels and annual reductions in personnel either through retirement, voluntary reductions, transfers to reserve status, and/or retraining of personnel for alternate career choices—all of which were done in post-Franco Spain.[56]

Participation in international organizations and international opportunities shift the military's attention from domestic politics, thus promoting new missions and roles.[57] African governments, for example, have been experimenting with various approaches to improving the nature and orientation of their militaries, including establishing regional intervention forces, enlisting private security companies, and/or co-opting Western states to educate and participate in joint manoeuvres.[58] (While the practice of sending military officers abroad to be educated in specialized military academies is not new, inviting foreign military officials into one's country to aid in training is beginning to gain popularity.) Organizations such as the African Crisis Response Initiative and the African Center for Strategic Studies increase military professionalism, strengthen civil-military boundaries, and lessen the political pressure for military intervention.[59]

Socialization of the armed forces continues through a process of "civilianization." Civilian supremacy can be achieved not only by removing the military from institutional positions irrelevant to defence planning but by placing civilians within the command and control structure of the armed forces. This is a deliberate process whereby the civilian authorities seek to replace military leaders with non-commissioned ones. Civilianization also involves replacing military intelligence services and security councils with civilian or at least civilian-led ones, as was done in Brazil under President Collor de Mello (1990–92). Participation in international military organizations, such as the North Atlantic Treaty Organization (NATO) and the Western European Union, often introduces civilian elements to the decision-making hierarchy of the armed forces.[60]

The most successful means by which control can be retained over the military is to combine aspects of institutionalization and socialization. Observing the changes in Eastern Europe's civil-military relations after the withdrawal of Soviet dominance, Huntington recorded a broad increase in civilian and parliamentary control. Security doctrines were replaced (including the abolition of the military's internal policing role), military defence ministers were replaced with civilians, and a participatory management style was introduced into the military. The numbers of military forces were downsized, and, presumably as part of a trade-off to prevent any possibility of military protest and armed repercussions, their equipment was modernized.[61]

Despite such advances in civilian control, Child suggests that these factors "make coups more difficult, but not impossible."[62] Certainly avoiding too quick a pattern of such changes may be prudent. For example, the first civilian government after Argentina's most recent democratization was that of President Raul Alfonsin (1983-89). This government passed legislation that redefined the mission of the military, restructured its organization, and placed civilians in charge of its defence bureaus.[63] Additionally—and perhaps going too far too fast—Alfonsin cut the military budgets and persecuted military officers for past involvement in coups and for human rights violations. As a result of his aggressive actions, there was a military backlash that threatened his regime.

Alfonsin's successor as president, Carlos Menem, took office in 1989 when the Argentine military was still politically powerful. While Menem consolidated his position, he allowed the armed forces to maintain their autonomy. Civilian officials drew up security guidelines but allowed the military to determine the details. Menem gradually earned the military's confidence by granting pardons to those officers who had committed past human rights violations. Once clearly established in his presidency, however, he cut expenditures to the armed forces, limited their financial resources, trimmed their acquisitions, and limited their recruitment. To compensate for his actions, he promoted confidence-building measures such as higher education for officers and involvement in international cooperative ventures, such as international peacekeeping and cooperative security organizations.[64]

Finally, at what point is civilian supremacy over the military achieved? Agüero suggests that there are four conditions that must be satisfied before the armed forces can be deemed subordinated.[65] First, there must be some regularity in the sense of repeated practice over time of civilian supremacy. Secondly, the roles and privileges of the military must be codified in the nation's constitution or other primary legal documents. Third, there must not have been any explicit challenges on the part of the military toward civilian authorities for an extended period of time. Finally, the military must demonstrate their subordination by willingly accepting a major civilian decision that was previously refused by a politically active military.

MEASURING CONTEMPORARY CIVIL-MILITARY RELATIONS

Continua remain the commonly accepted practice for measuring the degree of military intervention into a state's political and civilian affairs. While political scientists offer a variety of different continua describing the character of military intervention, these all share a polarization between civilian governance on one side and military governance on the other, with a gradation of different levels

TABLE 4.1 :: THE CONTINUUM OF CIVIL-MILITARY RELATIONS

	Democratic Civil-Military Relations			Autocratic Civil-Military Relations		
	CIVILIAN SUPREMACY	CIVILIAN CONTROL	CONDITIONAL SUBORDINATION	MILITARY TUTELAGE	MILITARY CONTROL	MILITARY RULE
(NUMERICAL SCORE)	10	8	6	4	2	0
Military retains control over security policy	no (but minor influence)	maybe	maybe	yes	yes	yes
Military has control over other policy areas	no	no (but minor influence)	maybe	some	most	most/all
Military perceives a "right" to intervene in times of national crisis	no	no	yes	yes	n/a (de facto)	n/a
Head of government	civilian	civilian	civilian	civilian	civilian	military figurehead
Military defence minister	no	maybe	usually	usually	yes	yes
Other military ministers	no	no	maybe a few some	usually substantial minority	at least a majority	yes, a
Military has ability to appoint/ override civilian positions	no	no	maybe	some	most	most/all
Constitutionally entrenched military powers/prerogatives	no	no	maybe	yes	yes	yes
Military has "own resources"	no	maybe	maybe	yes	yes	yes
Military is accountable for [past] human rights violations	yes	no	no	no	no	no
Military controls its own internal processes	no	yes	yes	yes	yes	yes

of military involvement in between. Although Liebenow notes that "levels of military involvement in domestic politics do not shift gradually between the points on a scale, such tools remain useful for comparative analyses."[66]

Of the various continua that have been outlined and used by scholars to indicate the range of civil-military relations, for our purposes we shall use one largely based on that of Fitch, but with some modifications.[67] In categorizing degrees of military intervention, Fitch uses five degrees of measurement: demo-

101

cratic control, conditional subordination, military tutelage, military control, and military regime. As with the definitions of civilian control/supremacy offered previously, the notion of democratic control insists that the military is fully subordinate and accountable to elected officials as well as to the general rule of law. Conditional subordination exists when the military enjoys greater institutional autonomy from the civilian government and, as such, reserves the (formal constitutional or mere historical) right to intervene and impress their preferences on the civilian regime—or even remove said civilian regime in a crisis situation. Military tutelage means that the armed forces enjoy autonomy from political control, exercising oversight over civilian politicians in certain policy areas, and again retaining the express right to intercede when a crisis is perceived. Countries are also classified as having the "equivalent to military tutelage" if they are autocracies led by a monarch with the military loyal to this monarch but not to civilian officials per se. Under military control, the armed forces direct most policy areas, and the civilian government is subordinate to and exists only at the tolerance of the military. Finally, a military regime is a *de facto* military government, with full control over state policy and with cabinet and political figures drawn from the officer corps of the armed forces.

Our continuum is presented in Table 4.1; Fitch's analysis is modified in particular by adding the category of **civilian supremacy**, which we have taken from Agüero as outlined earlier.[68] For our purposes, the key differences between civilian supremacy and civilian control are that with civilian control rather than supremacy: (1) the civilians may lack (enough) expertise in military affairs, thus leaving the military largely with effective control over security policy; (2) the military is not seriously held to account for any past human rights violations; and (3) the military is basically in control of its own internal processes including personnel matters. That said, both civilian supremacy and civilian control preclude any constitutionally entrenched military powers, military control over civilian positions, and any military sense of a "right" to intervene in times of crisis.

Overall, it is important to stress (as Table 4.1 does) that for our purposes the first three categories—civilian supremacy, civilian control, and conditional subordination—are congruent with calling a country a democracy in the basic sense of a distinction between democracy and autocracy. However, to be

TABLE 4.2 :: LEVELS (scores) OF CIVIL-MILITARY RELATIONS AS OF THE END OF 2004

10 Albania	10 Taiwan	8 Jamaica	8 Solomon Islands	6 Madagascar
10 Antigua and Barbuda	10 Trinidad and Tobago	8 Kazakhstan	8 Sri Lanka	6 Malawi
10 Australia	10 United Kingdom	8 Kenya	8 Tanzania	6 Mali
10 Austria	10 United States of America	8 Kiribati	8 Thailand	6 Niger
10 Belgium		8 Kyrgyzstan	8 Timor-Leste (East Timor)	6 Rwanda
10 Belize		8 Lesotho		6 Sierra Leone
10 Canada	8 Afghanistan	8 Libya	8 Tonga	6 Suriname
10 China	8 Andorra	8 Liechtenstein	8 Tunisia	6 Syria
10 Costa Rica	8 Argentina	8 Macedonia	8 Turkmenistan	6 Tajikistan
10 Croatia	8 Armenia	8 Malaysia	8 Tuvalu	6 Turkey
10 Cyprus (Greek)	8 Azerbaijan	8 Maldives	8 Ukraine	6 Uganda
10 Czech Republic	8 Bahamas	8 Marshall Islands	8 United Arab Emirates	6 Venezuela
10 Denmark	8 Bahrain	8 Mauritania	8 Uruguay	
10 Finland	8 Barbados	8 Mauritius	8 Uzbekistan	4 Egypt
10 France	8 Belarus	8 Mexico	8 Vanuatu	
10 Germany	8 Bhutan	8 Micronesia	8 Vietnam	4 Brunei
10 Greece	8 Bosnia-Herzegovina	8 Moldova	8 Yemen	4 Kuwait
10 Hungary	8 Botswana	8 Monaco	8 Zambia	4 Nepal
10 Iceland	8 Bulgaria	8 Mongolia	8 Zimbabwe	~ 4 Oman
10 Ireland	8 Cameroon	8 Morocco		~ 4 Qatar
10 Italy	8 Cape Verde	8 Mozambique	6 Algeria	~ 4 Saudi Arabia
10 Japan	8 Chile	8 Namibia	6 Angola	~ 4 Swaziland
10 Jordan	8 Colombia	8 Nauru	6 Bangladesh	~
10 Korea, North	8 Ivory Coast (Côte d'Ivoire)	8 Nicaragua	6 Benin	~ 2 Guinea
10 Korea, South	8 Cuba	8 Nigeria	6 Bolivia	~ 2 Guinea-Bissau
10 Latvia	8 Djibouti	8 Palau	6 Brazil	2 Pakistan
10 Lithuania	8 Dominica	8 Panama	6 Cambodia	2 Togo
10 Luxembourg	8 Dominican Republic	8 Papua New Guinea	6 Central African Republic	
10 Malta	8 El Salvador	8 Paraguay	6 Chad	0 Burkina Faso
10 Netherlands	8 Eritrea	8 Peru	6 Comoros	0 Burma/ Myanmar
10 New Zealand	8 Estonia	8 Philippines	6 Congo, DR (Kinshasa)	0 Burundi
10 Norway	8 Ethiopia	8 Romania		0 Equatorial Guinea
10 Poland	8 Georgia	8 Russia	6 Congo, R (Brazzaville)	0 Somalia
10 Portugal	8 Grenada	8 Saint Lucia	6 Ecuador	0 Sudan
10 Saint Kitts and Nevis	8 Guatemala	8 Saint Vincent and the Grenadines	6 Fiji	
10 San Marino	8 Guyana		6 Gabon	
10 Singapore	8 Haiti	8 Samoa	6 Gambia	
10 Slovakia	8 Honduras	8 São Tomé and Príncipe	6 Ghana	
10 Slovenia	8 India	8 Senegal	6 Indonesia	
10 South Africa	8 Iran	8 Serbia and Montenegro	6 Laos	
10 Spain	8 Israel	8 Seychelles	6 Lebanon	
10 Sweden			6 Liberia	
10 Switzerland				

deemed a **liberal democracy** in the context of Chapter 2, a country must be in one of the top two categories. In other words, the category (and concept) of conditional subordination is congruent with, but also limits, a country to being an **electoral democracy**. On the other side of the spectrum, the three categories of military rule, military control, and military tutelage are all part of autocratic rule. Indeed, with the exception of the monarchies classified as the equivalent of military tutelage, all of the countries in the last three categories are examples of **military authoritarianism**—a regime type which will be outlined in Chapter 8.

Table 4.2 lists the countries of the world as of the end of 2004 in terms of where they place on this continuum, with countries listed using the 10 to 0 score given under the categories of Table 4.1. Countries listed as "~4" means that they have the "equivalent to military tutelage" noted above. One sees that most countries of the world now have either civilian supremacy or civilian control, although only a minority enjoy the highest category of civilian supremacy. Still, this is a definite increase in average civilian control (and a corresponding decrease in average military control) compared with a generation ago. This positive trend is due not only to the "third wave of democratization" (see Chapter 9) but also to the fact that assorted new democracies have implemented the various techniques to increase civilian control over the military discussed above. Indeed, today there are less than 20 countries where the military is dominant over the civilians (and thus are autocracies). Let us stress, however, that there are a large group of countries where the military is subordinate only conditionally to civilian control, making these (as noted) at best electoral democracies for the moment. Furthermore, in these cases the military by definition certainly could intervene and even overthrow the democratic regime in a future crisis, as happened most recently in Guinea-Bissau, until 2003 also one of the cases of conditional subordination.

NOTES

1 Muthiah Alagappa, "Investigating and Explaining Change: An Analytical Framework," *Coercion and Governance: The Declining Political Role of the Military in Asia*, ed. Muthiah Alagappa (Stanford, CA: Stanford University Press, 2001) 29.

2 Richard H. Kohn, "How Democracies Control the Military," *Journal of Democracy* 8:4 (1997): 142.

3 Harold A. Trinkunas, "Crafting Civilian Control in Argentina and Venezuela," *Civil-Military Relations in Latin America: New Analytical Perspectives*, ed. David Pion-Berlin (Chapel Hill, NC: The University of North Carolina Press, 2001) 163.

4 Felipe Agüero, *Soldiers, Civilians, and Democracy: Post-Franco Spain in Comparative Perspective* (Baltimore, MD: Johns Hopkins University Press, 1995) 19.

5 Agüero, *Soldiers, Civilians, and Democracy* 19.

6 J. Gus Liebenow, *African Politics: Crises and Challenges* (Bloomington and Indianapolis, IN: Indiana University Press, 1986) 251; Kohn 144–45.

7 Lyle N. McAlister, "The Military," *Continuity and Change in Latin America*, ed. John J. Johnson (Stanford, CA: Stanford University Press, 1964) 144.

8 Claude E. Welch, Jr., and Arthur K. Smith, *Military Role and Rule: Perspectives on Civil-Military Relations* (North Scituate, MA: Duxbury Press, 1974) 9–30.

9 Jack Child, "The Military and Democracy in Argentina," *Assessing Democracy in Latin America: A Tribute to Russell H. Fitzgibbon*, ed. Philip Kelly (Boulder, CO: Westview Press, 1998) 288–89.

10 Samuel P. Huntington, *The Soldier and the State: The Theory and Politics of Civil-Military Relations* (Cambridge, MA: Harvard University Press, 1957).

11 J. Samuel Fitch, *The Armed Forces and Democracy in Latin America* (Baltimore, MD: The Johns Hopkins University Press, 1998) 2–3.

12 Herbert M. Howe, *Ambiguous Order: Military Forces in African States* (Boulder, CO: Lynne Rienner, 2001) 9–10.

13 Howe 57.

14 Howe 9.

15 Agola Auma-Osolo, "Objective African Military Control: A New Paradigm in Civil-Military Relations," *Journal of Peace Research* 17:1 (1980): 29–46.

16 David Pion-Berlin, "Introduction," *Civil-Military Relations in Latin America: New Analytical Perspectives*, ed. David Pion-Berlin (Chapel Hill, NC: The University of North Carolina Press, 2001) 5–6; Alagappa 42.

17 Eric A. Nordlinger, *Soldiers in Politics: Military Coups and Governments* (Englewood Cliffs, NJ: Prentice-Hall, 1977) 195.

18 Paul W. Zagorski, *Democracy vs. National Security: Civil-Military Relations in Latin America* (Boulder, CO: Lynne Rienner, 1992) 74; Fitch 23 and 30–31.

19 Auma-Osolo 45.

20 Karen L. Remmer, *Military Rule in Latin America* (Boulder, CO: Westview Press, 1991) 33.

21 Janusz Onyszkiewicz, "Poland's Road to Civilian Control," *Civil-Military Relations and Democracy*, ed. Larry Diamond and Marc F. Plattner (Baltimore, MD: The Johns Hopkins University Press, 1996) 101.

22 Brian Loveman, "Historical Foundations of Civil-Military Relations in Spanish America," *Civil-Military Relations in Latin America: New Analytical Perspectives*, ed. David Pion-Berlin (Chapel Hill, NC: The University of North Carolina Press, 2001) 261.

23 Michael C. Desch, "Threat Environments and Military Missions," *Civil-Military Relations and Democracy*, ed. Larry Diamond and Marc F. Plattner (Baltimore, MD: The Johns Hopkins University Press, 1996) 12–13.

24 Fitch 5 and 17.

25 Liebenow 257 and 248.

26 Huntington, *Political Order in Changing Societies* 221.

27 Felipe Agüero, "Institutions, Transitions, and Bargaining: Civilians and the Military in Shaping Postauthoritarian Regimes," *Civil-Military Relations in Latin America: New Analytical Perspectives*, ed. David Pion-Berlin (Chapel Hill, NC: The University of North Carolina Press, 2001) 171–74.

28 Brian Loveman, *The Constitution of Tyranny* (Pittsburgh, PA: University of Pittsburgh Press, 1993).

29 Fitch 17.

30 James Ockey, "Thailand: The Struggle to Redefine Civil-Military Relations," *Coercion and Governance: The Declining Political Role of the Military in Asia*, ed. Muthiah Alagappa (Stanford, CA: Stanford University Press, 2001) 206.

31 Fred Riggs, *Thailand: The Modernization of a Bureaucratic Policy* (Honolulu, HI: East-West Center Press, 1964) 47.

32 Muthiah Alagappa, "Asian Civil-Military Relations: Key Developments, Explanations, and Trajectories," *Coercion and Governance: The Declining Political Role of the Military in Asia*, ed. Muthiah Alagappa (Stanford, CA: Stanford University Press, 2001) 460–61.

33 Alagappa, "Investigating and Explaining Change" 43–44.

34 David Pion-Berlin, "Military Autonomy and Emerging Democracies in South America," *Comparative Politics* 25:1 (1992): 85, 87-90.

35 Alagappa, "Investigating and Explaining Change" 42.

36 Zagorski 7-8.

37 Babar Sattar, "Pakistan: Return to Praetorianism," *Coercion and Governance: The Declining Political Role of the Military in Asia*, ed. Muthiah Alagappa (Stanford, CA: Stanford University Press, 2001) 401–05.

38 Separate from this (and the other) factors, one cannot discount the possibility of self-interested motivations for usurping civilian authority. While performance failures on behalf of civilian governments are often cited as reasons for overthrowing the regime, the true intent is often to improve the usurper's personal security, enrich material well-being, and enhance personal glory. What often appears externally as a military coup is in reality the establishment of a personalistic regime. Military involvement is simply the vehicle by which ambitious individuals attain political control.

39 Nordlinger, *Soldiers in Politics* 85, 193.

40 Ockey 206.

41 Alagappa, "Investigating and Explaining Change" 47.

42 Samuel E. Finer, *The Man on Horseback: The Role of the Military in Politics*, 2nd rev. ed. (Boulder, CO: Westview Press, 1962) 78.

43 Fitch 170, 140.

44 Finer 79–80.

45 Gerardo L. Munck, *Authoritarianism and Democratization: Soldiers and Workers in Argentina, 1976-1983* (University Park, PA: Pennsylvania State University Press, 1998) 26–31.

46 Finer 78.

47 Kohn 143–44.

48 Alagappa, "Asian Civil-Military Relations" 480–82.

49 Agüero, *Soldiers, Civilians, and Democracy* 222.

50 Zagorski 197.

51 Howe 279–80.

52 Wendy Hunter, "Civil-Military Relations in Argentina, Brazil, and Chile: Present Trends, Future Prospects," *Fault Lines of Democracy in Post-Transition Latin America*, ed. Felipe Agüero and Jeffrey Stark (Miami, FL: North-South Center Press, 1998) 304.

53 Agüero, *Soldiers, Civilians, and Democracy* 136, 150.

54 Agüero, *Soldiers, Civilians, and Democracy* 117.

55 Kohn 145.

56 Agüero, *Soldiers, Civilians, and Democracy* 206–07.

57 Agüero, *Soldiers, Civilians, and Democracy* 243–45.

58 Howe 17.

59 Howe 245, 263.

60 Agüero, *Soldiers, Civilians, and Democracy* 203.

61 Samuel P. Huntington, "Armed Forces and Democracy: Reforming Civil-Military Relations," *Journal of Democracy* 6:4 (1995): 11–12.

62 Child 289.

63 Agüero, *Soldiers, Civilians, and Democracy* 223–24.

64 Hunter 287–88.

65 Agüero, *Soldiers, Civilians, and Democracy* 21–22.

66 Liebenow 251.

67 Fitch 39. For other continua, see Alagappa, "Asian Civil-Military Relations"; Finer 77-78; Liebenow 251-52; and Nordlinger, *Soldiers in Politics* 22.

68 Agüero, *Soldiers, Civilians, and Democracy* 19.

CHAPTER FIVE

Factors Conducive to Democracy

IN THIS CHAPTER YOU WILL LEARN:

» *what factors facilitate democracy as opposed to autocracy;*

» *where quantifiable, the current differences between democracies and autocracies on these factors;*

» *which factors collectively matter most in terms of where countries rank on the four-category scale of liberal democracy, electoral democracy, semi-liberal autocracy, and closed autocracy; and*

» *which countries are thus the most "logical" extremes of this scale.*

OVERVIEW

Our discussion of military intervention placed a key role on national political culture. Indeed, this point can be broadened to a general discussion of the factors that facilitate democracy. Consequently, building on the classifications of Chapter 3, in this chapter we shall assess why some (groups of) countries are more democratic than others based on various independent variables, that is, historical, socio-economic, cultural, and demographic causal factors. (Note that we cannot assess why a country is in one category or another based on the political factors used to *define* the categories; to do so would be to commit a tautology.) Our first overall distinction is that between democracies, be they liberal or electoral, and autocracies, be they semi-liberal or closed. In other words, we are collapsing the four categories of Table 3.3 into two.

COMPARING POLITICAL REGIMES

Our second overall distinction of interest is that between liberal democracies and electoral democracies.

POLITICAL DEVELOPMENT AND DEMOCRATIZATION

In Chapter 1, we discussed historical sequences, in particular Dahl's argument about the advantages of establishing (free and fair) competition before full (male) participation. This distinction does seem relevant for prewar developments. Table 5.1 lists the 71 sovereign states that existed at the start of 1938, that is, just before Nazi Germany's territorial expansion. These are grouped into the two categories of the first distinction above, democracies versus autocracies. Of the countries that were (still) democracies at that time, the vast majority developed according to Dahl's recommended route. The only major exception was France. In terms of the second column, Austria, Italy, and Uruguay stand out as the only places that established (or at least attempted) free and fair competition before full participation and yet still wound up as autocracies. Besides those three, various other countries in the second column did have periods of electoral democracy prior to 1938, but in none did free and fair competition precede full (male) participation; instead, participation came before (Germany, Greece) or at the same time as (Argentina, Estonia, Japan, Latvia, Lithuania, Poland, Spain) competition. So, in summary, although having competition come before participation in the prewar era was neither completely necessary nor completely sufficient to maintain (electoral) democracy, it certainly made it likely. Conversely, taking an alternate route—France excepted—was associated with subsequent democratic failure.

However, as Dix shows, in the postwar era the pattern is less clear.[1] Certainly, many places—mostly former British colonies—became sovereign (electoral) democracies at independence after having had colonial competition without (or before) full participation. Dix lists India, Trinidad and Tobago, Jamaica, and Mauritius,[2] to which one could add other places in the Caribbean. However, other countries which did follow this route could not maintain democracy, such as Burma, Lebanon, and the Philippines. Democracy also broke down in Chile in 1973 even though it had taken the competition

110

TABLE 5.1 :: THE WORLD AT THE START OF 1938

DEMOCRACIES (Liberal and Electoral) N = 21

Australia	Denmark	Luxembourg	Switzerland*
Belgium*	Finland	Netherlands	United Kingdom
Canada	France*	New Zealand	United States**
Chile*	Iceland	Norway	
Costa Rica*	Ireland	South Africa**	
Czechoslovakia	Liechtenstein*	Sweden	

* suffrage restricted by gender   ** suffrage restricted by race

AUTOCRACIES N = 50

Afghanistan	Egypt	Latvia	Portugal
Albania	El Salvador	Liberia	Romania
Argentina	Estonia	Lithuania	San Marino
Austria	Ethiopia	Mexico	Soviet Union
Bhutan	Germany	Monaco	Spain
Bolivia	Greece	Mongolia	Thailand
Brazil	Guatemala	Nepal	Tibet
Bulgaria	Haiti	Newfoundland	Turkey
China	Honduras	Nicaragua	Uruguay
Colombia	Hungary	Panama	Venezuela
Cuba	Iran	Paraguay	Yugoslavia
Dominican Republic	Italy	Peru	
Ecuador	Japan	Poland	

preceding participation route (and was an electoral democracy before the war). Conversely, the establishment and maintenance of (electoral) democracy was not fatally hindered by having participation come at the same time as competition in countries such as Israel (1948) and Papua New Guinea (1975). More critically, as Dix points out, by the 1970s the most common pattern for new democracies was neither competition preceding participation nor the direct opposite, but what he calls an "interrupted" pattern where there was an *earlier* period of some level of competition preceding full participation, but then a shift to autocracy, followed by a new attempt at democratization.[3] Various countries in Southern Europe, post-communist Central and Eastern Europe, and Latin America fit here. Moreover, many of these places also became democracies after the collapse or overthrow of the old autocratic regime, rather than through the slow, evolutionary process which Dahl saw as most favourable.[4] Dahl did not deal with interrupted patterns, but they hardly seemed implied in his model. Thus, the competition preceding participation "advantage" does seem less crucial in the modern era, as does the slow inauguration "advantage." Finally, competition preceding participation is also a route that is nowadays practically impossible, inasmuch as many autocracies have granted universal suffrage despite (or in some/many cases because of) the lack of competition and/or the rigging of elections. Indeed, of today's democracies, the last one to follow the competition preceding participation route was South Africa, where the suffrage was restricted based on race. Of course, by the 1960s South Africa was being condemned, not praised, for restricting the expansion of its suffrage.

In this context we can also note the concept of getting "democratization backwards," by which is meant that Western countries had (most) civil liberties and the rule of law before full participation and often before any competition. In contrast, many countries today have competition and participation without (having first established) the rule of law—Russia, for example.[5] The rule of law may be (one of) the hardest part(s) of a liberal democracy to create, so perhaps the West was "lucky" to have developed it early on. Of course, we should not necessarily assume the Western sequence to have been anything like a conscious strategy. Moreover, it is not clear that the rule of law itself is easier to establish if suffrage is restricted rather than universal. Thus, the notion of getting "democratization backwards" may be more an issue of whether the "hardest part" of democracy was established early on or still remains to be done.

CONTEMPORARY FACTORS

Returning to the contemporary classifications of Table 3.3, the reasons advanced as to why some countries are more democratic than others can be divided into eight areas: (1) political culture and political leadership, (2) the military, (3) the level of development, (4) the nature of the economic system, (5) the cultural-historical legacy, (6) the extent of homogeneity (or mitigating factors), (7) population size, and (8) regional and international factors. Let us stress in advance that no one of these factors is sufficient to ensure a democracy, nor does any one of these prove to be absolutely necessary, since exceptions exist for each factor. Consequently, the most crucial factor(s) for why one specific country is a democracy (or an autocracy) may well differ from that (those) of another democracy (or autocracy).[6] Furthermore, to use phrases like "precondition(s)," "prerequisite(s)," or "requirement(s)" for democracy is incorrect; indeed, the strongest term most social scientists would use is "requisite(s)"; however, this term still implies a (parallel) necessity, just not one in advance. Since there do seem to be exceptions for each of the following factors, we shall use the more cautious term of "conducive factor(s)."

POLITICAL CULTURE AND POLITICAL LEADERSHIP

We will begin with the self-evident fact that the greater the belief in democracy, its institutions, and its values by political leaders (and others), the more likely a country is to be democratic.[7] In other words, a democratic political culture—that is, one which stresses civility, tolerance for opposing views, moderation, pragmatism, and a willingness to compromise—is conducive to democracy, whereas a non-democratic (or indifferent) political culture makes democracy less likely, both in an immediate context and over the long term.[8] What appears to be particularly crucial is the political culture of a society's political leaders and activists, since they are more likely than the average person to have a clearly developed set of political beliefs, to be actually guided in their actions by their beliefs, and to have a greater influence on political events.[9] It is not a gross oversimplification to note that democracies are usually led by people who believe in democracy and who may well expound on their beliefs, whereas autocracies are led by people who do not believe in democracy and whose actions and words aim to keep their countries autocratic. Thus, what is crucial in individual cases is the nature of political leadership, particularly the post-independence and/or post-democratization leadership. Where this has been respectful of democratic principles—even at the price of policy goals—and competent, democracy has been more likely to survive. India is a classic example, inasmuch as a major reason for India's democratic development was that elites reached out to mass society to raise political consciousness, develop democratic practices, and mobilize participation—both in electoral politics and in a wide range of voluntary organizations. Political leadership and [democratic] ideology were crucial in this process, particularly in the person of Mahatma Gandhi, who emphasized the values of liberty, nonviolent and consensual resolution of conflict, and continuous incorporation of excluded groups.[10]

Gandhi's successor, Jawaharlal Nehru, Costa Rica's José Figueres (who, after winning the 1948 civil war, held free and fair elections for a Constituent Assembly, accepted defeat therein and consequently of his proposed constitution, and then handed power over to his opponents), and South Africa's Nelson Mandela are other classic examples of leaders who demonstrated effectively their democratic values at a crucial point in their country's development.

THE MILITARY

As the previous chapter showed, the military has been a political actor at some time or another in many nations, and remains a potential threat in most of Africa and Latin America. So, to "do something" about the military would definitely be conducive to preserving democracy. Basically, three successful options have been followed. (These are in no way mutually exclusive.) First, the armed forces of a country may be so small as to have what Dahl calls "virtual insignificance" in a political sense.[11] At the extreme, this means having no armed forces. Iceland, for example, has never had any armed forces of its own (even though it is a NATO member). Costa Rica abolished its army in 1948–49, and Panama did likewise in 1994. Of the world's larger countries, the key example is Japan; after World War II the United States effectively imposed a constitution that forbade Japan from maintaining land, sea, or air forces. Japan has since created a small "self-defence force," but it is both militarily and politically insignificant, most certainly in comparison with prewar Japan. More generally, even if one's armed forces are large enough to deter what

114

CHAPTER FIVE :: FACTORS CONDUCIVE TO DEMOCRACY

few enemies one has, they can still be small or "insignificant" enough as a share of the population that they could not effectively take over, occupy, and administer the country in the face of civilian opposition or even lack of cooperation. Canada's small armed forces (now around 60,000 in a country of 31 million) are an obvious example here. In fact, the peacetime armed forces of both the United Kingdom and the United States prior to World War II were never significant in a numerical sense. Moreover, to the end of the nineteenth century the armed forces of the United States were essentially local militias, lacking any central control. Central control is needed for a military regime. Citizen militias also played such a decentralizing role in the modern histories of other countries such as Canada, the United Kingdom, and Switzerland.[12]

However, many countries have, or have had, significant armed forces for security reasons, especially since the rise of large standing armies in eighteenth-century Europe. Consequently, if the first option of an insignificant army is not chosen, and would be foolish to choose given hostile enemies, then the maintenance of democracy requires ensuring that the armed forces are not individually and psychologically apart from, and with feelings of superiority over, the rest of society. One way to achieve this—and the second option overall—is to have an armed force (even a large one) composed of the "population as a whole." This involves (random) citizens called into the armed forces, normally through universal (male) conscription. These citizens serve a term in the military and may (as in Switzerland) go back annually for manoeuvres, but through their lives they are definitely citizens and not professional soldiers. The proto-democracy of ancient Athens was certainly facilitated by having such a citizen-militia (from the seventh century B.C. onwards). In contrast, nineteenth-century continental Europe tended to create professional armies with less democratic consequences—a pattern that remains to this day in much of Latin America. Finally, if (indeed, especially if) the armed forces are in fact an organization of lifetime professionals "cut off" socially from the rest of society, then democracy requires providing them with a democratic indoctrination. This third option can be done as part of military training, inculcating loyalty to the constitution and civilian authorities—something which, in their own way, communist countries were and are highly successful in doing. Conversely, as we saw in the previous chapter, if the constitution establishes the armed

TABLE 5.2 :: DIFFERENCES IN EXPLANATORY FACTORS BETWEEN CATEGORIES

1. ALL DEMOCRACIES VERSUS ALL AUTOCRACIES

	TOTAL N	MEAN FOR ALL DEMOCRACIES	MEAN FOR ALL AUTOCRACIES	T-TEST (EQUAL VARIANCES NOT ASSUMED)	SIGNIFICANCE LEVEL
Military participation ratio per 1000 population, 2002	192	4.617	9.886	−3.930	0.000
GDP per capita, 2002 (U.S.$ at PPPs)	174	11713	5173	4.980	0.000
HDI value, 2002	175	0.755	0.613	5.524	0.000
Life expectancy, 2002 (years)	182	68.961	59.275	5.299	0.000
Urbanization, 2002 (percentage)	175	57.695	47.593	2.803	0.006
Adult literacy (population 15 and above), 2002 (percentage)	181	87.119	72.285	4.848	0.000
Average years of schooling (population 25 and above), 2000	181	6.917	3.870	7.910	0.000
Effective number of ethnic groups	191	1.859	2.509	−2.512	0.014
Total population, 2002 (logged)	192	0.558	0.894	−2.615	0.010
Equivalent in millions		(3.613)	(7.830)		

2. LIBERAL DEMOCRACIES VERSUS ELECTORAL DEMOCRACIES

	TOTAL N	MEAN FOR ALL LIBERAL DEMOCRACIES	MEAN FOR ALL ELECTORAL DEMOCRACIES	T-TEST (EQUAL VARIANCES NOT ASSUMED)	SIGNIFICANCE LEVEL
Military participation ratio per 1000 population, 2002	117	4.998	4.157	0.933	0.353
GDP per capita, 2002 (U.S.$ at PPPs)	104	18205	4426	8.480	0.000
HDI value, 2002	105	0.848	0.653	7.324	0.000
Life expectancy, 2002 (years)	107	73.673	63.786	5.123	0.000
Urbanization, 2002 (percentage)	105	66.727	47.760	4.959	0.000
Adult literacy (population 15 and above), 2002 (percentage)	109	93.572	80.046	4.083	0.000
Average years of schooling (population 25 and above), 2000	107	8.553	4.980	7.367	0.000
Effective number of ethnic groups	116	1.638	2.131	−2.632	0.010
Total population, 2002 (logged)	117	0.295	0.876	−3.075	0.003
Equivalent in millions		(1.972)	(7.509)		

forces as the ultimate political "umpire" (as has been the case in Latin America), then such indoctrination is next to impossible; instead, an opposite anti-democratic indoctrination is likely to occur. And, as we saw, even if military intervention is not a constitutional "duty," when a professional military is a separate social order which feels superior to civilian authorities (in part due to their very professionalism), then they may resist civilian control and claim a "right" to intervene, as in Pakistan, Thailand, Turkey, and much of Africa.[13] Therefore, an antecedent factor in facilitating democracy is a democratic political culture, especially attitudes in favour of civilian rule and democracy held by political elites and activists. Such beliefs may have little to do with the level of a country's socio-economic development (and thus are a separate factor), although they may arise from historical patterns.[14]

Empirically, we can measure the "military participation ratio" of a country, that is, the size of armed forces per 1000 population. The most recent global figures that can be calculated are for 2002 (using data on the size of armed forces from *The Military Balance* and *The Statesman's Yearbook*). As in shown in Table 5.2, the mean military participation ratio for all democracies is 4.617, whereas for all autocracies it is 9.886. A *t*-test here, with equal variances not assumed, yields a value of -3.930; this is significant at the .000 level. Thus, autocracies are found to be significantly more militarized. However, in terms of the distinction between liberal democracies and electoral democracies, no significant distinction exists. Indeed, liberal democracies have a slightly higher military participation rate than do electoral democracies: 4.998 versus 4.157.

THE LEVEL OF DEVELOPMENT

Looking at Table 3.3, perhaps the most obvious distinction between democracies and autocracies is that democracies tend to be wealthier. For decades a linkage between wealth and democracy has been made by social scientists, especially Seymour Martin Lipset.[15] Moreover, the causal linkage is clearly from wealth to democracy, not the other way around;[16] autocracies can often deliver economic growth just as well as democracies can, and sometimes better (think of China in recent decades). However, what this emphasis on wealth really means is not just wealth *per se* but broader related aspects of development: industrialization, urbanization, and consequent economic diversity; literacy and advanced education; and low infant mortality and resulting long life expectancy. These various factors produce a society which is not just developed but also *dynamic* (in the sense of having economic growth and social mobility) and *pluralist* (in the sense of having many groups and independent organizations, especially in the economy).[17] However, such dynamism and pluralism will not flow from development if a wealthy country has its wealth concentrated in a few hands; the oil-rich Organization of Petroleum Exporting Countries (OPEC) of the Middle East are the clearest examples of this qualification. Nor does such pluralism exist under a communist economic system where individuals and most groups lack independent economic resources.

These various factors of development lead to a broad distribution (as opposed to a concentration) of what Tatu Vanhanen calls "**power resources**," that is, the economic, intellectual, and organizational resources that an individual or group can bring to bear in the struggle for political power.[18] In social terms, this means a society with a large middle class, rather than a sharp divide between a small elite and impoverished masses—in Barrington Moore's classic phrase, "no bourgeois, no democracy."[19] Developed societies with deconcentrated power resources facilitate democracy for two reasons: first, this diversity of power resources means that more people and groups can demand a say in the system, resist domination by others, and engage in competition and bargaining with other groups—all while having the resources to do such things effectively.[20] Conversely, it is that much harder for an individual or a small group to suppress its competitors and establish an autocracy. As Vanhanen summarizes, "The concentration of power resources leads to autocratic political structures, whereas the wide distribution of the same resources makes the sharing of power and democracy possible."[21] Second, in developed societies the greater equality of conditions and socio-economic opportunities fosters the existence of ideologies of equality (rather than hierarchy and deference) and positive-sum (rather than zero-sum) behaviour, which in turn make it more likely that most people are willing to share power with others and see the point of cooperation (the aforementioned notions of a democratic political culture).[22] Generally, as noted in Chapter 2, those with the most power (the traditional elites) have to feel that they will not lose everything in a more open system; such a feeling is more likely if most of the rest of society consists of people with something to lose and with moderate attitudes rather than having nothing to lose and radical or revolutionary attitudes.

Although such diversity of power resources is most likely to occur in urban industrial societies, it is still possible in more rural ones. The central economic issue is the pattern of land ownership. Where a society is (still) predominantly rural, and where most land is owned by relatively few large landowners, then the power resources are too concentrated to favour democracy; autocratic rule is more likely to exist. If the pattern of land ownership is one where most land is held by independent family farmers rather than large landowners, then a large middle class and consequent diversity of economic resources can arise. Democratic development was facilitated by the typical pattern of land ownership by independent family farms in the British settler societies of Australia, Canada, New Zealand, and the United States, as well as some of the smaller European countries (those of Scandinavia, plus Switzerland).[23] In contrast, in most of nineteenth-century Europe, land was highly concentrated, with consequent anti-democratic effects; consider, for example, the role of the Junkers in Prussia and Imperial Germany. Similar concentrations of landownership has been the norm in most of the developing world, with rare exceptions (Costa Rica is one). It is worth stressing that, besides demilitarizing postwar Japan, the United States also effected a major land reform there.

Table 5.2 summarizes the statistical analyses of differences between groups in terms of varying measures of socio-economic development. First is income per capita in 2002 (the Gross Domestic Product, or GDP), which is highly significant not only in terms of the distinction between all democracies and all autocracies, but also in terms of the distinction between liberal democracies and electoral democracies. In short, wealth is related to both democracy and to liberal democracy. However, a broader and thus presumably better measure of development is the UN's Human Development Index (HDI), which, as noted in Chapter 1, is a combination of income, education, and life expectancy.[24] Table 5.2 shows that, for the 175 countries with scores, average

HDI values are highly significant in terms of the distinction between all democracies and all autocracies, as well as in terms of the distinction between liberal democracies and electoral democracies. Moreover, at least for the overall distinction between democracies and autocracies, the data show an even stronger relationship (t score) than for just GDP per capita. We can also look at life expectancy where there is a highly significant difference in terms of the means for all democracies and all autocracies, and also in terms of the means for liberal democracies versus electoral democracies. Next, we can look at urbanization, that is, the percentage of the population living in urban areas. Urbanization is likewise significant in terms of the distinction between all democracies and all autocracies, and also highly significant in terms of the distinction between liberal democracies and electoral democracies.

Let us now turn to literacy, since this is argued by Axel Hadenius to be the most central factor in explaining the differing levels of democracy in developing countries.[25] Of course, in our analysis we are looking at all countries for which there is data on literacy for those 15 and above. As Table 5.2 shows, literacy is indeed statistically highly significant in terms of the distinction between all democracies and all autocracies, and also in terms of the distinction between liberal democracies and electoral democracies. However, literacy can be considered a problematic measure. First of all, we are talking about basic reading and writing ability, not the complex expression of ideas. Second and more crucially, because literacy is defined as a basic concept in many societies, most everyone is deemed to be literate; that is, a value of 99 per cent is used. Indeed, no less than 41 countries claim this value for 2002, with many others close to it. Consequently, the median literacy score for 181 countries is 90.0—making this a very skewed variable.

However, an alternative and superior measure of education does exist, namely, the total years of schooling, normally averaged for the population 25 and above.[26] This measure, by allowing us to assess individuals on an interval scale rather than with a yes/no dichotomy, suggests that ever more schooling (rather than basic literacy) makes people more likely to feel informed, efficacious, and politically engaged rather than apathetic. Data on average years of schooling are, however, much less common than for literacy. The last major cross-national measurement was done by the UN in its 1993 *Human*

Development Report, with the data themselves being for 1990. However, the work of Barro and Lee on this measure now contains data through to 2000, albeit for appreciably fewer countries than the UN data. Consequently, for our analysis, the UN data is used as a starting point and then updated to 2000 using either the specific country increase according to Barro and Lee or, failing this, the average regional increase as they reported.[27] Thus, we have data for almost all countries, although for a few less than for literacy. As Table 5.2 shows, the statistical relationship (*t* score) for average years of schooling between all democracies and all autocracies is higher than for any other socio-economic variable. It is also very high for the difference between liberal democracies and electoral democracies, although not quite as high as for GDP per capita. Finally in this regard, it should be noted that the six variables in Table 5.2 in varying ways tap into the same matter: the level of socio-economic development. It is not surprising that all of these variables are highly inter-correlated (all at the .000 level). Given such inter-correlation, we can simplify matters by focussing on what both theoretically and empirically seems to be the most crucial aspect of socio-economic development, namely, the average years of schooling.

In terms of measuring socio-economic equality, most data on family farms are not up-to-date enough to make a credible cross-national analysis across regime types. However, an alternative measure of equality—and one more crucial for urbanized societies—is the GINI index, which measures income distribution in a country. This ranges from 0 to 1, where 0 indicates a completely equal distribution of income across households and 1 indicates a single household having the entire national wealth and everyone else having absolutely nothing. However, although earlier cross-national analyses have shown a link between (relative) economic equality and democracy, there does not seem to be a global pattern any longer. The mean GINI index (based on the most recent year of data) for all democracies is 40.739, almost exactly the same as that for all autocracies at 40.302. A similar analysis looking at the share of income or wealth of the top 20 per cent of the population also shows no overall differences between democracies (47.606) and autocracies (47.505). Of course, these data are available for only 123 countries, almost two-thirds of all countries. Two different conclusions are possible. The first is that there is no relationship between equality and democracy. The second is that the relationship is more long term between equality and democratic *survival*.[28] In this sense, many contemporary democracies could well be at risk of breakdown if they remain highly inegalitarian. We shall return to this point in Chapter 10.[29]

The link between development and democracy may be strong, but it is not completely perfect. India is the classic example of a longstanding (electoral) democracy that is underdeveloped in various socio-economic ways. Newer examples of such "outliers" include Kiribati, Mali, and the Solomon Islands. In contrast, Singapore has a high level of socio-economic development and Malaysia a moderately high one, but both are still (semi-liberal) autocracies.

THE NATURE OF THE ECONOMIC SYSTEM

Classical liberalism was concerned as much about advocating property rights, free markets, and free trade as it was about advocating political freedoms and responsible government—and certainly more so than it was about advocating universal suffrage. To the extent that democracy involves freedom, and freedom has both political and economic dimensions, then we would expect democracies to have market economies. However, autocracies can have market economies as well, since these allow an autocratic elite to enrich itself.[30] Such an economic system presumably would be more likely to lead ultimately to democracy than a statist economic system in which economic resources are controlled by the state.

To this end, we can measure the role of the state in contemporary economies in terms of the public sector share of GDP, state-owned enterprises as a share of total industry (industrial production or investment), combined government and state-owned industry employment as a share of total employment, and/or the extent of government regulation of the economy. Data on such variables are not always available for every country, and sometimes there are differences in assessment, but generally most analyses agree in terms of basic national classifications and comparative patterns.[31] Consequently, we shall use here not a single continuous variable but rather two different dummy variables reflecting three categories. The first dummy variable, that of a capitalist market economy, is for economies with a predominance of private ownership and low-to-moderate government regulation of the economy. No exclusion is made for having a large welfare state. There are currently 71 countries which are deemed to have such capitalist market economies. This number is higher than what it would have been a couple of decades ago given that many countries have undergone a policy of privatization, starting in some cases as far back as the 1980s. The contrasting dummy variable is for a statist economy, that is, an economy with significant levels of government ownership, regulation, and/or overall control of the economy. Of the contemporary world economies, only 17 are clearly statist. All of the remaining economies—the majority—fall in between these extremes, having a mixed (capitalist-statist) economy or being in transition away from a statist economy (as is true of most post-communist countries). They are thus a residual category.

The patterns are quite striking. Of the 71 capitalist market economies, 66 are democracies (liberal or electoral) and only 5 are autocracies. Of the 17 statist economies, *every one* is an autocracy. In each case a statistical test (chi-square) confirms the significance of the dummy variable. In contrast, the residual economies divide more or less evenly: 50 are democracies and 54 are autocracies.

THE CULTURAL-HISTORICAL LEGACY

It has been argued that British colonialism was more favourable for later democratic development than that of other imperial powers. For example, in seeking to explain the strength and durability of liberal democracy in the Commonwealth Caribbean, Sutton has argued that "[t]he Westminster model, which was bequeathed to all Caribbean countries on independence, has taken root in the Caribbean and enjoyed widespread support. Its persistence is the single most important explanation for the comparative success of democracy in the region."[32] By the "Westminster model," Sutton does not mean single-member plurality elections and one-party governments (although these are also the "norm" in the Caribbean) but the democratic principles of constitutionalism, limited government, civilian supremacy, competitive elections (which

TABLE 5.3 :: **COLONIAL LEGACY AND DEMOCRACY VERSUS AUTOCRACY**
(for ex-colonies that became independent starting in 1945)

COLONIAL LEGACY	TOTAL DEMOCRACIES END 2004	TOTAL AUTOCRACIES END 2004	TOTAL EX-COLONIES END 2004
Anglo-American	36	22	58
Other	13	29	42
TOTALS	49	51	100

Pearson chi-square is 9.438 (significance level of 0.002).

began before independence), and civil liberties.[33] British colonialism generally left behind such features and much greater political institutionalization than was the case for the former colonies of other European powers. France comes second in this regard, followed by the Netherlands; Belgium and Portugal were "the worst" in terms of imperial legacies. We shall assess this point by looking at the entire list of ex-colonies (and ex-protectorates) that have become independent since 1945, that is, all countries outside of Europe that gained their independence from 1945 onwards. These can be found in Table 1.1. The total is 100 countries. We divide these into former Anglo-American colonies and protectorates (which includes those of Australia, New Zealand, and the United States as well as the United Kingdom) and all other former colonies or protectorates. Table 5.3 shows the two-by-two breakdown for colonial power and the dichotomy between democracy versus autocracy. As can be seen, there is a statistically significant greater percentage of democracies within the categories of former Anglo-American colonies or protectorates. That said, there are many non-democracies among the former Anglo-American colonies or protectorates. Thus, Sutton's point about the Westminster model "taking root" is crucial: British colonialism seemed to plant more democratic roots first in the white settler countries of Australia, Canada, New Zealand, and the United States, and then later on in the Caribbean and Pacific, than it did in most of Africa and Asia.

In this vein of culture, we can also speak of religious distinctions. The key factor appears to be the extent to which a religion is hierarchical and dogmatic, traits which do not lend themselves to questioning authority or demanding participation. Certainly, future Canadian Prime Minister Pierre Trudeau felt in the 1950s that the hierarchical nature of Catholicism was part of the reason why

Quebec up through that time was less democratic than other parts of Canada. As he wrote then:

> French Canadians are Catholics; and Catholics have not always been ardent supporters of democracy. They are authoritarian in spiritual matters; and since the dividing line between the spiritual and the temporal may be very fine or even confused, they are often disinclined to seek truth in temporal affairs through the mere counting of heads. If this be true in general, it is particularly so in the case of the clergy and laity of Quebec, influenced as they were by the Catholicism of nineteenth-century France, which largely rejected democracy as the daughter of the [French] Revolution.[34]

In contrast, Protestantism has been argued to be much more individualistic a religion, and thus Protestant countries are more likely to be democratic. As is the case with historical sequences of democratization, this point was certainly once empirically valid. Looking again at the two lists in Table 5.1, of the various democracies at the start of 1938, almost two-thirds were either Protestant or mixed Protestant-Catholic (usually with the Protestants politically dominant). There were seven Catholic democracies then (Belgium, Chile, Costa Rica, France, Ireland, Liechtenstein, and Luxembourg), although most of these had not yet granted women the vote (nor, for its part, had Switzerland). In any case, these seven were much fewer than the many Catholic autocracies of the time. In contrast, only three of the 1938 autocracies were (dominantly) Protestant—Estonia, Germany, and Latvia. It is still the case today that almost all Protestant countries (except for Liberia and Tonga) are democracies, and most are liberal democracies. However, the list of liberal and electoral democracies today contains many Catholic, Orthodox, and non-Christian countries. Certainly, it no longer seems the case that Catholicism tends to work against democracy, in large part due to changes in the Catholic Church in the 1960s that made it much more sympathetic to the poor and oppressed. Religious distinctions now centre more on Islam, since the vast majority of today's 47 majority-Islamic states are (semi-liberal or closed) autocracies, except for the electoral democracies of Albania, Bangladesh, Indonesia, Mali,

Niger, Nigeria, Senegal, Sierra Leone, and Turkey. Autocracy in the Muslim world may relate to such religious features as fundamentalist Islam's sexism and lack of separation between church and state, but equally if not even more so to the fact that these societies are generally either underdeveloped or have highly concentrated oil-based wealth—neither of which are socio-economic situations which favour democracy.[35]

SOCIAL HOMOGENEITY

All other things being equal, it is reasonable to assume that the agreements and compromises needed to make democracy work and survive are easier if the society is not sharply divided, with each side feeling that the other threatens its goals and underlying values. Although such polarization can be conceived of in class terms, it is important to remember that many economic issues can be dealt with by "splitting the difference," that is, by setting program spending, tax levels, or specific tariffs at the halfway level between what two opposing groups want. Compromise can be achieved if there is the collective will. In contrast, one cannot split the difference in terms of the number of official languages or religions in a country. Consequently, where the society is very heterogeneous in ethno-cultural terms we expect democracy to be less likely to survive. To this end, we can calculate a measure of the "effective number of ethnic groups" for 191 countries and assess whether there is a pattern with the regime classification of Table 3.3. Indeed, as Table 5.2 shows, the mean effective number of ethnic groups for all democracies is 1.859, whereas for all autocracies it is 2.509, a statistically significant difference. In other words, autocracies are more heterogeneous than democracies, as are electoral democracies compared to liberal democracies. Of course, the causality is far from prefect. There are certainly many "homogeneous autocracies"; for example, one cannot get much more homogeneous than North Korea. Conversely, one can find various cases of heterogeneous democracies, such as Canada.

In this regard, it is important to note that there are ways to mitigate ethno-cultural pluralism, if the political elites (including the constitution drafters) are willing to do so. The most comprehensive has been argued to be a system of

126

consociational democracy (or consociationalism). This is a political system based around power sharing as opposed to majoritarianism and which involves four aspects: (1) rule by a grand (broad) coalition; (2) mutual and thus minority vetoes on all sensitive issues; (3) proportionality not just in the cabinet but also in the civil service and/or official agencies and boards; and (4) local autonomy, including ultimately federalism where the various groups are geographically concentrated.[36] The classic cases of consociationalism are the small but divided European countries of Austria, Belgium, the Netherlands, and Switzerland, all of which reached their "high point" of consociational development in the late 1950s.[37] Key aspects of consociationalism still exist today in Belgium and Switzerland, but Austria and the Netherlands have become much more homogeneous as previous cleavages (divisions) have lessened or even vanished. Arend Lijphart has argued that there are many elements of consociationalism in India, which helps to explain the survival of democracy in that diverse, continental country.[38] Even where full-blown consociational democracy is not implemented, the use of some of its more flexible aspects— such as federalism or at least some form of regional government where the minorities are a local majority—can accommodate ethno-cultural divisions.

POPULATION SIZE AND ISLAND STATUS

One factor relating to democracy which did not receive much emphasis by social scientists in the postwar era but has been stressed in the past couple of decades is population size. Many countries which became independent in the 1970s and 1980s are small, and democracy has survived in most of these. Smallness is normally defined by population, as opposed to area. Still, scholars differ somewhat on what is meant by small. The most common procedure is to use a population cut-off of 1 million, as Anckar does.[39] However, Ott uses a cut-off of 1.5 million.[40] For his part, Diamond uses both 1 million and 0.5 million.[41] Diamond appears correct to use multiple cut-offs, since the frequency of contemporary democracies increases even more with a small cut-off, a point Ott also notes.[42] In summary, it is better to use population per se rather than any single unit of smallness. However, because national population levels are so skewed, in Table 5.2 we log the population values (in millions) for 2002. This shows that the average logged population for all democracies is 0.558, whereas the average logged population for all autocracies is 0.894. As noted in the table, the equivalent "real" numbers are averages of 3.613 million people for all democracies and 7.830 million people for all autocracies; thus, autocracies have on average over double the population of democracies. The t-test of the logged population, with equal variances not assumed, shows that this difference in size between democracies and autocracies is statistically significant. This statistical relationship is even stronger for the difference between liberal democracies and electoral democracies. Liberal democracies have an average logged population of 0.295 (that is, 1.972 million), whereas electoral democracies have an average logged population of 0.876 (that is, 7.509 million). In summary, democracies and, more specifically, liberal democracies tend to have small populations.

The relationship of size to democracy has been demonstrated to exist regardless of income (except, presumably, at the very highest income levels where all countries are democracies). In other words, if there are two countries at the same level of income (development) but with a clear difference in size, then the smaller one is more likely to be democratic and to maintain democracy.[43] Moreover, Ott's analysis stresses that, separately, "island countries were found to be far more likely to be democratic than non-island countries."[44] Since many island countries are also small, this is a possible reinforcing relationship; that is, democracy may be particularly likely in small island states.

Small size, and small islands, are seen to favour democratization for four reasons, some of which are antecedent factors of previous points. First, there is the assumption that small island states (small countries) are more likely to be homogeneous than other countries. Of course, there are some small island states which are heterogeneous, such as Fiji, Mauritius, and Trinidad and Tobago[45]—and certainly in Fiji, ethnic heterogeneity is at the centre of its inability to maintain democracy. Overall, though, the data in fact show that the global correlation between logged population and the effective number of ethnic groups is a statistically insignificant 0.099, so this pattern of homogeneity may exist only for small *island* states. Secondly, in small states people have a greater chance of reaching and influencing decision-makers, so they develop feelings of political efficacy and are more participatory. (Although this is not the central explanatory factor for voter turnout, turnout in elections is indeed higher in smaller countries than in larger ones.) Political leaders, in turn, are more attentive to individual citizens in small states.[46] It is for this reason that Diamond stresses political decentralization in large states as a desirable policy in and of itself, although Ott is more sceptical here.[47] Thirdly, elites in small states are more likely to be cooperative than confrontational.[48] This occurs in part because the smaller number of elites makes it likely that they all know each other and in part because the country does not want to appear vulnerable to outsiders. Indeed, small size is one of the factors seen to facilitate consociationalism.[49] Fourth and finally, small island states have no direct neighbours and thus no hostile neighbours; therefore, they can spend less on defence and undertake one of the options for taming military coercion. With the exception of Fiji, the military has never staged a coup in a small island state. Beyond this, even where a small country is not an island, it may see little point in military spending since it cannot defend itself against a hostile enemy without help (or, more charitably, it will be unlikely to have an aggressive military posture *vis-à-vis* its neighbours). This assumes that there is less militarization in small states regardless of island status.[50] In fact, a correlation between population size (logged) and military participation ratios for 2002 yields a statistically insignificant value of 0.055, so there is no relationship between population size and (the lack of) militarization. To repeat, then: in today's world, small size alone does not directly relate to either ethnic homogeneity or small armed forces, so these other factors remain as separate explanations for the level of democracy.

On this point, Diamond argues that the greater frequency of democracy (both electoral and liberal) in former Anglo-American colonies is a spurious result of the fact that these are more likely to be smaller than the former colonies of other powers. He argues that countries of less than 1 million are as likely to be democracies (and, as noted, they are likely to be so) whether they are former Anglo-American colonies or not.[51] Indeed, looking at the 100 former colonies discussed above under the notion of colonial legacy, we find that the group of former Anglo-American colonies and protectorates have a significantly smaller mean logged population (0.202) than the other former colonies and protectorates

TABLE 5.4 :: REGRESSION ON REGIME TYPE (1 to 4 scale)

	B	STANDARD ERROR	T	SIGNIFICANCE LEVEL
Military participation ratio, 2002	0.025	0.006	3.882	0.000
Capitalist market economy (dummy)	−0.841	0.129	−6.509	0.000
Statist economy (dummy)	0.845	0.187	4.524	0.000
Population logged, 2002	0.193	0.060	3.218	0.002
Mean years of schooling for population 25 and above, 2000	−0.135	0.020	−6.911	0.000
Constant	2.943	0.120	24.500	0.000

$N = 182$ Adjusted $r^2 = 0.631$

(0.748). The t score here, with equal variances not assumed, is −2.929, which has a significance level of 0.004. Moreover, going back to the discussion above, the former Anglo-American colonies and protectorates of Africa and Asia are generally much more populous than the former Anglo-American colonies and protectorates of the Caribbean and the Pacific.

REGIONAL AND INTERNATIONAL FACTORS

A final observation from Table 3.3 is that the countries that are autocracies tend to be surrounded largely, if not wholly, by other autocracies. This allows them to avoid pressure to democratize both from their neighbours and from their own populations who, especially in a semi-liberal autocracy, could well be aware of the situation in neighbouring countries. (Such access to information, of course, is easier today with the spread of communications such as satellite dishes and the Internet).[52] Conversely, there have been "positive regional outliers"—that is, democracies in (more or less) a sea of autocracies, such as India and Israel today (although India is big enough not to be affected easily by its neighbours) or Czechoslovakia in the late 1930s.

If a region has an organized body *and* if most members of this body are democratic, then they may use the regional organization to try and encourage the remaining countries to become democratic or at least discourage internal

130

attempts to overthrow current democracies in the region. We see this pattern today in two continents: Europe, via the Council of Europe and the Organization for Security and Co-operation in Europe, and Latin America, via the Organization of American States (OAS). The OAS, along with the United States and others, intervened to neutralize coups in both Guatemala in 1993 and Paraguay in 1996.[53] Even in Africa, two coups in São Tomé and Príncipe—in 1995 and 2003—each fizzled out after about a week due to opposition from neighbouring West African countries.

A different type of regional/international effect has been the foreign pressure/influence of what is now the European Union (EU) on would-be members, since EU membership is conditional on being a liberal democracy (not that the EU uses that precise phrase, but that is the reality). This requirement has acted as an incentive to EU neighbours wishing to join, but only if they have felt that there is a reasonable chance for admission, which is less so the further East or Southeast one is in Europe.

Finally, one should also reflect on the changing role of the United States as the key Western superpower in terms of "caring" about whether countries are democratic or not. This concern was greater in the late 1940s, the late 1970s (under President Carter), and since the end of the Cold War than *during* most of the Cold War, when United States foreign policy was concerned only that a country was anti-communist.

A MULTIVARIATE ANALYSIS

To keep the analysis simple (or simpler) we have focussed so far on dichotomies, first between all democracies and all autocracies and then between liberal democracies and electoral democracies. We have also generally looked at the variables in turn without too much focus on the ones that matter most. However, by classifying the categories of Table 3.3 into a four-point scale (with liberal democracy as "1," electoral democracy as "2," semi-liberal autocracy as "3," and closed autocracy as "4"), we can make a multiple regression analysis of all the quantifiable and dummy variables. The result of this is reported in Table 5.4. We see that there are five key variables: (1) the

TABLE 5.5 :: **VALUES OF RELEVANT DATA**

LIBERAL DEMOCRACY = 1
ELECTORAL DEMOCRACY = 2
SEMI-LIBERAL AUTOCRACY = 3
CLOSED AUTOCRACY = 4

COUNTRY	REGIME CATEGORY	MILITARY PARTICIPATION RATIO, 2002 (per 1000 population)	MARKET CAPITALIST ECONOMY DUMMY	STATIST ECONOMY DUMMY	POPULATION 2002 (millions)	LOGGED POPULATION 2002 (millions)	AVERAGE YEARS OF SCHOOLING, POPULATION 25 AND ABOVE
AFGHANISTAN	3	4.32	0	0	22.900	1.360	1.0
ALBANIA	2	8.71	0	0	3.100	0.491	6.0
ALGERIA	3	10.16	0	1	31.300	1.496	4.3
ANDORRA	1	0.00	1	0	0.069	−1.161	9.0
ANGOLA	3	10.61	0	1	13.200	1.121	2.5
ANTIGUA AND BARBUDA	2	2.00	0	0	0.069	−1.161	5.4
ARGENTINA	2	2.70	1	0	38.000	1.580	9.4
ARMENIA	3	14.71	0	0	3.100	0.491	5.0
AUSTRALIA	1	2.61	1	0	19.500	1.290	11.9
AUSTRIA	1	4.27	1	0	8.100	0.908	11.7
AZERBAIJAN	4	10.49	0	0	8.300	0.919	5.0
BAHAMAS	1	2.87	1	0	0.314	−0.503	7.0
BAHRAIN	3	29.86	0	1	0.672	−0.173	5.1
BANGLADESH	2	1.39	0	0	143.800	2.158	2.3
BARBADOS	1	2.03	1	0	0.269	−0.570	9.8
BELARUS	4	19.17	0	1	9.900	0.996	7.0
BELGIUM	1	3.81	1	0	10.300	1.013	11.0
BELIZE	1	3.50	0	0	0.253	−0.597	5.4
BENIN	1	1.07	0	0	6.600	0.820	1.3
BHUTAN	3	0.00	0	0	2.200	0.342	1.1
BOLIVIA	2	7.98	1	0	8.600	0.934	4.8
BOSNIA-HERZEGOVINA	3	4.83	0	0	4.100	0.613	7.0
BOTSWANA	1	5.83	1	0	1.800	0.255	3.6
BRAZIL	2	3.82	0	0	176.300	2.246	4.7
BRUNEI	4	35.67	0	0	0.351	−0.455	6.2
BULGARIA	2	12.80	0	0	8.000	0.903	7.5
BURKINA FASO	3	4.78	0	0	12.600	1.100	1.1
BURMA/MYANMAR	4	11.13	0	1	48.900	1.689	2.8
BURUNDI	4	13.18	0	0	6.600	0.820	1.3
CAMBODIA	3	13.91	0	0	13.800	1.140	3.2
CAMEROON	3	2.04	1	0	15.700	1.196	2.4
CANADA	1	1.97	1	0	31.300	1.496	13.0
CAPE VERDE	1	2.40	0	0	0.458	−0.339	3.2
CENTRAL AFRICAN REP.	3	0.67	0	0	3.800	0.580	1.4
CHAD	3	3.66	1	0	8.300	0.919	1.2

COUNTRY	REGIME CATEGORY	MILITARY PARTICIPATION RATIO, 2002 (per 1000 population)	MARKET CAPITALIST ECONOMY DUMMY	STATIST ECONOMY DUMMY	POPULATION 2002 (millions)	LOGGED POPULATION 2002 (millions)	AVERAGE YEARS OF SCHOOLING, POPULATION 25 AND ABOVE
CHILE	1	7.31	1	0	15.600	1.193	8.2
CHINA	4	2.91	0	0	1294.900	3.112	5.3
COLOMBIA	2	7.38	0	0	43.500	1.638	7.7
COMOROS	3	0.00	0	0	0.586	−0.232	2.0
CONGO, DR (Kinshasa)	4	2.71	0	0	51.200	1.709	2.5
CONGO, R (Brazzaville)	3	3.33	0	0	3.600	0.556	2.9
COSTA RICA	1	2.05	1	0	4.100	0.613	6.1
CROATIA	2	13.86	0	0	4.400	0.643	7.5
CUBA	4	6.42	0	1	11.300	1.053	8.6
CYPRUS (Greek)	1	12.63	1	0	0.765	−0.116	7.9
CZECH REPUBLIC	1	5.39	1	0	10.200	1.009	9.2
DENMARK	1	4.20	1	0	5.400	0.732	10.4
DJIBOUTI	3	17.64	0	0	0.657	−0.182	1.3
DOMINICA	1	0.00	1	0	0.072	−1.143	5.5
DOMINICAN REPUBLIC	2	4.59	0	0	8.600	0.934	5.2
ECUADOR	2	4.67	0	0	12.800	1.107	6.2
EGYPT	4	10.96	0	0	70.500	1.848	4.3
EL SALVADOR	2	4.30	1	0	6.400	0.806	5.0
EQUATORIAL GUINEA	4	2.64	0	0	0.481	−0.318	1.8
ERITREA	4	51.30	0	0	4.000	0.602	1.3
ESTONIA	1	6.23	1	0	1.300	0.114	9.2
ETHIOPIA	3	2.36	0	0	69.000	1.839	2.1
FIJI	3	4.38	0	0	0.823	−0.085	5.7
FINLAND	1	6.71	1	0	5.200	0.716	11.2
FRANCE	1	6.05	1	0	59.800	1.777	12.4
GABON	3	3.62	1	0	1.300	0.114	3.6
GAMBIA	3	0.57	0	0	1.400	0.146	1.5
GEORGIA	2	5.62	0	0	5.200	0.716	5.0
GERMANY	1	3.59	1	0	82.400	1.916	11.4
GHANA	2	0.34	0	0	20.500	1.312	4.5
GREECE	1	16.51	1	0	11.000	1.041	7.8
GRENADA	1	1.00	0	0	0.102	−0.991	5.5
GUATEMALA	2	4.20	0	0	12.000	1.079	4.6
GUINEA	4	2.30	0	0	8.400	0.924	1.8
GUINEA-BISSAU	3	8.04	0	0	1.400	0.146	1.3
GUYANA	1	3.88	0	0	0.772	−0.112	5.7
HAITI	4	0.65	0	0	8.200	0.914	2.0

continues...

COUNTRY	REGIME CATEGORY	MILITARY PARTICIPATION RATIO, 2002 (per 1000 population)	MARKET CAPITALIST ECONOMY DUMMY	STATIST ECONOMY DUMMY	POPULATION 2002 (millions)	LOGGED POPULATION 2002 (millions)	AVERAGE YEARS OF SCHOOLING, POPULATION 25 AND ABOVE
HONDURAS	2	2.94	0	0	6.800	0.833	4.3
HUNGARY	1	4.79	1	0	9.900	0.996	9.7
ICELAND	1	0.33	1	0	0.284	−0.547	8.7
INDIA	2	2.28	0	0	1049.500	3.021	3.5
INDONESIA	2	2.27	0	0	217.100	2.337	5.3
IRAN	3	8.22	0	0	68.100	1.833	5.2
IRAQ	3	18.31	0	1	24.500	1.389	5.9
IRELAND	1	2.69	1	0	3.900	0.591	9.2
ISRAEL	1	26.90	1	0	6.300	0.799	10.2
ITALY	1	8.19	1	0	57.500	1.760	8.1
IVORY COAST (Côte d'Ivoire)	3	1.68	1	0	16.400	1.215	2.9
JAMAICA	2	1.09	1	0	2.600	0.415	6.0
JAPAN	1	1.98	1	0	127.500	2.106	11.2
JORDAN	3	20.79	0	0	5.300	0.724	7.0
KAZAKHSTAN	4	6.10	0	0	15.500	1.190	5.0
KENYA	2	0.92	1	0	31.500	1.498	3.3
KIRIBATI	1	0.00	0	0	0.087	−1.060	
KOREA, NORTH	4	54.78	0	1	22.500	1.352	6.0
KOREA, SOUTH	1	14.57	1	0	47.400	1.676	10.0
KUWAIT	3	9.21	0	1	2.400	0.380	6.5
KYRGYZSTAN	4	3.12	0	0	5.100	0.708	5.0
LAOS	4	23.47	0	1	5.500	0.740	4.1
LATVIA	1	3.78	1	0	2.300	0.362	9.5
LEBANON	3	23.56	0	0	3.600	0.556	5.7
LESOTHO	2	1.11	1	0	1.800	0.255	3.8
LIBERIA	4	6.06	0	0	3.200	0.505	2.3
LIBYA	4	14.17	0	1	5.400	0.732	4.7
LIECHTENSTEIN	2	0.00	1	0	0.033	−1.481	
LITHUANIA	1	7.80	1	0	3.500	0.544	9.3
LUXEMBOURG	1	3.75	1	0	0.444	−0.353	10.5
MACEDONIA	2	9.95	0	0	2.000	0.301	7.0
MADAGASCAR	2	1.28	0	0	16.900	1.228	3.2
MALAWI	2	0.57	1	0	11.900	1.076	1.7
MALAYSIA	3	5.00	0	0	24.000	1.380	7.7
MALDIVES	3	16.67	0	0	0.287	−0.542	5.4
MALI	2	1.20	0	0	12.600	1.100	0.5
MALTA	1	5.25	1	0	0.397	−0.401	6.9
MARSHALL ISLANDS	1	0.00	0	0	0.052	−1.284	

COUNTRY	REGIME CATEGORY	MILITARY PARTICIPATION RATIO, 2002 (per 1000 population)	MARKET CAPITALIST ECONOMY DUMMY	STATIST ECONOMY DUMMY	POPULATION 2002 (millions)	LOGGED POPULATION 2002 (millions)	AVERAGE YEARS OF SCHOOLING, POPULATION 25 AND ABOVE
MAURITANIA	3	7.39	0	0	2.800	0.447	1.3
MAURITIUS	1	1.67	1	0	1.200	0.079	4.5
MEXICO	2	2.00	0	0	102.000	2.009	5.6
MICRONESIA	1	0.00	1	0	0.108	−0.967	
MOLDOVA	2	2.47	0	0	4.300	0.633	6.0
MONACO	2	0.00	0	0	0.034	−1.469	
MONGOLIA	2	6.27	0	0	2.600	0.415	7.5
MOROCCO	3	8.18	0	0	30.100	1.479	4.1
MOZAMBIQUE	2	0.44	0	0	18.500	1.267	1.9
NAMIBIA	2	7.50	0	0	2.000	0.301	
NAURU	1	0.00	0	0	0.013	−1.886	
NEPAL	3	3.57	0	0	24.600	1.391	3.0
NETHERLANDS	1	3.29	1	0	16.100	1.207	11.2
NEW ZEALAND	1	2.29	1	0	3.800	0.580	10.7
NICARAGUA	2	2.64	0	0	5.300	0.724	5.1
NIGER	2	0.93	1	0	11.500	1.061	0.4
NIGERIA	2	1.33	0	0	120.900	2.082	2.2
NORWAY	1	5.91	1	0	4.500	0.653	12.6
OMAN	4	16.46	0	1	2.800	0.447	2.2
PAKISTAN	3	6.06	0	0	149.900	2.176	2.0
PALAU	1	0.00	1	0	0.020	−1.699	
PANAMA	2	3.81	0	0	3.100	0.491	7.3
PAPUA NEW GUINEA	2	0.55	1	0	5.600	0.748	1.6
PARAGUAY	2	5.86	0	0	5.700	0.756	4.9
PERU	2	6.60	0	0	26.800	1.428	7.8
PHILIPPINES	2	1.91	0	0	78.600	1.895	7.9
POLAND	1	4.78	1	0	38.600	1.587	8.3
PORTUGAL	1	9.00	1	0	10.000	1.000	6.6
QATAR	3	20.67	0	0	0.610	−0.215	6.9
ROMANIA	2	8.00	0	0	22.400	1.350	7.3
RUSSIA	3	9.70	0	0	144.100	2.159	9.0
RWANDA	4	7.59	0	0	8.300	0.919	1.6
SAINT KITTS AND NEVIS	1	2.50	1	0	0.046	−1.337	6.8
SAINT LUCIA	1	0.00	1	0	0.159	−0.799	4.7
SAINT VINCENT AND THE GRENADINES	1	0.00	1	0	0.117	−0.932	5.4

continues...

COUNTRY	REGIME CATEGORY	MILITARY PARTICIPATION RATIO, 2002 (per 1000 population)	MARKET CAPITALIST ECONOMY DUMMY	STATIST ECONOMY DUMMY	POPULATION 2002 (millions)	LOGGED POPULATION 2002 (millions)	AVERAGE YEARS OF SCHOOLING, POPULATION 25 AND ABOVE
SAMOA (Western)	1	0.00	1	0	0.176	−0.754	6.9
SAN MARINO	1	33.33	1	0	0.027	−1.569	9.0
SÃO TOMÉ AND PRÍNCIPE	2	4.00	0	0	0.154	−0.812	3.3
SAUDI ARABIA	4	9.15	0	0	23.500	1.371	5.0
SENEGAL	2	1.88	1	0	9.900	0.996	1.2
SERBIA AND MONTENEGRO	2	11.64	0	0	10.500	1.021	7.5
SEYCHELLES	2	7.00	0	0	0.084	−1.076	5.6
SIERRA LEONE	2	2.92	0	0	4.800	0.681	1.6
SINGAPORE	3	37.33	1	0	4.200	0.623	6.5
SLOVAKIA	1	5.72	1	0	5.400	0.732	8.9
SLOVENIA	1	6.75	1	0	2.000	0.301	9.4
SOLOMON ISLANDS	2	0.00	0	0	0.443	−0.354	2.2
SOMALIA	4	3.59	0	0	9.500	0.978	1.2
SOUTH AFRICA	1	1.24	1	0	44.800	1.651	6.6
SPAIN	1	6.13	1	0	41.000	1.613	8.0
SRI LANKA	2	13.04	1	0	18.900	1.276	7.7
SUDAN	4	3.48	0	0	32.900	1.517	1.5
SURINAME	1	4.60	0	0	0.423	−0.374	5.0
SWAZILAND	4	2.73	0	0	1.100	0.041	4.6
SWEDEN	1	7.81	1	0	8.900	0.949	12.9
SWITZERLAND	1	3.83	1	0	7.200	0.857	11.6
SYRIA	4	24.54	0	1	17.400	1.241	5.6
TAIWAN	1	17.63	1	0	22.400	1.350	8.3
TAJIKISTAN	4	1.16	0	0	6.200	0.792	5.0
TANZANIA	3	0.78	0	0	36.300	1.560	3.0
THAILAND	2	6.74	0	0	62.200	1.794	4.6
TIMOR-LESTE (East Timor)	2	0.00	0	0	0.711	−0.148	
TOGO	4	1.94	0	0	4.800	0.681	2.1
TONGA	3	1.00	0	0	0.101	−0.996	
TRINIDAD AND TOBAGO	2	2.08	0	0	1.300	0.114	9.0
TUNISIA	4	4.85	0	0	9.700	0.987	3.3
TURKEY	2	9.46	0	0	70.300	1.847	4.4
TURKMENISTAN	4	3.65	0	1	4.800	0.681	5.0
TUVALU	1	0.00	1	0	0.010	−2.000	
UGANDA	3	2.47	0	0	25.000	1.398	1.5
UKRAINE	3	8.48	0	0	48.900	1.689	6.0
UNITED ARAB EMIRATES	4	14.31	0	0	2.900	0.462	6.4
UNITED KINGDOM	1	3.56	1	0	59.100	1.772	12.1

COUNTRY	REGIME CATEGORY	MILITARY PARTICIPATION RATIO, 2002 (per 1000 population)	MARKET CAPITALIST ECONOMY DUMMY	STATIST ECONOMY DUMMY	POPULATION 2002 (millions)	LOGGED POPULATION 2002 (millions)	AVERAGE YEARS OF SCHOOLING, POPULATION 25 AND ABOVE
UNITED STATES	1	5.04	1	0	291.000	2.464	12.6
URUGUAY	1	7.33	1	0	3.400	0.531	8.4
UZBEKISTAN	4	2.80	0	1	25.700	1.410	5.0
VANUATU	1	1.50	0	0	0.206	−0.686	4.9
VENEZUELA	2	3.27	0	0	25.200	1.401	7.0
VIETNAM	4	6.53	0	1	80.300	1.905	5.8
YEMEN	3	7.07	0	0	19.300	1.286	2.1
ZAMBIA	3	1.82	0	0	10.700	1.029	4.0
ZIMBABWE	4	3.97	0	1	12.800	1.107	3.7
MEAN		6.67				0.689	5.7

military participation ratio (armed forces per 1000 population), (2) the capitalist market economy dummy variable, (3) the statist market economy dummy variable, (4) the logged value of the population, and (5) the mean years of schooling of those 25 and above. These five variables explain over 60 per cent of the variance in the level of democracy versus autocracy across our four categories. Of these five variables the single most important one is the average years of schooling. Table 5.5 provides the values on each of these five variables for all countries. One can see, for example, how all of the Nordic countries are "logical liberal democracies" given their limited militarization, their capitalist market economies, their small populations, and their high levels of education in terms of average years of schooling. On the other hand, North Korea can serve as a "logical closed autocracy" given especially its extreme militarization (the highest in the world) and its statist economy.

NOTES

1 Robert H. Dix, "History and Democracy Revisited," *Comparative Politics* 27:1 (October 1994): 91–105.

2 Dix 94.

3 Dix 95.

4 Dix 96–98.

5 Richard Rose and Doh Chull Shin, "Democratization Backwards: The Problem of Third-Wave Democracies," *British Journal of Political Science* 31 (2001): 331–54.

6 Samuel P. Huntington, *The Third Wave: Democratization in the Late Twentieth Century* (Norman, OK: University of Oklahoma Press, 1991) 38.

7 Robert A. Dahl, *Democracy and its Critics* (New Haven, CT: Yale University Press, 1989) 262.

8 Larry Diamond, Juan J. Linz, and Seymour Martin Lipset, "Introduction: What Makes for Democracy?" *Politics in Developing Countries: Comparing Experiences with Democracy*, 2nd ed., ed. Larry Diamond *et al.* (Boulder, CO: Lynne Rienner, 1995) 19.

9 Dahl, *Polyarchy* 126–28.

10 Diamond, Linz, and Lipset 20.

11 Dahl, *Democracy and its Critics* 248.

12 Dahl, *Democracy and its Critics* 248–49.

13 Dahl, *Democracy and its Critics* 246–50.

14 Dahl, *Democracy and its Critics* 260–62.

15 Seymour Martin Lipset, "Some Social Requisites of Democracy: Economic Development and Political Legitimacy," *American Political Science Review* 53 (1959): 69–105; and Seymour Martin Lipset, "The Social Requisites of Democracy Revisited," *American Sociological Review* 59 (1994): 1–22.

16 On this causal sequence, see Adam Przeworski and Fernando Limongi, "Modernization: Theories and Facts," *World Politics* 49 (1997): 155–83.

17 Dahl, *Democracy and its Critics* 251.

18 Tatu Vanhanen, *The Process of Democratization: A Comparative Study of 147 States, 1980–88* (New York, NY: Crane Russak, 1990) 50–65.

19 Barrington Moore, *Social Origins of Dictatorship and Democracy: Lord and Peasant in the Making of the Modern World* (Boston, MA: Beacon Press, 1966) 418.

20 Dahl, *Democracy and its Critics* 252.

21 Vanhanen 50.

22 Dahl, *Democracy and its Critics* 252.

23 Dahl, *Democracy and its Critics* 253–54.

24 On the superior utility of using the HDI as opposed to just per capita wealth as a causal explanation for democracy, see Larry Diamond, "Economic Development and Democracy Reconsidered," *American Behavioral Scientist* 35:4–5 (March/June 1992): 457–60.

25 Axel Hadenius, *Democracy and Development* (Cambridge, UK: Cambridge University Press, 1992) 86–91.

26 For an analysis of levels of democracy (using Freedom House scores) which includes average years of schooling as a variable, see Henry S. Rowen, "The Tide Underneath the 'Third Wave,'" *Journal of Democracy* 6:1 (January 1995): 52–64.

27 Robert J. Barro and Jong-Wha Lee, "International Data on Educational Attainment: Updates and Implications," Working Paper No. 42 (Cambridge, MA: Harvard University, Center for International Development, April 2000) data appendix.

28 See for example Edward N. Muller, "Democracy, Economic Development, and Income Inequality," *American Sociological Review* 53:1 (February 1988): 50–68. Specifically, Muller found that, of countries that were (electorally) democratic as of 1961 and for which inequality data existed, those with high levels of income inequality all failed to maintain stable democracy through 1980. In contrast, most of the sample countries with intermediate levels of income inequality maintained stable democracy, as did all of the countries with low levels of income inequality (Muller 63).

29 Of course, income equality can be seen as an aspect of development to the extent that wealthier countries are more likely to have less inequality. For the available data (123 countries), the correlation between per capita income and the GINI index is -0.410, which is indeed significantly negative (significant at the .000 level).

30 Charles E. Lindblom, *Politics and Markets: The World's Political-Economic Systems* (New York, NY: Basic Books, 1977) 164–65.

31 The analyses used for these purposes are primarily those of Freedom House (*Freedom in the World* and *Nations in Transit*), but also those of the Heritage Foundation (its Index of Economic Freedom), the Fraser Institute, and the United States Government Trade Office (its Country Commercial Guides).

32 Paul Sutton, "Democracy in the Commonwealth Caribbean," *Democratization* 6:1 (Spring 1999): 68.

33 Sutton 68–69.

34 Pierre Elliott Trudeau, "Some Obstacles to Democracy in Quebec," *The Canadian Journal of Economics and Political Science* 24:3 (August 1958): 300.

35 Adrian Karatnycky, "The 2001 Freedom House Survey: Muslim Countries and the Democracy Gap," *Journal of Democracy* 13:1 (January 2002): 99–112.

36 Dahl, *Democracy and its Critics* 256–57; Arend Lijphart, *Democracy in Plural Societies: A Comparative Exploration* (New Haven, CT: Yale University Press, 1977).

37 Lijphart, *Democracy in Plural Societies* 1–2.

38 Arend Lijphart, "The Puzzle of Indian Democracy: A Consociational Reinterpretation," *American Political Science Review* 90:2 (1996): 258–68.

39 For example, Dag Anckar, "Democratic Standard and Performance in Twelve Pacific Micro-states," *Pacific Affairs* 75:2 (Summer 2002): 208.

40 Dana Ott, *Small is Democratic: An Examination of State Size and Democratic Development* (New York, NY and London, UK: Garland Publishing, 2000).

41 Diamond, *Developing Democracy* 117–19.

42 Diamond, *Developing Democracy* 117–19; Ott 209, note 1.

43 Ott 197.

44 Ott 200.

45 H.E. Chehabi, "Small Island States," *The Encyclopedia of Democracy*, ed. Seymour Martin Lipset (Washington, DC: Congressional Quarterly, 1995) 1136.

46 Ott 203.

47 Diamond, *Developing Democracy* 119ff.; Ott 208.

48 Ott 203.

49 Lijphart 65–68.

50 See Lijphart 69–70.

51 Diamond, *Developing Democracy* 118.

52 In this regard one can note the regional domino effect of democratization in the 1980s and 1990s and also of the democratic breakdowns in the 1930s (in East-Central Europe) and the 1960s (in Latin America).

53 Morton H. Halperin and Kristen Lomasney, "Guaranteeing Democracy: A Review of the Record," *Journal of Democracy* 9:2 (April 1998): 137–39.

CHAPTER SIX

Institutional Variations of Democracies

IN THIS CHAPTER YOU WILL LEARN:

» *what is the precise definition of a presidential system and the precise definition of a parliamentary system;*

» *what are the strengths and weakness of each of these systems, and how the weaknesses might be mitigated;*

» *how democratic systems can be neither fully presidential nor fully parliamentary, but rather "mixed";*

» *what are the differing types of heads of state in parliamentary systems;*

» *what are the reasons for bicameralism;*

» *how lower houses and upper houses differ;*

» *what precisely is federalism in terms of both inter-state and intrastate factors; and*

» *how does federalism differ from other spatially based political structures.*

CONTEXT

As determined in Chapter 3, there are today 116 independent countries which are either liberal democracies or at least electoral democracies. This chapter will outline how these systems vary in terms of their institutional features. First, we shall make a distinction between presidential and parliamentary systems. Then we shall note some variations in the roles and natures of legislatures. Finally, we shall outline what is meant by federalism and look at alternatives to this. Note that the analysis applies only to the liberal and electoral democracies in the world; for example, many non-democracies are run by presidents, but they are not our concern here.

PRESIDENTIAL AND PARLIAMENTARY SYSTEMS

Although students undoubtedly have a "gut" understanding of these variations, the full definitions need to be noted. Let us start with a **presidential system**. There are five aspects to such a system:

» the position of head of government (the one who runs the country) and head of state (the symbolic national head) are fused in the single office of the president;

» this is a one-person executive office which cannot be shared, thus making the presidency a "winner-take-all" position;

» the president is chosen separately from the legislature (even if on the same day), making the president independent from the legislature in terms of political survival (and vice-versa);

» the president is elected for a fixed term of a specified number of years, as are legislators for their own fixed terms; and

» the head of government (the president) is elected directly by the voters or possibly by an **electoral college** which is itself directly elected for this specific purpose and no other (so it is not an ongoing body).

In short, this system provides a definite stability for the position of president. Table 6.1 lists the 30 current democracies which meet the above criteria. Of these 30, a majority (16) are in Latin America, with eight others being in Africa. Presidential systems are thus far and away the most common political system in Latin America. One can see that the length of presidential terms

TABLE 6.1 :: LIBERAL AND ELECTORAL DEMOCRACIES, PRESIDENTIAL SYSTEMS

COUNTRY	LENGTH OF PRESIDENTIAL TERM (years)	MAXIMUM CONSECUTIVE TERMS	ELECTORAL FORMULA
ARGENTINA	4	2	plurality of 45%, otherwise runoff *
BENIN	5	2	absolute majority, otherwise runoff
BRAZIL	4	2	absolute majority, otherwise runoff
CHILE	6	1	absolute majority, otherwise runoff
COLOMBIA	4	1	absolute majority, otherwise runoff
COSTA RICA	4	1	plurality of 40%, otherwise runoff
CYPRUS	5	unlimited	absolute majority, otherwise runoff
DOMINICAN REPUBLIC	4	1	absolute majority, otherwise runoff
ECUADOR	4	1	absolute majority, otherwise runoff **
EL SALVADOR	5	1	absolute majority, otherwise runoff
GHANA	4	2	absolute majority, otherwise runoff
GUATEMALA	4	1	absolute majority, otherwise runoff
HONDURAS	4	1	simple plurality
INDONESIA	5	2	absolute majority plus regional minimums, otherwise runoff
KENYA	5	2	simple plurality plus regional minimums, otherwise runoff
MALAWI	5	2	simple plurality
MEXICO	6	1	simple plurality
NAMIBIA	5	2	absolute majority, otherwise repeated
NICARAGUA	5	1	plurality of 40%, otherwise runoff ***
NIGER	5	2	absolute majority, otherwise runoff
NIGERIA	4	2	simple plurality plus regional minimums, otherwise runoff
PALAU	4	2	?
PANAMA	5	1	simple plurality
PARAGUAY	5	1	simple plurality
PHILIPPINES	6	1	simple plurality
SEYCHELLES	5	3	?
SIERRA LEONE	5	2	qualified majority of 55%, otherwise runoff
UNITED STATES	4	2	absolute majority in electoral college, otherwise election by House of Representatives
URUGUAY	5	1	absolute majority, otherwise runoff
VENEZUELA	6	2	simple plurality

 * In Argentina, 40% is sufficient to win outright on the first ballot if this is also 10% above the second-place candidate.

 ** In Ecuador, 45% is sufficient to win outright on the first ballot if this is also 10% above the second-place candidate.

 *** In Nicaragua, 35% is sufficient to win outright on the first ballot if this is also 5% above the second-place candidate.

vary from four to six years. Analyses have linked a shorter term to greater political stability, since six years is a long time to wait for a head of government to leave office or face the voters again. However, not all presidents will or even can face the voters again. This is because almost all presidential systems (Cyprus being the one exception) place a limit on the number of consecutive terms one can be president—and some presidential systems go further by limiting individuals to one term only, that is, a president cannot *ever* run for re-election.[1] This constraint has been particularly common in Latin America, existing, for example, in Colombia, Costa Rica, and Mexico. Although this rule obviously prevents someone being in office too long, it also lessens the incentive to do a good job since one cannot be re-elected. Of course, even if a president can serve two terms—the most common pattern for presidencies outside of Latin America[2]—he or she will still be a "lame duck" in the second (or final) term.

The most common method of electing a president is requiring someone to win an absolute majority of the votes (on the first ballot); otherwise, there is a runoff election of the top two candidates. Several presidents, however, are elected by simple plurality; that is, there is only one ballot and the candidate with the most votes wins. Of course, under any plurality system, there is no guarantee of high, let alone majority, support if there are multiple candidates. In 1970, under such a system, the leftist Salvador Allende won the presidency of Chile with only 36 per cent of the vote. Three years later, just over halfway into his term, he was overthrown in a military coup.[3] Some countries have qualified this plurality method by insisting that a candidate win a certain percentage of the vote, even if not an absolute majority. The United States uses a very unique system to elect its president, based not on total votes (as, most recently, 2000 showed) but on candidates winning votes in an electoral college which is determined state-by-state.

There is much less variation in presidential powers across systems. All of these presidents hand-pick their cabinets, make a range of other appointments (in both cases possibly subject to confirmation by the legislature), chair the cabinet meetings (and thus set the agenda), are in charge of foreign policy, and have a veto on legislation (with varying thresholds to overturn). Of course, a legislative veto is a negative power; that is, it stops or delays change. In terms of bringing forth new legislation, most presidents must rely on their political skills to sell this to their legislature. Only a very few presidents (Argentina, Brazil, Chile) have decree powers, whereby they can effectively proclaim something to take effect (unless or until there is actual legislation on the issue).

A **parliamentary system** can also be viewed as having five aspects, listed so as to contrast it point-by-point with a presidential system:

» the key day-to-day political position is that of the head of government (prime minister or equivalent); however, this person is not the head of state; instead, there is almost always a separate head of state;

» the cabinet is much more of a collegial body than in presidential systems, making parliamentary cabinets amenable to coalition governments (and thus parliamentary elections not necessarily winner-take-all);

» the government is continually dependent for its survival on maintaining the confidence, or at least the acquiescence, of the parliament;

» failing the last point, the government can fall at any time (when parliament is sitting, anyway) through a motion of non-confidence; and

» the head of government is not chosen directly by the voters but is ultimately selected by the legislature (in effect by its partisan composition).

The nature and role of parliamentary heads of state vary significantly; we shall return to this point. (Successful) non-confidence motions mean that a parliamentary head of government does not have any constitutionally fixed minimum term of office, so in some cases people have lasted as prime minister for only a matter of days or weeks. In terms of the final point, following Arend Lijphart, we use the broad term "selected" because there is a key difference here:[4] in some parliamentary systems, there is a formal vote by the parliament on a would-be government/prime minister, which/who must then win this **vote of investiture**. Such a procedure is called *positive parliamentarianism*, since there must be a positive endorsement of a new, or continuing, government (even if the voters apparently did so). In contrast, under *negative parliamentarianism* there is no vote of investiture that one must win. A prime minister and government are simply appointed, and they are assumed to be acceptable ("negative" confirmation) unless or until there is a successful motion of non-confidence. In situations where no party wins a majority, positive parliamentarianism is likely to lead to a majority coalition (so it has the votes to be invested), whereas negative parliamentarianism is likely to lead to a minority government of the largest party. Related to this variation, it is also generally the case that it takes longer to form a government under positive parliamentarianism,[5] usually a month and sometimes several months. Broadly speaking, positive parliamentarianism is the more common version globally; however, the United Kingdom, Canada, and other former British colonies use negative parliamentarianism, as do Austria, France, Portugal, and most Nordic countries.[6]

We can now note the various strengths and weaknesses of presidential and parliamentary systems, which tend to be the mirror image of each other. Parliamentary systems can be unstable, with governments collapsing or changing frequently (such as in Weimar Germany or postwar Italy). However, if a parliamentary government has both a majority and policy consensus, then it is quite likely to get its legislation passed. In contrast, presidential systems are stable in the sense of the individual president remaining in office, but there is no guarantee of any desired legislation occurring if the president's party has little strength in the legislature. Thus, presidential systems are prone to a gridlock which has no parliamentary equivalent. Indeed, a president may not even be able to count on members of her/his own party. In a parliamentary system, deputies almost never vote against a government of their own party, since this would bring down the government; however, in a presidential system there is no such constraint.

That said, within each system there are procedures one can use to mitigate the likelihood of dysfunctional outcomes. In a parliamentary system, one effective procedure is to require a "constructive vote of non-confidence"; that is, when (before) a government is removed, there must be majority support for an alternate government (or prime minister) to take over. Given its interwar parliamentary instability, postwar Germany chose this system, and there has been only one successful non-confidence vote in postwar Germany (in 1982). Similar requirements for a "constructive vote of non-confidence" now exist in Belgium, Hungary, and Spain. A weaker but still useful variant of this procedure occurs in Portugal and Sweden, where an absolute majority of all deputies (not merely those present and voting) is needed for a successful non-confidence motion. In a presidential system, in order to increase the president's support in the legislature, scholars have argued for having the entire legislature elected at the same time as the president, so as to maximize the president's "coat-tails effect." Certainly, when and where the legislature is elected at a different time, this tends to go against the president. For example, in the United States the president's party almost always loses support in midterm Congressional elections.

MIXED SYSTEMS

Currently there are some 73 pure parliamentary systems among the world's liberal democracies and electoral democracies. Before subdividing these further, let us note that there are also several systems that are neither presidential nor parliamentary, but which we are calling "mixed." Figure 6.1 lists these. The first type has a dual executive, but the prime minister is elected directly, using a vote separate from that of the legislature. This was the situation in Israel from 1996 through 2001, and it was also seriously discussed in the Netherlands in the 1960s and 1970s. Such a system is meant to counteract the instability that comes from a fragmented multi-party system. However in Israel, if anything, this system exacerbated party fragmentation, since people no longer had to vote for one of the larger parties in the hopes that its leader would become prime minister. The second type has a dual executive but is effectively presidential, since neither the president nor the prime minister are accountable to the legislature, and the president has the usual range of presidential powers. In these systems (Guyana, South Korea, and Sri Lanka), the prime minister is more of a "house leader" for the president, aiming to get legislation passed, than an independent political leader. The third and fourth types of mixed systems have a single executive, which at first glance might make them seem fully presidential. However, in the third type (Botswana, Kiribati, the Marshall Islands, and Nauru) the president is accountable to the legisla-

147

FIGURE 6.1 :: LIBERAL AND ELECTORAL DEMOCRACIES, SYSTEMS OF GOVERNMENT

PARLIAMENTARY

(dual executive, with head of government accountable to legislature)

MONARCHY		REPUBLIC		
parliamentary system with indigenous monarch	parliamentary system with governor general	parliamentary system with a figurehead president	parliamentary system with a presidential corrective	parliamentary system with presidential dominance

PRESIDENTIAL

(single executive, not accountable to legislature)

MIXED

MIXED 1: dual executive, with prime minister directly elected (Israel 1996–2001)
MIXED 2: dual executive, with prime minister not accountable (Guyana, South Korea, Sri Lanka)
MIXED 3: single executive, accountable to legislature (Botswana, Kiribati, Marshall Islands, Nauru)
MIXED 4: single executive, chosen by but not accountable to legislature (Bolivia [usually], Micronesia, South Africa, Suriname, Switzerland)
MIXED 5: co-executives, chosen by but not accountable to legislature (San Marino)

ture and can be removed by a simple vote of non-confidence. Thus, they are more parliamentary than presidential. With the exception of Kiribati, these presidents are chosen by the legislatures and not directly by the voters. In the fourth type of mixed system, the single executive president is chosen by the legislature but thereafter is not accountable to it. These systems enjoy presidential-like stability, but their presidents lack the legitimacy of direct election. Such a system is found in Micronesia, South Africa,[7] Suriname, and Switzerland (although Swiss presidents serve only a one-year rotating term). In Bolivia the system is a bit more complicated: candidates there run in a direct election for president, but unless there is a majority winner on the first and only ballot, the legislature will pick among the top finishers and do not have to confirm the plurality leader (indeed, they rarely have). Finally, San Marino is analogous to Switzerland in that it has a rotating executive, except that the leadership term is only six months and there are *two* joint "captains-regent" (one each representing the city and the countryside).

148

FURTHER VARIATIONS WITHIN PARLIAMENTARY SYSTEMS

Parliamentary systems obviously vary in terms of the strength of their heads of government. However, such variations relate more to contextual factors, such as whether the head of government is a party leader, how many seats the government has, and how many parties are in the government. Where there is a coalition of two or more parties, key policies and cabinet positions are worked out beforehand, leaving the head of government much less freedom to change policies or shuffle ministers than if it were a one-party government. These contextual variations can be shaped by institutions, such as positive versus negative parliamentarianism, but the key antecedent institution is probably the electoral system—which we shall get to later.

Two key distinctions can be made concerning the head of state. The first is the nature of the position. In a relatively small group of 13 democracies, largely in Western Europe, there is an indigenous monarch as head of state (Belgium, Denmark, Japan, Lesotho, Liechtenstein, Luxembourg, the Netherlands, Norway, Samoa, Spain, Sweden, Thailand, and the United Kingdom). With some electoral democratic exceptions, such as Liechtenstein, these monarchs have basically no political power; they "reign but do not rule" in constitutional monarchies. The 15 Commonwealth countries that recognize the British monarch as head of state (as of the end of 2004) are also formally constitutional monarchies (Antigua and Barbuda, Australia, Bahamas, Barbados, Belize, Canada, Grenada, Jamaica, New Zealand, Papua New Guinea, Saint Kitts and Nevis, Saint Lucia, Saint Vincent and the Grenadines, the Solomon Islands, and Tuvalu). In each of these cases, a local governor-general (appointed for a fixed term) serves as the British monarch's representative and can be argued to be the country's effective head of state. However, those who wish to "cut the British link" want an indigenous president as head of state, as is the case in the remaining Commonwealth countries.[8]

The other parliamentary liberal democracies and electoral democracies are all republics with a president as head of state. Some of these presidents are popularly elected by the voters; others are chosen by the national legislature (or the national legislature combined with regional politicians). These presidents, especially when elected, may exercise political power; this could amount to any or all of the aforementioned powers of presidents in presidential systems,

149

plus also the power to dissolve the legislature (which does not exist in pure presidential systems). Obviously, the more power exercised by the president, the less there is for the prime minister or equivalent, making the latter a weak head of government. Many scholars refer to the political systems of countries like France and Russia (when Russia was democratic, anyway) as being "semi-presidential," which is normally defined as having a directly elected president with various political powers but also a prime minister and cabinet account-able to the legislature (as well as to the president). Such a term is problematic, however, since such systems retain the most central feature of parliamentary democracy: the ability to remove the prime minister and cabinet through a vote of non-confidence. Thus, these systems can all be considered parliamentary, albeit with qualifications relating to the role of the president (our second key distinction for the majority of parliamentary democracies and electoral democ-racies). Consequently, a three-fold distinction is offered here,[9] as shown in Figure 6.1. First of all, there are some 22 parliamentary systems with a fig-urehead president, who plays only a symbolic role analogous to the afore-mentioned monarchs and governors-general (Albania, Austria, Bangladesh, the Czech Republic, Dominica, Estonia, Finland since its 2000 constitution, Germany, Greece, Hungary, Iceland, India, Israel once again, Italy, Latvia, Malta, Mauritius, Moldova, Slovakia, Slovenia, Trinidad and Tobago, and Vanuatu).[10] It is reasonable to assume that any future president of, say, Australia or Canada would fall into this category. However, in other parlia-mentary systems, the president does have political powers, usually some com-bination of appointment powers, chairing of cabinet meetings, veto power over legislation, and/or the central role in foreign policy. These systems can be called "parliamentary systems with a presidential corrective," inasmuch as the president is able to intervene politically from time to time or control selected areas. There are now 12 of these systems, largely in Europe (Bulgaria, Croatia, Ireland, Lithuania, Macedonia, Mongolia, Poland, Portugal, Romania, Taiwan, Timor-Leste, and Turkey, with all but the Turkish president being popularly elected). Finally, despite the apparent contradiction, there are systems which are parliamentary with (the possibility of) coalition governments, motions of non-confidence, and the like, but where the majority of political power is usually exercised by the president. These can be called "parliamentary systems with presidential dominance," but one should not forget that they are ultimately parliamentary, and if parties hostile to the president gain control of the legislature, the president will be "demoted" to a corrective role. Currently, there are 9 of these systems, basically in Africa and Europe (Cape Verde, France, Georgia, Madagascar, Mali, Mozambique, Peru, São Tomé and Príncipe, and Senegal). Of the African cases of this system, there are just as many former Portuguese colonies as there are former French colonies; this becomes understandable if one notes that after democratization Portugal had this type of parliamentary regime for a few years.

COMPARING LEGISLATURES: STRUCTURAL DISTINCTIONS

Let us now turn to variations across democratic legislatures. Table 6.2 provides information on these for all liberal and electoral democracies. In terms of more formal variations across legislatures, the first structural distinction to note is whether the legislature can exert independent policy-making, normally through a system of numerous standing committees which match government departments and which assess (or can introduce) legislation early on in the process. Such powerful committees are standard in presidential systems but exist in only a minority of parliamentary systems, such as those of (most of) continental Western Europe and Japan. In contrast, the parliaments of the United Kingdom and its former colonies, as well as France under the Fifth Republic, are known for weak committees and for legislatures that are more focussed on debating and "grandstanding" than on policy details. In these latter cases, it is rare for any legislation to be changed greatly from the wishes of the cabinet.

Another structural distinction regarding legislatures, and our central one here, is whether the legislature is *unicameral* (has one chamber) or *bicameral* (has two chambers). Most of the current liberal and electoral democracies are unicameral, but close to 40 per cent are bicameral. It is extremely rare for a country to add a new upper house to a unicameral legislature, although South Africa did this when it adopted a fully democratic constitution in 1994. Newly democratic Indonesia likewise added an upper house in 2004. In contrast, several countries have abolished their upper houses: Denmark (in 1953), New

151

TABLE 6.2 :: LIBERAL AND ELECTORAL DEMOCRACIES, NATIONAL LEGISLATURES

COUNTRY	LOWER HOUSE NAME	NUMBER OF MEMBERS	TERM (YEARS)
ALBANIA	People's Assembly	140	4
ANDORRA	General Council of the Valleys	28	4
ANGOLA	National Assembly	220	4
ANTIGUA AND BARBUDA	House of Representatives	19	5
ARGENTINA	Chamber of Deputies	257	4
AUSTRALIA	House of Representatives	150	3
AUSTRIA	National Council	183	4
BAHAMAS	House of Assembly	40	5
BANGLADESH	National Parliament	300	5
BARBADOS	House of Assembly	30	5
BELGIUM	House of Representatives	150	4
BELIZE	House of Representatives	29	5
BENIN	National Assembly	83	4
BOLIVIA	Chamber of Deputies	130	5
BOTSWANA	National Assembly	57	5
BRAZIL	Chamber of Deputies	513	4
BULGARIA	National Assembly	240	4
CANADA	House of Commons	301	5
CAPE VERDE	National People's Assembly	72	5
CENTRAL AFRICAN REPUBLIC	National Assembly	109	5
CHILE	Chamber of Deputies	120	4
COLUMBIA	Chamber of Representatives	166	4
COSTA RICA	Legislative Assembly	57	4
CROATIA	House of Representatives	151	4
CYPRUS (Greek)	House of Representatives	80	5
CZECH REPUBLIC	Chamber of Deputies	200	4
DENMARK	Parliament	179	4
DOMINICA	Chamber of Assembly	31	5
DOMINICAN REPUBLIC	House of Deputies	150	4
ECUADOR	Chamber of Representatives	123	4
EL SALVADOR	Legislative Assembly	84	3
ESTONIA	State Assembly	101	4
ETHIOPIA	House of People's Representatives	550	5
FINLAND	Parliament	200	4
FRANCE	National Assembly	577	5
GEORGIA	Parliament	235	4
GERMANY	Federal Diet	666	4
GHANA	National Assembly	230	4
GREECE	Parliament	200	4
GRENADA	House of Representatives	15	5

UPPER HOUSE NAME	NUMBER OF MEMBERS	TERM (YEARS)	DIRECTLY/INDIRECTLY APPOINTED/ ELECTED?
n/a	n/a	n/a	n/a
n/a	n/a	n/a	n/a
n/a	n/a	n/a	n/a
Senate	17	5	appointed
Senate	72	6	directly elected
Senate	76	6	directly elected
Federal Council	64	5 to 6	indirectly elected
Senate	16	5	appointed
n/a	n/a	n/a	n/a
Senate	21	5	appointed
Senate	71	4	40 direct / 21 appointed / 10 co-opted
Senate	8	5	appointed
n/a	n/a	n/a	n/a
Chamber of Senators	27	5	directly elected
n/a	n/a	n/a	n/a
Federal Senate	81	8	directly elected
n/a	n/a	n/a	n/a
Senate	105	until age 75	appointed
n/a	n/a	n/a	n/a
n/a	n/a	n/a	n/a
Senate of the Republic	48	8	38 direct / 9 appointed *
Senate of the Republic	102	4	directly elected
n/a	n/a	n/a	n/a
n/a	n/a	n/a	n/a
n/a	n/a	n/a	n/a
Senate	81	6	directly elected
n/a	n/a	n/a	n/a
n/a	n/a	n/a	n/a
n/a	n/a	n/a	n/a
n/a	n/a	n/a	n/a
n/a	n/a	n/a	n/a
n/a	n/a	n/a	n/a
House of the Federation	120	5	both directly and indirectly elected
n/a	n/a	n/a	n/a
Senate	321	9	indirectly elected
n/a	n/a	n/a	n/a
Federal Council	69	varies	appointed
n/a	n/a	n/a	n/a
n/a	n/a	n/a	n/a
Senate	13	5	appointed

continues…

COUNTRY	LOWER HOUSE NAME	NUMBER OF MEMBERS	TERM (YEARS)
GUATEMALA	Congress of the Republic	158	4
GUYANA	National Assembly	65	5
HONDURAS	National Congress	128	4
HUNGARY	National Assembly	386	4
ICELAND	Althing	63	4
INDIA	House of the People	543	5
INDONESIA	People's Representative Council	550	5
IRELAND	House of Representatives	166	5
ISRAEL	Assembly of the Republic	120	4
ITALY	Chamber of Deputies	630	5
JAMAICA	House of Representatives	60	5
JAPAN	Diet	480	4
KENYA	National Assembly	224	5
KIRIBATI	House of Assembly	42	4
KOREA, SOUTH	National Assembly	273	4
LATVIA	Parliament	100	4
LIBERIA	House of Representatives	64	6
LIECHTENSTEIN	Diet	25	4
LITHUANIA	Parliament	141	4
LUXEMBOURG	Chamber of Deputies	60	5
MACEDONIA	Assembly	120	4
MADAGASCAR	Parliament	150	5
MALAWI	National Assembly	193	5
MALI	National Assembly	147	5
MALTA	House of Representatives	65	5
MARSHALL ISLANDS	House of Representatives	33	4
MAURITIUS	National Assembly	70	5
MEXICO	Chamber of Deputies	500	3
MICRONESIA	Congress	14	2
MOLDOVA	Parliament	101	4
MONGOLIA	State Great Hural	76	4
MOZAMBIQUE	Assembly of the Republic	250	5
NAMIBIA	National Assembly	72	5
NAURU	Parliament	18	3
NETHERLANDS	First Chamber	150	4
NEW ZEALAND	House of Representatives	120	3
NICARAGUA	National Assembly	92	5
NIGER	National Assembly	113	5
NIGERIA	House of Representatives	360	4
NORWAY	Parliament	165	4
PALAU	House of Delegates	16	4
PANAMA	Legislative Assembly	71	5

UPPER HOUSE NAME	NUMBER OF MEMBERS	TERM (YEARS)	DIRECTLY/INDIRECTLY APPOINTED/ELECTED?
n/a	n/a	n/a	n/a
n/a	n/a	n/a	n/a
n/a	n/a	n/a	n/a
n/a	n/a	n/a	n/a
n/a	n/a	n/a	n/a
Council of States	245	6	233 elected / 12 appointed
Regional Representatives Council	128	5	directly elected
Senate	60	5	49 elected / 11 appointed
n/a	n/a	n/a	n/a
Senate of the Republic	321	5	315 elected / 4 appointed / 2 ex-officio
Senate	21	5	appointed
House of Councillors	247	6	directly elected
n/a	n/a	n/a	n/a
n/a	n/a	n/a	n/a
n/a	n/a	n/a	n/a
n/a	n/a	n/a	n/a
Senate	26	9	directly elected
n/a	n/a	n/a	n/a
n/a	n/a	n/a	n/a
n/a	n/a	n/a	n/a
n/a	n/a	n/a	n/a
Senate	90	6	60 directly elected / 30 appointed
n/a	n/a	n/a	n/a
n/a	n/a	n/a	n/a
n/a	n/a	n/a	n/a
n/a	n/a	n/a	n/a
n/a	n/a	n/a	n/a
House of Senators	128	6	directly elected
n/a	n/a	n/a	n/a
n/a	n/a	n/a	n/a
n/a	n/a	n/a	n/a
n/a	n/a	n/a	n/a
National Council	26	6	indirectly elected
n/a	n/a	n/a	n/a
Second Chamber	75	4	indirectly elected
n/a	n/a	n/a	n/a
n/a	n/a	n/a	n/a
n/a	n/a	n/a	n/a
Senate	109	4	directly elected
n/a	n/a	n/a	n/a
Senate	9	4	directly elected
n/a	n/a	n/a	n/a

continues...

COUNTRY	LOWER HOUSE NAME	NUMBER OF MEMBERS	TERM (YEARS)
PAPAU NEW GUINEA	National Parliament	109	5
PARAGUAY	House of Deputies	80	5
PERU	Congress of the Republic	120	5
PHILIPPINES	House of Representatives	214	3
POLAND	Chamber of Deputies	460	4
PORTUGAL	Assembly of the Republic	230	4
ROMANIA	Chamber of Deputies	345	4
SAINT KITTS AND NEVIS	National Assembly	15	5
SAINT LUCIA	House of Assembly	18	5
SAINT VINCENT AND THE GRENADINES	House of Assembly	22	5
SAMOA	Legislative Assembly	49	5
SAN MARINO	Grand General Council	60	5
SÃO TOMÉ AND PRÍNCIPE	National Assembly	55	4
SERBIA AND MONTENEGRO	Chamber of Citizens	138	4
SEYCHELLES	National Assembly	34	5
SIERRA LEONE	Parliament	124	5
SLOVAKIA	National Council	150	4
SLOVENIA	National Assembly	90	4
SOLOMON ISLANDS	National Parliament	50	4
SOUTH AFRICA	National Assembly	400	5
SPAIN	Congress of Deputies	350	4
SRI LANKA	Parliament	325	6
SURINAME	National Assembly	51	5
SWEDEN	Riksdagen	349	4
SWITZERLAND	National Council	200	4
TAIWAN	Legislative Yuan	164	3
THAILAND	House of Representatives	500	4
TIMOR-LESTE (East Timor)	National Parliament	88	5
TRINIDAD AND TOBAGO	House of Representatives	36	5
TURKEY	Grand National Assembly	550	5
TUVALU	Parliament	15	4
UNITED KINGDOM	House of Commons	659	5
UNITED STATES	House of Representatives	435	2
URUGUAY	Chamber of Representatives	99	5
VANUATU	Parliament	52	4
VENEZUELA	National Assembly	165	5

Source: Inter-Parliamentary Union <http://www.ipu.org>.

UPPER HOUSE NAME	NUMBER OF MEMBERS	TERM (YEARS)	DIRECTLY/INDIRECTLY APPOINTED/ ELECTED?
n/a	n/a	n/a	n/a
House of Senators	45	5	directly elected
n/a	n/a	n/a	n/a
Senate	24	6	directly elected
Senate	100	4	directly elected
n/a	n/a	n/a	n/a
Senate	140	4	directly elected
n/a	n/a	n/a	n/a
Senate	11	5	appointed
n/a	n/a	n/a	n/a
n/a	n/a	n/a	n/a
n/a	n/a	n/a	n/a
n/a	n/a	n/a	n/a
Chamber of Republics	40	4	indirectly elected
n/a	n/a	n/a	n/a
n/a	n/a	n/a	n/a
n/a	n/a	n/a	n/a
National Council	40	5	elected by interest organizations
n/a	n/a	n/a	n/a
National Council of Provinces	90	5	indirectly elected
Senate	259	4	208 directly / 51 indirectly elected
n/a	n/a	n/a	n/a
n/a	n/a	n/a	n/a
n/a	n/a	n/a	n/a
Council of States	46	4	directly elected
National Assembly	334	4	directly elected
Senate	200	6	directly elected
n/a	n/a	n/a	n/a
Senate	31	5	appointed
n/a	n/a	n/a	n/a
n/a	n/a	n/a	n/a
House of Lords	713	life	hereditary/appointed
Senate	100	6	directly elected
House of the Senate	31	5	directly elected
n/a	n/a	n/a	n/a
n/a	n/a	n/a	n/a

Zealand (in 1951), Sweden (in 1971), and Venezuela (in 2000). Since bicameral systems are the minority, we should ask the question "why bicameralism?" rather than "why unicameralism?" Two reasons can be offered here. First, upper houses can provide a vehicle for regional interests, especially those of less populated regions that would be outvoted in the lower house. Secondly, upper houses can act as a counterbalance to the lower house, independent of any regional concerns. This counterbalancing has taken differing forms. Historically, upper houses were composed of nobles or of people elected on a more restricted franchise than the lower house. These upper houses served as a conservative "check" on the popularly elected lower houses. Nowadays, such a rationale would be seen as unacceptably undemocratic. So the issue today is not so much that a lower house produces excessively radical legislation as it is that the lower house may produce hasty or ill-thought out legislation that needs modification. Hence the expression in Canada that the Senate is the chamber of "sober second thought."

An alternative way of looking at the question of "why bicameralism?" is to note which types of countries are bicameral. Two factors are relevant here. The first is size: small countries (in the sense of population) tend to be unicameral, larger and presumably more diverse countries bicameral. The second factor is federalism; as we shall see shortly, federal systems are invariably bicameral. One factor that might seem relevant here is presidentialism and its logic of "checks and balances"; however, this is not the case. Of the 30 presidential systems in Table 6.1, only half are federal—hardly a strong relationship.

VARIATIONS ACROSS THE TWO CHAMBERS

What variations occur between the lower and upper house in bicameral liberal and electoral democracies? Five main differences are worth noting. The first difference is chamber size: lower houses are almost always larger than their corresponding upper houses. Only in the United Kingdom is this not the case (in fact, its House of Lords used to be even bigger until most of the hereditary lords were removed from it). The second difference is length of term: here it is the upper house where the value is normally greater. For example, United

158

States senators serve terms of six years, three times the two-year term of House members. Canadian senators used to be appointed for life; now they must resign at age 75, but this is still certainly job security. However, one should not be too biased by these North American figures; in many countries the term length is the same for both houses (for example, Bolivia, Colombia, Ireland, Nigeria, Poland, and Switzerland). The third difference is selection procedure: members of the lower house are invariably directly elected, but one gets to be a member of an upper house through a variety of ways: direct election, indirect election by a regional assembly (itself directly elected), being appointed, and in some cases being an ex-officio member (such as Royal princes in Belgium or former presidents in Chile). Where indirect election occurs, often the regional assemblies will select some of their own to this additional job. The fourth difference is that, at least for the elected upper houses, these elections tend to be staggered so that only some of the senators or equivalent are elected at any one time (year).[11] Staggered elections do not occur as such in lower houses (Luxembourg until 1954 being the exception). At best, elections may be spread over a couple of weeks such as in India or nineteenth-century Canada; however, this would be a matter of logistics and not a "check and balance."

The fifth and final difference is that upper houses are normally weaker than lower houses in two senses—government formation and legislative power. In terms of government formation, the norm in parliamentary systems is that only the lower house selects the government, and so only lower house elections matter for coming to office (Italy is an exception to this situation; both houses matter there). Of course, this is irrelevant in presidential systems. The second point is that whereas lower houses have to pass legislation for it to become law, the consent of the upper house is not always required. Objections (or modifications) to legislation by the upper house can often be overcome by the lower house passing the legislation again after a set period of time. This is the pattern in the United Kingdom, for example. Obviously, then, an upper house that cannot actually stop or modify anything significantly is much weaker than one that can.

Arend Lijphart has argued that for bicameralism to be **strong bicameralism**, where the upper house truly matters, three factors must be present:[12] first, both houses must be equal or relatively equal in terms of legislative powers.

Second, the upper house must have the legitimacy to use its powers. Legitimacy normally comes from direct elections, but this could also involve, as in Germany, the upper house representing elected regional governments. In any case, Canada's appointed Senate is a perfect counter-example here. Finally, the upper house must be composed, or (s)elected, in a different way from the lower house; most commonly, this involves a change in the allocation of members, which is to the benefit of the less populated regions, but this may also involve a different electoral system for each chamber (assuming the upper house is elected). If the upper house is chosen in more or less the same way as the lower house, and at the same time, it should be no surprise that its partisan composition will look the same; thus, a party (or coalition) would presumably control both houses. In this sense—Italy and (usually) Japan are examples here—a seemingly important upper house is basically superfluous. Relatively few democracies—Argentina, Australia, Brazil, Colombia, Germany, Mexico, Switzerland, and the United States—meet these three criteria of strong bicameralism. One can note that a majority of these are presidential systems. Yet in a parliamentary system with strong bicameralism and where different parties (or alliances) control the lower and upper houses, the lower house-based government may be stable but will often find it very difficult to get legislation through. In Australia when legislation fails to get through the upper house twice, the prime minister may dissolve both houses. Of course, the resulting *"double dissolution"* election puts the government—and the prime minister's job—on the line. Should such an Australian government be re-elected, yet still be unable to get the legislation through the new Senate, then a *joint sitting* of the House of Representatives and the Senate takes place, where the numerical superiority of the House is usually decisive. In Germany, there are no such options of a "double dissolution" (since the German upper house is indirectly elected) or a joint sitting, and the Germans have taken to using the term *Reformstau* ("political gridlock") to describe a situation of differing partisan control of the chambers.

COMPARING LEGISLATURES: GENDER VARIATIONS

Another way in which legislatures vary is in terms of the dominant demographic characteristics of their members: age, education, gender, and occupational background. In turn, as noted in Chapter 3, one can assess these patterns in comparison to the broader society as a whole. Of these characteristics, the one most thoroughly studied in a global sense is gender; that is, to what extent is a legislature (relatively) balanced between men and women?[13] Again as noted, women are less than half of the deputies in every national parliament in the world—and thus less that half in every national parliament in the world's democracies. However, in Sweden, they are a near-parity minority; as of Sweden's 2002 elections, 45.3 per cent of the deputies in the (unicameral) Swedish *Riksdag* are women. At the other extreme, as of 2004 there are no women in the parliaments of several democracies in Oceania: Micronesia, Nauru, Palau, the Solomon Islands, and Tuvalu. Besides looking at the extremes, we can also dichotomize the world's legislatures in terms of whether the female minority nevertheless amounts to a **critical mass** of around 30 per cent—the scholarly consensus suggests that when women reach such a critical mass, they will have a clear effect on legislatures in terms of both general behaviour (it becoming less antagonistic) and policy priorities and resulting policies. Looking at the legislatures of the world's democracies, or more precisely looking only at the lower chambers in the bicameral systems—since as noted this is almost always the more important chamber—we see that, as of the end of 2004, such a critical mass of female deputies existed in only 15 of the 116 (liberal and electoral) democracies. In descending order of female percentages, these democracies are Sweden, Denmark, Finland, the Netherlands, Norway, Spain, Belgium, Costa Rica, Argentina, Austria, South Africa, Germany, Iceland, and Mozambique. We can note that *all* of these countries use list proportional representation (see Chapter 7); this they generally combine with political leftism—both as a broader national ideology and in terms of the strength of leftist parties—and with non-traditional cultural values.

FEDERALISM

The previous discussion of upper houses leads us to an analysis of federalism. Nearly every liberal democracy or electoral democracy, unless it is very tiny, has local governments, that is, city governments, counties, communes, and/or municipalities. These need not be elected; even if they are, such governments are not constitutionally guaranteed. In any case, the real issue is the level(s) of government between the national and the local one. At one extreme are unitary states: ones where there are no regional governments, just a national government with most of the power (and all of the sovereignty) and usually some local governments. **Federalism** goes well beyond this by: (1) having regional governments and (2) giving these regional governments constitutionally entrenched powers and some sort of national role. In other words, federalism involves a combination of "elements of *shared-rule* through common institutions and *regional self-rule* for the governments of the constituent units."[14] Table 6.3 gives the 15 liberal or electoral democracies that are constitutionally federal or effectively federal. One should note that these are a very small percentage of all liberal and electoral democracies. In short, federalism is a rare political phenomenon. Considered as a group, these countries tend to be large (in area) or diverse or both, again with the diversity regionally concentrated.

A full definition of federalism has no less than five features, as follows:

» two autonomous levels of government—central (federal) and regional—with each being directly elected and accountable;

» a formal division of authority specifying the powers and sources of revenue held by each level of government (each level thus in some ways acts directly on the citizens), as well as the level which holds the residual powers;

» a written constitution which, among other things, sets out the respective powers of each level of government and which can only be changed with some difficulty (or with broad agreement);

TABLE 6.3 :: LIBERAL AND ELECTORAL DEMOCRACIES, FEDERAL SYSTEMS

COUNTRY	FEDERAL SINCE	KEY CONSTITUENT PARTS TODAY	ORIGINS
ARGENTINA	1853	22 provinces, 1 national territory, and 1 federal district	coming together
AUSTRALIA	1901	6 states, 2 territories, and 1 capital territory	coming together
AUSTRIA	1918	9 Länder (provinces)	coming together
BELGIUM	1993	3 regions and 3 cultural communities [overlapping]	holding together
BRAZIL	1891	26 states and 1 federal capital district	mixed
CANADA	1867	10 provinces and 3 territories	mixed
GERMANY	1871/1919/1949	16 Länder (states)	mixed
INDIA	1950	28 states, 6 union territories, and 1 national capital territory	holding together
INDONESIA*	2004	30 provinces, 2 special regions, and 1 special capital city district	holding together
MEXICO	1917	31 states and 1 federal district	holding together
NIGERIA	1947	36 states	holding together
SOUTH AFRICA*	1994	9 provinces	holding together
SPAIN*	1978	17 autonomous communities	holding together
SWITZERLAND	1848	26 cantons	coming together
UNITED STATES	1789	50 states and 1 federal district	coming together

* borderline cases of federalism

» a supreme court to, among other things, arbitrate between the central and regional governments when there are disputes over whether one level of government may act in a certain way; and

» a bicameral legislature in which the lower house represents the people as a whole but the upper house represents the regions or the people in each region. Normally, the composition of the upper house will be weighted to a lesser or greater extent in favour of the less populous regions, whereas the lower house is based more purely on population (which is obviously to the advantage of the more populous regions).

The first four of these features speak to what is called *inter-state federalism*, that is, the divisions and relations *between* the two levels of government. The last feature, in contrast, speaks to what is called *intrastate federalism*, that is, the role of the regions (or regional governments) *within* the national political institutions (or, if one prefers, in the national capital). If we view federalism

163

in terms of the component parts, then strong inter-state federalism is where the regions as regions "matter" in terms of policy areas, taxing and spending, and generally affecting the lives of those who live there. In contrast, strong intrastate federalism would be where the regions, especially the smaller ones, are important in a powerful upper house, thus producing national policy outcomes that differ from what one would get if power rested solely on the population-based lower house. Figure 6.2 gives a crude attempt to situate the federal systems on these two dimensions. Thus in Canada, for example, the provinces as provinces matter within their borders, but provincial voters are unable to use an effective Senate to counteract the weight of Ontario and Quebec in the House of Commons. This "incompleteness" is also found in some other systems. However, the most common subgroup of federalism are those systems (such as the United States) where there are both relevant regional governments and strong bicameralism (to use the earlier term), with the upper house weighted towards the less populous areas. The least common pattern is found in Mexico, which has strong bicameralism but weak states. Of course, Mexico is a relatively recent electoral democracy, so its situation may well evolve. Still, for the moment it provides the one polar opposite example to Canadian federalism. Finally, it is worth noting that the countries that are stronger on intrastate federalism tend to be more homogeneous than those that are weaker. This is perhaps because in more heterogeneous societies the emphasis has been on regional autonomy, often asymmetrically in favour of the more "distinct" regions, rather than checking and balancing the national government per se.

Alfred Stepan has noted that federalism evolved in three different ways, which he calls "coming together," "holding together," and "putting together" federations.[15] Under "coming together" federalism, which incorrectly has often been seen as the only way to this political system, various distinct parts—which may be sovereign entities or simply separate colonies—more or less freely agree to form a single political entity. This involves some sort of conference or convention at which the "founding fathers" of the country work out the details. Since unanimity is required, even the smallest component parts will have a lot of say in the initial set up. The United States is the classic example of this route to a federal structure, but it also occurred in various other coun-

FIGURE 6.2 :: LIBERAL AND ELECTORAL DEMOCRACIES, COMPARATIVE FEDERAL SYSTEMS

		INTRASTATE FEDERALISM (regions, especially the smaller ones, are important via a strong upper house)	
		LESS SO	**MORE SO**
INTERSTATE FEDERALISM (regional governments have policy importance, especially re taxing and spending)	**MORE SO**	Canada India Nigeria South Africa	Argentina Australia Brazil Germany Switzerland United States
	LESS SO	Austria Belgium Indonesia Spain	Mexico

tries (see Table 6.3). The second variant, "holding together" federalism, begins with a sovereign, unitary state. However, centrifugal tendencies and demands for regional autonomy (if not outright independence) from certain regions push the system towards federalism as an alternative to the (partial) break-up of the country. Thus, federalism is a means to "hold together" a polity, hence the term. Obviously, regional demands must not only exist but reach a certain undefined level for the centre to "give in" and agree to this change. Both the amount of time for the change and the amount of time as a unitary state beforehand can vary. Belgium is a good example of the slowness of these processes. Changes towards federalism began in 1971 but were not completed until its constitutional accord of 1993. Yet for a century and a half before 1970 (from 1830 onwards, to be precise), Belgium existed as a centralized unitary state. On the other hand, the creation of federalism in India occurred only three years after its independence, with federalism more the result of foresight by national leaders. Finally, "putting together" federalism is the non-democratic variant where sovereign entities are conquered or forced into a theoretically federal entity. The creation in 1922 of the Union of Soviet Socialist Republics, to use its full name, is Stepan's standard example of this. Of course, as Stepan notes, countries can combine some or all of these routes;

for example, elements of all three existed in Canada from the conquest of Quebec in 1759 through 1867.

ALTERNATIVES TO FEDERALISM

Federalism is but one of many forms of (potentially) multi-level political organization. As Figure 6.3 shows, the nine different types of such political organization relate to each other on two different dimensions. The first—more centralized (to the left) versus more decentralized (to the right)—is fairly self-evident. However, there is a second dimension, which we shall call "population-based completeness," that is, the extent to which the specific political organization applies on all levels to the entire population.

Let us start by looking at situations where this "completeness" is perfect or close to it. We have already distinguished between a *federation*, with its two levels of government and related features, and a *unitary state*, with but one level of government (above the local one). Examples of unitary states countries are Estonia, Greece, Iceland, and New Zealand—all rather small places. In between a federation and a unitary state, though, are countries with regional governments, and even elected regional governments (like a federation), but where these regional governments and their powers are not "protected" by being entrenched in the constitution. As such, these regions could be abolished, merged, or have their powers reduced without any legal right to prevent such changes. Of course, central governments may rarely choose to do such things if that will annoy public opinion, but they could. Countries with this type of political organization are Colombia, France, Italy, Japan, Poland, Slovakia, and Sweden. In Sweden, regional governments have existed for centuries; in the other cases, they are much more recent. In fact, Italy seems to be moving somewhat towards full federalism, but is not there yet.

Moving away from a federation towards more decentralization brings us to a **confederation**. A confederation is where a group of sovereign entities form a common government for specific and limited purposes (such as defence or economics); this common government has no independent sovereignty, relies upon the constituent governments (who normally work by unanimity) to take

FIGURE 6.3 :: FEDERALISM AND ITS ALTERNATIVES

← ——— MORE CENTRALIZED ——— ——— MORE DECENTRALIZED ———→

POPULATION-BASED "COMPLETENESS" TOTAL OR VERY HIGH	Unitary state	Unitary state with non-constitutionally entrenched regional governments	Federation	Hybrid	Confederation
POPULATION-BASED COMPLETENESS LOW		Devolution	Federacy	Self-governing territory in bilateral free association, with right to independence	Associated state (in a bilateral customs union or treaty or "compact")

Note: Everything within the shaded area involves only one sovereign polity.

all key decisions, and leaves matters of implementation to the constituent governments. Thus, the "central government" (and this is definitely stretching the term) does not act directly on the citizens, and each constituent government retains ultimate sovereignty. Two standard historical examples of a confederation are Switzerland for most of the period before 1848 and the United States between 1776 and 1789. Another confederation was the German *Zollverein* (customs union) of the nineteenth century. Confederalism seems to be an unstable type of organization over the long run, often evolving into federations (as in these examples) or collapsing and dissolving (like the post-Soviet Commonwealth of Independent States). The European Union is often called a confederation, although this does not seem appropriate, especially since the Maastricht Treaty of 1993, if not indeed earlier. On the other hand, the EU is clearly not yet a federation (and there is strong debate on this goal), and its component countries still retain considerable sovereignty, even if they have "pooled this" in an ever-increasing number of areas. One can best consider the EU to be some sort of *hybrid* between confederation and federation, as indicated in Figure 6.3.

Turning now to situations of low "population-based completeness," the first variant is now called *devolution* (and until the 1920s was known as "home rule") in the United Kingdom. Historically, this involved demands by the Celtic peripheral areas—Ireland (especially), Scotland, and Wales—for their own assemblies so they would not be so dependent on the English-dominated government in London. The separation of the Catholic-controlled parts of Ireland in 1922, after decades of trying to find a "solution" to Irish demands, largely pushed this issue off the table, although Northern Ireland retained its own assembly from 1921 until 1972. In the latter year the government in London first prorogued the Northern Irish Assembly (seeing it as contributing to the local political violence) and then abolished it, something that obviously could not occur under true federalism. In the 1970s demands for local assemblies resurfaced, although now these were stronger in Scotland and Wales. In 1978 referenda on devolution were held in those two areas, but were unsuccessful. Further such demands were largely resisted, however, by the Conservative governments of Margaret Thatcher (1979–90) and John Major (1990–97). By the end of the 1990s, however, an elected Scottish parliament and elected Welsh and Northern Irish assemblies were (re-)established under a Labour government. These bodies, though, especially in Wales and Northern Ireland, are quite weak compared to, say, a provincial legislature in Canada.

Where is the low "population-based completeness" in all of this? The reader should remember that under federalism, every citizen also lives in a constituent part of the federation. For example, all Canadians live in either a province or a territory. Likewise, each and every constituent part (1) has its own legislature *and* (2) is represented in the national legislature. These patterns are also true for the polities with non-constitutionally entrenched regional governments everywhere. Under devolution, however, the "main part" normally does not have its own legislature. There is no separate assembly or parliament for England the way there is for Scotland, Wales, and Northern Ireland. Consequently, over 80 per cent of the United Kingdom's population is not represented by any regional government. (This figure leaves aside the elected Greater London Assembly, but even if one generously calls this a regional parliament, still the rest of England—some 70 per cent of the total United Kingdom population—has only the national government and local government.)

The next variation of political organization is called a *federacy*. This also involves a smaller region (at least in the sense of population), but one with considerable entrenched autonomy from the larger whole of which it is a constituent part. On the other hand, often the federacy (or its residents) have little input into the larger whole. The relationship can be changed only by mutual agreement between the federacy and the central government, which resembles federalism. Examples of federacies are the Faroe Islands and Greenland with Denmark; the Åland Islands with Finland; and Guernsey, Jersey, and the Isle of Man with the United Kingdom. All of these have very small populations. A somewhat larger federacy is Puerto Rico *vis-à-vis* the United States. Puerto Rico as an area functions similarly to a state of the United States, with an elected governor and so on, and its residents are United States citizens. However, Puerto Rico only has a single commissioner in the United States House of Representatives (who is free to speak but can only vote in committees) and no senators. Equally, its residents cannot vote for president (unless they move to the United States mainland).

Even more autonomy can be granted to a small region by giving it the right to determine its own future, including independence if and when it wishes. Such a territory is self-governing (except for defence, foreign affairs, and usually some other areas), but it is not sovereign. In Figure 6.3 we call this a situation of "a self-governing territory in bilateral free association, with a right to independence." Some sort of treaty or equivalent will define this situation. Most eastern Caribbean islands went through this stage prior to independence from the United Kingdom. Current examples are the Cook Islands with New Zealand (since 1965), Niue Island with New Zealand (since 1974), and Aruba with the Netherlands (since 1986). In theory, this is also the situation of Jammu and Kashmir with India; however, India has never recognized that region's right to self-determination.

Finally, a small sovereign country may wish to have formal links with a larger country, have the larger country take care of its defence, and/or use the currency of the larger country. Said "larger country" may or may not be the former colonial power. This small sovereign territory becomes an *associated state* of the larger country. The two countries will have a formal bilateral treaty or customs union if this is merely an economic relationship. Formal sovereignty is retained by each part, and either can end the relationship (as in a confederation). However, the relationship is clearly asymmetrical in that one speaks of the smaller country being associated with the larger country, never the other way around. Given this asymmetry, this is effectively a relationship of low "popu-

169

lation-based completeness." Long-lasting examples of associated states are Bhutan with India (associated since 1949), Liechtenstein with Switzerland (associated since 1923), Monaco with France (associated since 1919), and San Marino with Italy (associated since 1862). Interestingly, neither Bhutan nor Monaco is a democracy, although of course India and France respectively are. More recent examples of associated states are the Marshall Islands and Micronesia, each of which signed a Compact of Free Association with the United States to define their post-independence relationship. These "Compacts" took effect in 1986. A similar Compact was reached with Palau in 1993. Their main benefit to the United States is the maintenance of military bases in these countries; in return, the associate states each receive substantial funds.[16]

NOTES

1 The weaker version of restrictions on re-election is where the president has to wait a term before being able to run again. Chile, the Dominican Republic, and Uruguay are examples here. In Panama, two terms (10 years) must elapse before one can run again.

2 This pattern has also become more common in Latin America; in the 1990s Argentina, Brazil, and Venezuela all changed their respective constitutions to permit immediate re-election to a second term.

3 As Table 6.1 shows, since re-democratization in Chile, one requires an absolute majority to be elected president.

4 Arend Lijphart, *Patterns of Democracy: Government Forms and Performance in Thirty-Six Countries* (New Haven, CT: Yale University Press, 1999) 117.

5 Torbjörn Bergman, "Constitutional Design and Government Formation: The Expected Consequences of Negative Parliamentarianism," *Scandinavian Political Studies* 16 (1993): 287–89.

6 Some clarification is needed here on Portugal and Sweden. Formally, both appear to involve positive parliamentarianism in that there is an actual vote of investiture. However, in each case the government does not have to "win" the vote in the sense of having more votes in favour than against; it merely has to ensure (or hope) that there is not an absolute majority of votes (of the eligible deputies) against it. In other words, both formal abstentions and absences count on the government side. For example, in

Sweden in 1981 a government was invested with 102 votes in favour, 174 votes against, 62 abstentions, and 11 absences (of the 349 deputies). See Bergman 297. Consequently, then, both Portugal and Sweden should be considered to *effectively* have negative parliamentarianism. In contrast, Luxembourg and the Netherlands do not formally require a vote of investiture, but each invariably undertakes such a vote, so they *effectively* have positive parliamentarianism.

7 Despite the worldwide recognition of Nelson Mandela, he was never directly elected by South African voters (although he would have won). Mandela was elected unopposed by the National Assembly in 1994 and so was his successor as president, Thabo Mbeki, in both 1999 and 2004. Such outcomes have reflected the one-party predominance of the African National Congress (see Chapter 7).

8 Australia held a referendum on making such a change in 1999, but this was unsuccessful.

9 Taken from Alan Siaroff, "Comparative Presidencies: The Inadequacy of the Presidential, Semi-Presidential, and Parliamentary Distinction," *European Journal of Political Research* 42:3 (May 2003): 287–312.

10 Andorra effectively also fits here, even though it has *two* figurehead heads of state, representing respectively the president of France and the Bishop of Seo de Urgell in Spain..

11 Lijphart, *Patterns of Democracy* 205.

12 Lijphart, *Patterns of Democracy* 211.

13 The Inter-Parliamentary Union is an invaluable source of data and analysis on this issue.

14 Ronald L. Watts, *Comparing Federal Systems*, 2nd ed. (Montreal, QC and Kingston, ON: McGill-Queen's University Press, 1999) 7.

15 Alfred Stepan, "Toward a New Comparative Politics of Federalism, (Multi)Nationalism, and Democracy: Beyond Rikerian Federalism," *Arguing Comparative Politics* (New York, NY: Oxford University Press, 2001) 320–23.

16 One should note that some scholars use the term "associate state" to apply to the last two categories; however, we wish to make a distinction based on the key difference of sovereignty and are thus reserving the term for the last category.

CHAPTER SEVEN

Electoral Systems and Party Systems in Democracies

IN THIS CHAPTER YOU WILL LEARN:

» *what are the components of an electoral system;*
» *what are the various electoral systems used in the world's democracies, and how their individual mechanics differ;*
» *how electoral systems vary in terms of (dis)proportionality;*
» *what are some precise ways of measuring party system fragmentation;*
» *what are the six main types of party systems defined in terms of fragmentation and competition, and what are the differences between them;*
» *what are the differences between more and less institutionalized party systems, and how democracies divide in terms of this distinction; and*
» *how and why party system institutionalization matters for democratic performance and stability.*

ELECTORAL SYSTEMS

Regardless of the institutional distinctions outlined in the previous chapter, all democracies have legislatures elected in (more or less) free and fair elections. But how exactly are these legislatures elected? In the first part of this chapter we shall examine the various electoral systems used to elect the lower house (or single chamber) in all the liberal and electoral democracies in the world. Electoral systems have enormous consequences for what government is formed, or at least which party dominates the chamber (if it is a presidential system).

TABLE 7.1 :: TYPES OF ELECTORAL SYSTEMS (for the lower house where bicameral)

MAJORITARIAN SYSTEMS	single-member plurality	Antigua and Barbuda Bahamas Bangladesh Barbados Belize Botswana Canada Dominica Ghana	Grenada India Jamaica Kenya Lesotho Malawi Micronesia Mongolia Nigeria	Palau Papua New Guinea St. Kitts and Nevis St. Lucia St. Vincent and the Grenadines Solomon Islands Trinidad and Tobago United Kingdom United States
	single-member majority-plurality	France	Kiribati	
	single-member majority (alternative vote)	Australia		
	mixture of single-member, dual-member, and/or multi-member plurality	Marshall Islands Tuvalu	Mauritius*	Samoa
	single non-transferable vote	Vanuatu		
PROPORTIONAL SYSTEMS	single transferable vote	Ireland	Malta	
	party list proportional representation	Argentina Austria Belgium Benin Brazil Bulgaria Cape Verde Chile Colombia Costa Rica Croatia* Cyprus Czech Republic Denmark Dominican Republic Ecuador El Salvador Estonia Finland	Greece Guyana Honduras Iceland Indonesia Israel Latvia Liechtenstein Luxembourg Moldova Mozambique Namibia Netherlands Nicaragua Niger* Norway Panama Paraguay Peru	Poland Portugal Romania* San Marino Serbia and Montenegro Sierra Leone Slovakia Slovenia São Tomé & Príncipe South Africa Spain Sri Lanka Suriname Sweden Switzerland Turkey Uruguay
	mixed member proportional (fully compensatory)	Bolivia Venezuela	Germany	New Zealand
IN-BETWEEN SYSTEMS	parallel	Albania Andorra Georgia Guatemala Japan Korea, South Lithuania	Macedonia Madagascar Senegal Seychelles Taiwan Thailand Timor-Leste	
	mixed member semi-compensatory	Hungary Philippines	Italy	Mexico

* includes some single member constituencies for ethnic minorities
Note: There are also idiosyncratic electoral systems in each of Mali and Nauru.

However, it is incorrect, or at least too broad, to consider an electoral system to be the method of electing a *government*. Rather, an **electoral system** determines the partisan composition of the legislature by establishing, in the words of Farrell, "*the means by which votes are translated into seats in the process of electing politicians into office.*"[1]

For analytical purposes, there are four aspects of an electoral system, although most central are the first three: district magnitude, electoral formula, and ballot structure.[2] By **district magnitude** we mean the number of seats to be filled in an electoral district. At one extreme, Israel and the Netherlands elect their parliaments in a single national calculation; thus, they each have only one district. Everywhere else, however, the country is divided into various electoral districts (or constituencies).[3] For each district in a country, then, we need to know how many members are being elected—this is the district magnitude. In the United Kingdom, each of its 659 constituencies elects one member to the House of Commons; thus, the district magnitude is one (as it is in Canada). Conversely, in Israel the district magnitude is 120 (the size of the *Knesset*), and likewise in the Netherlands it is 150. To the extent that the system is not winner-take-all, then for any given system (electoral formula) the larger the district magnitude the greater the proportionality.[4] Finally, it does not have to be the case that a country with multiple districts has the same district magnitude in each district; indeed, this will not be the case if the districts vary in population. Secondly, by the *electoral formula* we mean the precise calculation within each district (and, where relevant, regionally and/or nationally) that allocates the seats among the competing candidates and parties. Although in theory there could be an infinite number of such formulae, in reality there are only a few. Thirdly, by *ballot structure*, we mean whether the voter makes one choice or alternatively ranks in order a list of competing candidates. Lastly, some scholars note a fourth aspect of an electoral system—the total size of the legislature.[5] Very small legislatures, in particular, tend to be less proportional for any given system (that is, any given electoral formula).

Table 7.1 classifies the various electoral systems in today's liberal and electoral democracies, grouped into three categories based on their overall national effects. First are majoritarian electoral systems, so named because of their tendency to give a majority of seats to one party. To repeat, this is a tendency, not

175

TABLE 7.2 :: COMPARING TWO HUNG PARLIAMENTS IN CANADIAN HISTORY AND THEIR DISPROPORTIONALITY

	VOTE %	SEATS	SEAT %	PERCENTAGE DIFFERENCE
JUNE 2004 (total of 308 seats)				
Liberals	36.7	135	43.8	7.1
Conservatives	29.6	99	32.1	2.5
New Democratic Party	15.7	19	6.2	−9.5
Bloc Québécois	12.4	54	17.5	5.1
Greens	4.3	0	0.0	−4.3
No affiliation (Chuck Cadman)	0.1	1	0.3	0.2
Others and independents	1.2	0	0.0	−1.2

Total disproportionality was 15.0. As shown, the seat bonus for the leading party was 7.1, which—although important—was obviously not enough to manufacture a majority for the Liberals.

	VOTE %	SEATS	SEAT %	PERCENTAGE DIFFERENCE
OCTOBER 1925 (total of 245 seats)				
Conservatives	46.5	116	47.3	0.8
Liberals	39.9	99	40.4	0.5
Progressives	8.9	24	9.8	0.9
Others and independents	4.7	6	2.4	−2.3

Total disproportionality was only 2.3. As shown, the seat bonus for the leading party was only 0.8.
Ironically, a party with 46.5% of the vote would normally win a manufactured majority under such a national vote distribution.

a "guarantee." Such a majority of seats will often occur even if the party does not win a majority of the popular vote; this is what is known as a **manufactured majority**, since it has been "manufactured" by the electoral system. In these majoritarian electoral systems, there is no conscious attempt to make the final percentage of seats match the overall percentage of the vote won by each party. Sometimes (very rarely) this does happen—the Canadian federal election of 1925 for example—but this is more of a "fluke." Indeed, even if there is a **hung parliament** (where in fact no one party has a majority) under a majoritarian system, there is still normally a bias in favour of the largest party or parties. Table 7.2 shows this pattern for Canada's 2004 federal election, contrasting this with the "exceptional" 1925 election.

Second, in what are known as proportional electoral systems, there *is* an explicit goal of matching the share of seats won with the share of votes won, except perhaps for (very) tiny parties. Consequently, in these systems a single party should not win a majority of seats unless it has won a majority of the popular vote (or something very close to this). Third are systems which combine elements of each of the first two types to produce a pattern which is somewhat "in-between," that is, with some element(s) of proportionality but not the clear overall pattern found in the second category.

The most common type of majoritarian system by far is single-member plurality (SMP), which is used in the United Kingdom and many former British colonies, including Canada and the United States. In this system, the district magnitude is one, hence the single member (elected at a time) aspect. To win the seat, a candidate needs to have more votes than any other candidate; all that is required is a plurality of votes, not necessarily a majority. Of course, some victors will have won a majority of the votes in their constituency, but, again, this is not required. Indeed, there is *no* specific share of the vote required to win under SMP; this will vary with the number and strength of candidates. Consequently, the frequently used description of this system as "first-past-the-post" is incorrect and inappropriate: there is no actual "post." (A more accurate analogy would be the kind of set-time race in which whoever is leading when time runs out is declared the winner.) Under SMP, the election is a series of individual races in however many districts there are. There is no linkage between overall votes won and overall seats won, nor is there any consolation prize for coming second in a constituency. Indeed, a party that comes second everywhere wins the same number of seats—zero!—as a party which comes, say, last everywhere.

One criticism of such a system is that the winning candidate in a district may have won only a minority of the vote; in other words, most people did not vote for her or him. One solution to this "problem" could be to have a run-off vote between the top two candidates. In fact, although this is done in various presidential elections (see Chapter 6), the only democracy which actually does this at the legislative level is Lithuania, for the half of its parliament which consist of single-member seats. A related procedure is that of the French National Assembly, a single-member system which does have a run-off election in every constituency where nobody won a majority on the first ballot. However, rather than restricting the run-off to the top two candidates, any candidate who gets 12.5 per cent of the constituency's electorate—that is, the total potential vote—is allowed to contest the run-off. Candidates above this threshold are not *obliged* to contest the run-off, and parties will often make deals between the ballots (if not before) which involve candidates who clear the threshold withdrawing in favour of other, stronger candidates of allied parties. Such strategic withdrawal is necessary because only a plurality is needed to win the run-off, and a plurality may be all that is achieved when there are more than two candidates. Consequently, the French system is one of "single-member majority-plurality." So too is the Kiribati system, where if nobody wins a majority on the first ballot then the top three candidates go on to the run-off.

In the Australian House of Representatives there is an overall requirement of achieving majority support. In this case (and also in the semi-liberal autocracy of Fiji) this is done by means of the alternative vote using a *preferential ballot*. That is, rather than just indicating one's preferred choice, voters rank all the candidates 1, 2, 3, etc. Then a calculation is made of each candidate's "first preferences"—their number of "1"s. If this is a majority, the counting stops. However, if no candidate has a majority of first preferences, then the candidate with the least number of first preferences is dropped, and the second preferences of her or his voters are distributed. If this does not push anyone over the 50 per cent level, then the next least popular candidate is dropped, and so on. Of course, if a voter has unpopular tastes, it may be that her vote keeps being recounted until she is using, say, her fifth preference! Nevertheless, at some point a candidate will win a majority of preferences—even if this requires getting down to two final choices.

To repeat, all of these systems use single-member districts (district magnitudes of one). However, also classified as majoritarian systems are those which use a combination of SMP, dual member plurality, and multi-member plurality. Here we emphasize the plurality aspect, that is, the electoral formula. In such systems the voter gets as many votes as there are members to be elected in the constituency, and the parties normally also run that number of candidates. Assuming that voters vote for each and every candidate of their preferred party, then one party will win all the seats in the constituency with each of their candidates getting (basically) the same number of votes—but not necessarily a plurality. Of course, a voter may "mix and match" candidates across parties, but this is rare, or at least this is rare enough that it is seldom the case that candidates of more than one party are elected. Although this pattern of plurality voting in districts of varying magnitude (but none very large) exists today only in Mauritius and three Pacific islands (see Table 7.1), it should be stressed that it was used historically in some Canadian provinces.

The final type of majoritarian electoral system is called a single non-transferable vote (SNTV). As in the previous examples, deputies are elected in multi-member districts. However, the voter is given only *one* vote which must be cast for a specific candidate. The electoral formula is plurality, so that if it is a five member district then the top five candidates all get elected. Since voters get only one vote, they have to choose among the candidates of their preferred party, assuming that there are more than one of these. Voters cannot vote for all the candidates of a given party (since they only have one vote), nor can they rank order the candidates as in a preferential ballot. This means that multiple candidates of the same party have to compete against each other (on something other than party label, obviously). It also means that larger parties have to decide strategically how many candidates to run in a district: too many and they will divide the vote excessively; too few and an extra seat that could have been won will be lost. Generally, a party with overall majority support in a district will run, say, three candidates in a five member district and hope to elect all three. Conversely, small parties will run only one candidate in a district and hope to get about one-fifth (or whatever) of the vote to win one seat. Although SNTV is now used only in Vanuatu, from 1947 through 1993 it was the system used in Japanese lower house elections.

All of these majoritarian electoral systems can lead to manufactured majorities; even if this is not the case, there is generally an imbalance between the percentage of votes won and the percentage of seats won by individual parties. This imbalance amounts to a deviation from pure proportionality (wherein the seat percentage exactly equals the vote percentage for every party) and is more commonly phrased in terms of how *dis*proportional are the election results. Mathematically, we shall measure the disproportionality of elections (under any and all electoral systems) by the Loosemore-Hanby **index of disproportionality**, which sums the absolute value of each party's vote share to seat share difference and then divides this total by two (since some party's excessively high percentage of seats must be balanced by some other party's excessive low percentage) to get a value between zero and 100—the higher the number the greater the disproportionality.[6] For example, for the countries using SMP where there is relevant data, the average disproportionality value is 14.9; for all countries using majoritarian electoral systems and with relevant data the average disproportionality value is 16.1 (calculated from Table 7.3). In such majoritarian systems, parties whose support is broad geographically but not very deep locally (such as the federal Progressive Conservatives in Canada in 1993) will come up short with most of their votes "wasted" (not electing the desired candidate). Yet, it is also the case that parties who are extremely popular locally (such as the federal Liberals in urban Ontario or now the federal Conservatives in rural Alberta) will have candidates winning with well over half the vote; all of these "surplus" votes are also wasted.[7] Thus, by definition any single-member system is disproportional; so too are multi-member plurality systems.

Electoral systems which are proportional in their philosophy avoid both of these features: that is, they use multi-member rather than single-member districts, and they use a non-plurality electoral formula. One type of proportional system is that of the single transferable vote (STV). This has the moderate district magnitude (usually three to five) and the single vote of the SNTV system, but it not only allows but often requires voters to indicate their preferences (1, 2, 3, etc.) across all the candidates of all the parties. This preferential ballot structure is what we saw with the alternative vote, but there only one person gets elected. Under STV, a few people will get elected in each constituency. The key mechanism is the establishment of an electoral quota, known as the "Droop quota," which is one more than the total number of valid votes divided by the total number of district seats plus one. This quota is the smallest share of the vote needed to elect a full number of candidates, but no more. Consequently (in rounded-up terms) for a five member district the quota is 17 per cent, for a four member district the quota is 21 per cent, and for a three member district the quota is 26 per cent. Indeed, for a single-member district the quota is 51 per cent, which is the definition of single-member *majority* systems like that of the Australian lower house.[8] As is the case with the alternative vote, unpopular candidates get dropped from the ballot, and the second (and subsequent) preferences of their voters get transferred. Even more multiple rounds of counting take place to elect all the candidates. However, what is really different from the alternative vote (and SMP too, of course) is that under STV one can never win "too many" votes. Whenever a candidate reaches or exceeds the quota—be this on the first or a subsequent count—she is declared elected. At this stage any preferences she has which are above the quota are then redistributed (as a share of the next preferences of all her voters). These subsequent preferences will presumably help to elect someone else of the same party. And although parties do run only a reasonable number of candidates given their size, unlike in SNTV parties do not run the same danger of splitting their vote if they run excessive candidates under STV, since surplus preferences transfer.

Although the electoral formula used with STV is certainly proportional, the small district magnitude tends to prevent this system from achieving full proportionality. That is, although a quota of 17 per cent or 21 per cent is certainly better for smaller parties than 51 per cent or even being the plurality candidate, 17 per cent may still be too high for small parties. They would not win any seats in a given constituency; conversely, another party (usually the largest) will win, say, one too many. Such a problem is less the greater the district magnitude; however, since voters can or must rank multiple candidates of various parties, and since the more candidates to be elected the more rounds of counting are involved, for practical purposes STV is not normally used with a district magnitude of more than five or six. Indeed, in Ireland many constituencies have a district magnitude of only three or four. (However in Malta, all districts have a magnitude of five.) On the other hand, the small district magnitudes and constituency sizes mean that all deputies have clear local ties.

These patterns are essentially inversed in the main form of proportional representation, the party list system. Indeed, party list proportional representation is the single most common type of electoral system in the world's democracies, due to its dominance in continental Europe and Latin America (see Table 7.1). We have already noted that in Israel and the Netherlands there is only one district, and parties offer only national lists. However, the usual pattern for party list proportional representation is to divide the country into a few districts (normally the provinces or equivalents if there are regional governments), each of which elects perhaps 10 or 20 or 40 members who are no more locally based than at this regional level. Spain is an exception in that some of its districts have magnitudes as low as three. Under party list proportional representation there may also be some seats allocated at the national level to "correct" any imperfections at the regional level, such as in Sweden. Voters normally vote for the party list as a whole, although some systems allow (or in Finland require) the voter to express a preference within the list. Still, unlike STV, the voter in party list proportional representation does not rank everyone, nor is he expressing a series of preferences. Thus, the basic electoral formula is quite simple: a party that wins, say, 10 per cent of the votes gets 10 per cent of the seats. Of course, parties usually win fractional amounts whereas seat numbers are integers, so varying formulae exist to determine which party gets the last unclaimed seat (some formulae favour larger parties, some favour smaller ones). There is no quota per se, as in STV. However, what matters usually is a legal threshold of support that a party must meet in order to win any proportional seats at all. This threshold is often 4 or 5 per cent of the national vote, but it may be established regionally instead. The extreme cases of thresholds are Turkey at 10 per cent of the national vote (which in its last election eliminated all but two parties) and Denmark at 2 per cent (which eliminates only very marginal parties). Of course, even where there is no legal threshold there is an effective threshold based on the size of the legislature. For example, the Israeli Knesset has 120 members, so a party that cannot win about 1/120th of the vote (0.833 per cent) is out of luck.

One attempt to combine party list proportional representation with at least partial local constituency representation is called mixed member proportional (MMP) representation. This system has been used in Germany since its first postwar election in 1949 and has also been adopted in Bolivia, New Zealand, and Venezuela—in the case of New Zealand as a conscious change away from SMP. Under MMP a certain number of deputies (half in Germany) are elected in local constituencies using SMP voting. Thus, everyone can be said to have a local member of parliament, although this matters more in New Zealand than it ever has in Germany. The other half of deputies are elected from (regional) party lists. Voters have separate votes for the local candidate and for the party list, and can engage in "ticket-splitting" (although this was not the case in the 1949 German elections). Of these two votes, the party list one is by far the more important one, since the goal of the system is to make the final outcome of seats as proportionally close as possible to the party list share of the vote for all those parties above the legal threshold. For example, if a party gets 40 per cent of the party list vote, it should at the end of the process have 40 per cent of the total seats in the parliament. How many seats it gets from the party lists will vary inversely with how many it won in the single-member constituencies; effectively, this latter number is subtracted from 40 per cent, and the remainder are taken from the party lists. Of course, all of the usual biases of SMP apply to the local seats, so smaller parties such as the German Greens may *never* win a local seat and will get all of their seats from the party lists. Yet, as long as there are sufficient numbers of seats available in the list portion (such as under the German 50:50 ratio), the overall result will be quite proportional. Consequently, the MMP system can be said to be *fully compensatory*, in that the party list seats should fully compensate any party above the threshold that won too few seats in the local constituencies. Hence, it is clearly in the proportional category. Indeed, the average index of disproportionality for the four MMP systems is 9.7, essentially the same value as the average for the party list proportional representation systems, which is 9.2.

The final category of electoral systems involve those that are neither fully majoritarian nor fully proportional; instead, they fall "in between" as a compromise (or perhaps as an internal contradiction). The more common variant are usually called parallel systems. In these there are both locally elected deputies (usually by SMP) and deputies elected from regional and/or national lists. Voters usually have two separate votes. However, the electoral formulae for each component remain totally independent of each other; that is, the calculation of party list seats (only) is proportional to the party list vote, regardless of how well (or poorly) a party did in the local (single-member) constituencies. Since the seats determined by the locally elected constituencies will be disproportional, and since the party list seats in no way compensate for this, the overall result will not be fully proportional. However, it will be more proportional than if, say, all the seats were elected by SMP. Consequently, the ratio of locally elected seats to party list seats is crucial: where the system is heavily weighted towards the locally elected seats (as in South Korea), the result will be more disproportional than where the ratio is 50:50, all other things being equal. Overall, though, the average index of disproportionality for all parallel systems is 16.1, exactly the same as that for all majoritarian systems.

Finally, the few cases of what we shall call mixed-member semi-compensatory electoral systems fall basically between the parallel systems and the pure proportional representation ones, both conceptually and in terms of their average index of disproportionality (which is 12.0 for the three cases with data). These semi-compensatory systems do take into account the results of the single-member constituencies when allocating the party list seats, but not to the extent of aiming to achieve full proportionality. Instead, some compensation is achieved by looking at the strength of the runner-up party in a constituency (Italy), by limiting how many list seats any one party can get (the Philippines), or by "capping" the leading party so that it does not get an overall seat percentage more than 8 per cent above its party list vote percentage (Mexico).

PARTY SYSTEMS

A **party system** is the relationship among the various political parties in a territory, that is, their total number, relative size, competitiveness, and so on. For a party system to exist there must be at least two parties; one party by itself does not interact with any other party. Almost every democracy has a party system; the exceptions are six island states in the Pacific Ocean (Kiribati, the Marshall Islands, Micronesia, Nauru, Palau, and Tuvalu) which do not have political parties for cultural-traditional reasons.[9] (Similarly, there are no parties in the Northwest Territories or Nunavut.) To be clear, party-like alliances may form in their legislatures, but everyone is elected as an independent. (In contrast, if political parties did not exist because they were banned, then a system would not be democratic.)

Party systems can be assessed and compared in three ways. The two traditional ways are in terms of fragmentation and polarization.[10] By *fragmentation* we mean how many parties there are, both in an absolute sense and allowing for relative size. By *polarization* we mean the ideological spread among parties, or between the two most extreme ones, or perhaps between the two largest ones. Polarization is, however, very difficult to measure and compare globally, and we shall not attempt to do so in this analysis. In any case, the ending of communism in Eastern Europe and the decline of the far left has meant that left-right ideological gaps in most of the world are not what they were a generation ago.[11] The newest way in which scholars look at party systems is in terms of institutionalization. By *party system institutionalization* we mean the extent to which individual parties are well organized, have stable and deep roots in (segments of) society, are consistent in their ideological positions *vis-à-vis* each other, and experience relatively stable inter-party competition; also, political parties and elections have high legitimacy.[12] Scholarly concern with the organizational structure and capacity of individual parties goes back to the 1960s, but it originally focussed more on party institutionalization than on broader party *system* institutionalization.[13]

Measuring party system fragmentation is essentially objective since it involves "hard" numbers of votes and seats for various parties. Table 7.3 provides a range of data on the most recent elections (as of the end of 2004) in the world's democracies, based primarily on parliamentary seats. The actual measure of party system fragmentation used by scholars weights the parties by size, as is done for the effective number of parties (the next column). However, for party system fragmentation, the sum of the squared decimal values of all parties is subtracted from one rather than taking its inverse.[14] This means that party system fragmentation ranges from zero (0.000) where a single party has all the seats, to one (1.000) where no party has any seats. This latter situation cannot exist, of course, as long as there are parties being elected, so a value of 1.000 would only occur in those countries without political parties. As Table 7.3 shows, the most fragmented system with parties, that of Papua New Guinea, has a value of 0.941. (Perhaps the following scenario is more illustrative: in a 100-seat legislature, if 100 different parties each win one seat, then the fragmentation value is 0.990.)

Another way of looking at party system fragmentation is to count the effective number of parties, which, as noted, is the same procedure but expressed differently, on a scale with a minimum of 1 and no absolute maximum value. Finally, one can simply count all the parties without weighting them to give an integer value. However, should we consider a party with only one or two seats as being relevant? To measure the number of empirically rel-

TABLE 7.3 :: MOST RECENT ELECTIONS FOR ALL LIBERAL AND ELECTORAL
DEMOCRACIES (End of 2004)

YEAR: YEAR OF ELECTIONS
PFRG: PARLIAMENTARY FRAGMENTATION
ENPP: EFFECTIVE NUMBER OF PARLIAMENTARY PARTIES
P3%S: PARTIES WITH 3% OR MORE OF THE SEATS
2PSC: TWO-PARTY SEAT CONCENTRATION (combined seat percentage of the top two parties)
2PVC: TWO-PARTY VOTE CONCENTRATION (combined vote percentage of the top two parties)
1PSC: ONE-PARTY SEAT CONCENTRATION (seat percentage of the top party)

	YEAR	PFRG	ENPP	P3%S	2PSC	2PVC
ALBANIA	2001	0.616	2.61	3	85.0	78.3
ANDORRA	2001	0.554	2.24	3	82.1	76.1
ANTIGUA AND BARBUDA	2004	0.443	1.80	3	94.1	96.9
ARGENTINA	2001	0.648	2.84	4	79.5	60.5
AUSTRALIA	2004	0.583	2.40	3	90.0	78.5
AUSTRIA	2002	0.653	2.88	4	80.9	79.2
BAHAMAS	2002	0.444	1.80	2	90.0	92.7
BANGLADESH	2001	0.484	1.94	4	85.0	81.1
BARBADOS	2003	0.358	1.56	2	100.0	99.9
BELGIUM	2003	0.858	7.03	8	33.3	28.4
BELIZE	2003	0.366	1.56	2	100.0	98.8
BENIN	2003	0.791	4.79	6	55.4	
BOLIVIA	2002	0.799	4.96	7	48.5	38.8
BOTSWANA	2004	0.359	1.56	2	98.2	
BRAZIL	2002	0.882	8.48	9	34.3	34.3
BULGARIA	2001	0.657	2.92	4	71.2	60.9
CANADA	2004	0.670	3.03	4	76.0	66.3
CAPE VERDE	2001	0.517	2.07	2	97.2	90.0
CHILE	2001	0.507	2.03	2	99.2	92.2
COLOMBIA	2002	0.863	7.30	5	46.6	42.3
COSTA RICA	2002	0.728	3.68	4	63.2	56.9
CROATIA	2003	0.687	3.19	5	75.7	56.5
CYPRUS	2001	0.725	3.64	4	69.6	68.7
CZECH REPUBLIC	2002	0.727	3.67	4	64.0	54.7
DENMARK	2001	0.777	4.48	6	61.7	60.4
DOMINICA	2000	0.580	2.38	3	90.5	86.4
DOMINICAN REPUBLIC	2002	0.631	2.71	3	76.0	71.0
ECUADOR	2002	0.866	7.46	9	40.0	
EL SALVADOR	2003	0.717	3.54	5	69.0	65.8
ESTONIA	2003	0.786	4.67	6	55.4	50.0
FINLAND	2003	0.797	4.92	7	54.0	49.2
FRANCE	2002	0.558	2.26	4	85.8	57.2

1PVC: ONE-PARTY VOTE CONCENTRATION (vote percentage of the top party)
ED: ELECTORAL DECISIVENESS (EM = earned majority, MM = manufactured majority, HP = hung parliament)
SR 1:2: RATIO OF SEATS BETWEEN THE TOP PARTY AND THE SECOND-LARGEST PARTY
SR 2:3: RATIO OF SEATS BETWEEN THE SECOND-LARGEST PARTY AND THE THIRD-LARGEST PARTY
TVOL: TOTAL VOLATILITY (vote shares) BETWEEN THE GIVEN ELECTION AND THE PREVIOUS ONE [Loosemore-Hanby index]
DISP: DISPROPORTIONALITY BETWEEN SEAT PERCENTAGES AND VOTE PERCENTAGES (for all parties)

1PSC	1PVC	ED	SR 1:2	SR 2:3	TVOL	DISP
52.1	41.5	MM	1.59	7.67	15.1	10.6
60.7	46.1	MM	2.83	1.20	16.3	14.6
70.6	55.2	EM	3.00	4.00	11.5	20.3
52.0	37.4	MM	1.89	4.38	26.8	20.2
50.0	40.8	HP	1.25	5.00	8.2	13.6
43.2	42.3	HP	1.14	3.63	20.9	1.9
72.5	51.8	EM	4.14	7.00	16.1	23.4
64.3	41.0	MM	3.11	3.65		25.0
76.7	55.8	EM	3.29	∞	8.5	20.9
16.7	15.4	HP	1.00	1.04	12.8	11.1
75.9	53.2	EM	3.14	∞	6.5	22.7
37.3		HP	2.07	1.36		
27.7	26.9	HP	1.33	1.04	29.9	12.3
77.2		EM	3.67	12.00		
17.7	17.7	HP	1.07	1.15	15.0	0.2
50.0	42.7	HP	2.35	1.06	42.7	14.5
43.8	36.7	HP	1.36	1.83	12.7	15.0
55.6	49.5	MM	1.33	15.00	21.1	7.2
51.7	47.9	MM	1.09	57.00	7.9	7.0
33.5	31.3	HP	2.57	1.91	19.5	10.0
33.3	29.8	HP	1.12	1.21	19.1	10.1
45.8	33.9	HP	1.53	3.91	14.4	19.2
35.7	34.7	HP	1.05	2.11	4.5	2.9
35.0	30.2	HP	1.21	1.41	8.6	12.5
32.0	31.3	HP	1.08	2.36	13.3	2.5
47.6	43.1	HP	1.11	4.50	22.2	4.5
48.7	41.9	HP	1.78	1.14	10.7	6.8
24.0		HP	1.50	1.07		
36.9	33.8	HP	1.15	1.69	11.8	9.2
27.7	25.4	HP	1.00	1.47	34.1	6.6
27.5	24.7	HP	1.04	1.33	6.1	6.3
61.5	33.3	MM	2.54	4.83	23.0	28.9

continues...

	YEAR	PFRG	ENPP	P3%S	2PSC	2PVC
GEORGIA	2004	0.531	2.13	2	80.0	75.3
GERMANY	2002	0.643	2.80	4	82.8	77.0
GHANA	2004	0.523	2.10	2	96.5	
GREECE	2004	0.543	2.19	3	94.0	86.0
GRENADA	2004	0.498	1.99	2	100.0	90.8
GUATEMALA	2003	0.784	4.64	6	57.0	45.9
GUYANA	2001	0.552	2.23	3	93.8	94.8
HONDURAS	2001	0.585	2.41	4	90.6	87.3
HUNGARY	2002	0.543	2.19	3	95.3	83.1
ICELAND	2003	0.731	3.71	5	66.7	64.7
INDIA	2004	0.847	6.53	6	52.1	48.9
INDONESIA	2004	0.859	7.07	7	43.1	40.1
IRELAND	2002	0.706	3.41	6	67.5	64.0
ISRAEL	2003	0.838	6.17	8	47.5	43.9
ITALY	2001	0.511	2.04	2	96.8	81.2
JAMAICA	2002	0.491	1.965	2	100.0	99.5
JAPAN	2003	0.615	2.60	3	86.3	72.3
for comparison, Japan	*2000*	*0.683*	*3.15*	*7*	*75.0*	*53.5*
KENYA	2002	0.548	2.21	3	90.0	91.5
KIRIBATI	2003	1.000		NO PARTIES		
KOREA, SOUTH	2004	0.576	2.36	4	91.3	74.1
LATVIA	2002	0.801	5.04	6	50.0	42.8
LESOTHO	2002	0.537	2.16	4	83.1	77.3
LIECHTENSTEIN	2001	0.534	2.15	3	96.0	91.0
LITHUANIA	2004	0.837	6.13	7	45.4	43.2
LUXEMBOURG	2004	0.737	3.81	5	63.3	59.5
MACEDONIA	2002	0.653	2.88	4	77.5	64.9
MADAGASCAR	2002	0.565	2.30	3	78.1	43.1
MALAWI	2004	0.809	5.24	3	57.8	
MALI	2002	0.689	3.21	4	78.1	
MALTA	2003	0.497	1.99	2	100.0	99.3
MARSHALL ISLANDS	2003	1.000		NO PARTIES		
MAURITIUS	2000	0.231	1.30	3	90.9	88.3
MEXICO	2003	0.668	3.01	3	75.6	69.9
MICRONESIA	2003	1.000		NO PARTIES		
MOLDOVA	2001	0.459	1.85	3	89.1	63.4
MONGOLIA	2004	0.551	2.23	2	94.6	91.2
MOZAMBIQUE	2004	0.461	1.85	2	100.0	
NAMIBIA	2004	0.405	1.68	5	83.3	
NAURU	2004	1.000		NO PARTIES		
NETHERLANDS	2003	0.789	4.74	7	57.3	55.9
NEW ZEALAND	2002	0.734	3.76	6	65.8	62.4
NICARAGUA	2001	0.497	1.99	2	98.9	95.3

1PSC	1PVC	ED	SR 1:2	SR 2:3	TVOL	DISP
67.2	67.6	EM	5.27	∞		25.1
41.6	38.5	HP	1.01	4.51	6.3	6.7
55.7		EM	1.36	23.50		
55.0	45.4	MM	1.41	9.75	3.2	9.6
53.3	46.7	MM	1.14	∞	23.9	9.2
31.0	25.6	HP	1.20	1.37		13.1
52.3	53.1	EM	1.26	13.50		2.0
47.7	46.5	HP	1.11	11.00	8.8	3.4
48.1	42.0	HP	1.02	10.10	19.6	12.2
34.9	33.7	HP	1.10	1.67	8.1	3.3
26.7	26.7	HP	1.05	3.21	8.6	16.4
23.3	21.6	HP	1.17	1.88	24.8	12.2
48.8	41.5	HP	2.61	1.48	6.2	10.0
31.7	29.4	HP	2.00	1.27	27.2	6.0
58.4	42.5	MM	1.52	22.00	13.3	16.4
56.7	52.3	EM	1.31	∞	8.1	4.4
49.4	34.9	HP	1.34	5.21	19.8	18.0
48.5	*28.3*	*HP*	*1.83*	*4.10*	*7.6*	*25.7*
59.5	61.0	EM	1.95	4.57		0.9
50.8	38.3	MM	1.26	12.10	51.3	17.9
26.0	23.9	HP	1.08	1.14	42.9	16.0
65.3	54.9	EM	3.67	4.20	15.7	10.5
52.0	49.9	MM	1.18	11.00	10.9	5.0
27.7	28.6	HP	1.56	1.19	50.3	12.0
40.0	36.1	HP	1.71	1.40	10.4	4.5
50.0	40.5	HP	1.82	2.06	27.4	14.7
64.4	34.3	MM	4.68	4.40		36.8
31.6		HP	1.20	1.81		
41.3		HP	1.12	5.90		
53.8	51.8	EM	1.17	∞	0.5	2.0
81.8	51.7	EM	9.00	3.00		32.1
44.6	38.1	HP	1.44	1.61	9.7	7.5
70.3	50.1	EM	3.74	1.73	34.3	28.3
48.6	46.5	HP	1.06	34.00		3.9
64.0		EM	1.78	∞		
76.4	74.9	EM	11.00	1.25		
29.3	28.6	HP	1.05	1.50	15.8	2.4
43.3	41.3	HP	1.93	2.08	17.2	5.4
57.6	53.2	EM	1.39	38.00	12.8	4.4

continues…

	YEAR	PFRG	ENPP	P3%S	2PSC	2PVC
NIGER	2004	0.731	3.72	6	63.7	
NIGERIA	2003	0.538	2.16	3	89.0	81.9
NORWAY	2001	0.813	5.35	6	49.1	45.6
PALAU	2004	1.000	NO PARTIES			
PANAMA	2004	0.670	3.03	6	73.1	57.0
PAPUA NEW GUINEA	2002	0.941	17.02	6	28.4	
PARAGUAY	2003	0.685	3.18	4	72.5	61.0
PERU	2001	0.794	4.85	7	58.3	46.0
PHILIPPINES	2001	0.734	3.76	4	69.6	
POLAND	2001	0.717	3.53	6	61.3	53.7
PORTUGAL	2002	0.611	2.57	4	87.4	79.4
ROMANIA	2004	0.703	3.36	4	73.5	67.9
SAMOA	2001	0.709	3.43	3	73.5	68.3
SAN MARINO	2001	0.716	3.52	5	66.7	65.7
SÃO TOMÉ AND PRÍNCIPE	2002	0.614	2.59	3	85.5	79.0
SENEGAL	2001	0.433	1.76	3	83.3	65.7
SERBIA AND MONTENEGRO	2003	0.781	4.56	7	54.0	55.1
SEYCHELLES	2002	0.438	1.78	2	100.0	96.9
SIERRA LEONE	2002	0.392	1.65	2	98.2	89.7
SLOVAKIA	2002	0.837	6.12	7	42.7	34.6
SLOVENIA	2004	0.787	4.69	7	59.1	51.9
SOLOMON ISLANDS	2001	0.699	3.32	4	67.3	
SOUTH AFRICA	2004	0.491	1.97	3	82.3	82.1
SPAIN	2004	0.600	2.50	2	89.1	80.3
SRI LANKA	2001	0.638	2.76	4	82.7	82.8
ST. KITTS AND NEVIS	2004	0.545	2.20	4	81.8	59.4
ST. LUCIA	2001	0.291	1.41	2	100.0	90.8
ST. VINCENT AND THE GRENADINES	2001	0.320	1.47	2	100.0	97.4
SURINAME	2000	0.561	2.28	5	82.4	62.4
SWEDEN	2002	0.763	4.23	7	57.0	55.0
SWITZERLAND	2003	0.800	4.99	5	53.5	49.9
TAIWAN	2001	0.714	3.50	5	68.9	67.9
THAILAND	2001	0.672	3.05	5	75.2	67.3
TIMOR-LESTE	2001	0.591	2.44	4	70.5	66.1
TRINIDAD AND TOBAGO	2002	0.494	1.976	2	100.0	97.3
TURKEY	2002	0.460	1.85	2	98.4	53.7
TUVALU	2002	1.000	NO PARTIES			
UNITED KINGDOM	2001	0.537	2.16	3	87.9	74.9
UNITED STATES	2004	0.500	2.00	2	99.8	
URUGUAY	2004	0.585	2.41	3	87.9	84.7
VANUATU	2004	0.893	9.36	8	36.5	
VENEZUELA	2000	0.710	3.45	5	67.9	60.3

1PSC	1PVC	ED	SR 1:2	SR 2:3	TVOL	DISP
41.6		HP	1.88	1.14		
61.6	54.5	EM	2.24	3.06		7.1
26.1	24.4	HP	1.13	1.46	15.5	7.4
51.3	37.8	MM	2.35	1.89		16.1
17.4		HP	1.58	1.50		
46.3	35.3	HP	1.76	2.10	37.1	11.5
34.2	26.3	HP	1.41	1.93	24.0	13.2
40.7		HP	1.40	3.10		
47.6	41.0	HP	3.48	1.19	41.5	9.8
45.6	40.9	HP	1.09	6.86	8.6	8.0
39.8	36.6	HP	1.18	2.33	19.4	10.1
46.9	44.8	HP	1.77	13.00	5.6	5.2
41.7	41.5	HP	1.67	1.25	5.8	1.1
43.6	39.6	HP	1.04	2.86	23.4	6.5
74.2	49.6	MM	8.09	1.10	43.3	25.0
38.9	39.1	HP	2.58	1.12	36.7	0.3
67.6	54.3	EM	2.09	∞	16.5	13.3
74.1	69.9	EM	3.07	13.50	48.1	8.7
24.0	19.5	HP	1.29	1.12	37.5	18.2
33.0	29.1	HP	1.26	2.30	21.6	9.7
40.8		HP	1.54	1.08		
69.8	69.7	EM	5.58	1.79	8.3	0.9
46.9	42.7	HP	1.11	14.80	10.1	9.3
48.4	45.6	HP	1.42	4.81	11.4	7.0
63.6	50.6	EM	3.50	2.00	1.9	24.0
82.4	54.2	MM	4.67	∞	5.9	28.2
72.5	54.6	EM	4.00	∞	13.5	23.3
62.7	47.3	MM	3.20	3.33		20.0
41.3	39.8	HP	2.62	1.15	13.9	3.0
27.5	26.6	HP	1.06	1.44	8.0	4.8
38.7	36.6	HP	1.28	1.48	19.3	6.3
49.6	40.6	HP	1.94	3.12	40.6	12.1
62.5	57.4	EM	7.86	1.17		6.4
55.6	50.7	EM	1.25	∞	4.2	4.8
66.0	34.3	MM	2.04	∞	41.4	46.3
62.7	42.2	MM	2.49	3.19	4.3	20.6
53.3		EM	1.15	∞		
53.5	50.4	EM	1.56	3.40	25.2	3.4
19.2		HP	1.11	1.13		
48.5	44.2	HP	2.50	1.78	26.0	14.5

evant parties, we shall use Ware's cut-off of 3 per cent (or more) of the seats.[15] Although the maximum value could be 33 (100 per cent divided by 3 per cent), the real world maximum at the moment is nine parties in Brazil and Ecuador.[16]

Table 7.3 presents various measures of looking at the top party, or the top two. Of central concern is whether any one party has won a majority of seats, which would give it control of the legislature and (outside of presidential systems) the government. Alternatively, if no one party has a majority, there is a hung parliament, necessitating legislative compromise and likely producing (outside of presidential systems) a coalition government. At the moment (as of the end of 2004) there are 46 cases of single-party majorities in the world's democracies, clearly fewer than the 64 hung parliaments. The subsequent issue is whether those majority governments are **earned majorities**, that is, "earned" by winning a majority of the popular vote, or are "manufactured" by the electoral system. Of the 46 majorities, 27 are earned and 19 are manufactured. Interestingly, although the 19 manufactured majorities include SMP systems like the United Kingdom, there are also manufactured majorities in party list proportional representation systems (such as Turkey, whose electoral system uniqueness has been noted above) and in in-between systems. Thus a (purely) majoritarian electoral system is hardly an absolute necessity in order to have a manufactured majority. What is largely eponymous about majoritarian electoral systems is the fact that, leaving aside those without political parties, around two-thirds currently have single-party majorities. Some of these are manufactured, the rest are by definition earned. And although the earned ones could involve little "seat bonus" for the largest party (as in the United States) it is often the case that a party with 50-something per cent of the vote gets around 80 per cent of the seats (as in many Caribbean systems). So, we return to the general high level of disproportionality in majoritarian electoral systems. For (comparative) information, the last column of Table 7.3 gives the index of disproportionality wherever possible for all democracies.

The previous descriptions of party systems have involved either a continuum (such as for fragmentation) or a dichotomy (such as for a single-party majority or not). That said, we can also group the various party systems of democracies into a few types based on long-term patterns of the number of relevant parties (P3%S) and certain key relative sizes. Arguably there are six such types of party systems:

» First, there is a *competitive two-party system*. This involves only two relevant parties, which have alternated in power at various times. In any given election, or at least most of them, each of the two parties has a reasonable chance of winning. The United States is a clear example of this, although more for its Senate than its House of Representatives (which has been less competitive for long periods of time).[17] Even better examples of competitive two-party systems are Malta and most of the ex-British colonies of the Caribbean.

» In contrast, in an *imbalanced two-party system* there are only two relevant parties, but one of them is in power for a very long time with the other having little chance of winning. Botswana until recently (when it became multiparty) was a definite example of this type; some state legislatures in the United States still fit this pattern.

» A *moderate multiparty system* has anywhere from three to five relevant parties, but usually has four or five, still a moderate number. The party system is fairly deconcentrated, in that the top two parties have less than 80 per cent of the seats (2PSC is below 80.0). With no one party winning an outright majority, coalition government is the norm (if it is a parliamentary system). Examples include Austria, Bulgaria, and the Czech Republic in Europe, and Argentina and Mexico in Latin America.

» A distinctive subtype of moderate multiparty systems is a *two-and-a-half-party system*. This also involves from three to five relevant parties, although usually only three or four. Of these, two parties are much larger than the rest, making a clear distinction between the two main parties and the "half" party or parties. In contrast to a moderate multiparty system, in a two-and-a-half-party system the top two parties will together have 80 per cent or more of the seats. There is also only a small gap in size between the top two parties, a feature measured by SR1:2 in Table 7.3. It is possible, but never cer-

193

tain, in this type of party system for one of the main parties to win an outright majority of seats. If such a single-party majority does not occur, then the likely government is a coalition between one of the main parties and a smaller party. Consequently, the smaller or "half" party (or one of these) in this system could wind up with disproportionate influence, especially if it is an acceptable coalition partner to both main parties and can play these off against each other. Longstanding examples of such a party system are Australia and Germany; a more current one is South Korea.[18] We can note that Canada had this type of party system through 1980, with the Liberals and Progressive Conservatives as the two main parties with the NDP and, for a time, Social Credit each as a smaller "half." One difference in the Canadian version of this party system was that hung parliaments led to minority governments and early elections rather than to coalition governments.

» The *extreme multiparty system* is highly fragmented, with more than five relevant parties. There are rarely any large parties, usually medium-sized and small ones. Not only are coalition governments the norm (in non-presidential systems), as in moderate multiparty systems, but the coalition governments in extreme multiparty systems often involve four or more parties, so they can be quite difficult to hold together. We have already noted Brazil and Ecuador as current illustrations of such a party system type; other examples are Belgium, Poland, and Switzerland in Europe, and Israel. As its name suggests, an extreme multiparty system is so fragmented that, unless there is cooperation among the parties, governance can be difficult and the quality of government will suffer. Weimar Germany was an historical example of such a party system without such cooperation—indeed, with clearly antagonistic and polarized parties—which as noted earlier ultimately broke down.

» Finally, there are what are known as *one-party predominant systems*. These should not be confused with pure one-party systems, as in China or Cuba, which by definition are non-democratic. Rather, one-party predominant systems are multiparty systems, in that they have at least three relevant parties. However, one of these parties is much larger than the rest, as evidenced by a large gap between the first and second party in both votes and seats (on seats, again see SR1:2 in Table 7.3). This one large party is so big that it both predominates in parliament and controls the government for decades (or at a minimum for a long period of time). Such long-lasting control may involve outright single-party majorities, but, even when it fails to win an outright majority, the predominant party can either form a minority government or lead a coalition—and in doing so it usually has a pick of willing coalition partners. This is the key difference with imbalanced two-party systems: there if the traditionally dominant party fails to win a majority, this presumably means that the traditional opposition party has done so and will take over power. In a one-party predominant system, displacing the dominant party from power not only involves it failing to win a majority but having most if not all of the traditional opposition band together—a coalition that is usually not very durable. Japan since 1955, with the predominance of its Liberal Democratic Party (LDP), remains (or at least was) the main long-established example of this type of party system.[19] Other key historical examples are Italy, whose Christian Democrats (DC) had one-party predominance from 1946 until 1992 (or at least up until 1983), and Sweden, whose Social Democrats predominated from 1932 until 1976.[20] Beginning in 1994, the Swedish Social Democrats appear to have re-established their predominance. One-party predominance definitely has existed in Namibia since 1991 with its predominant South-West Africa People's Organization (SWAPO) and in South Africa since 1994 with its predominant African National Congress (ANC). And, of course, the reader may well have already guessed that one-party predominance is the appropriate term to describe Canadian federal elections from 1993 through 2000, not just because the Liberals won three straight majorities, but because the various Official Opposition parties had such limited support that they presented no real competition for first place. With the merger of the Progressive Conservative and Canadian Alliance parties into one Conservative Party, however, Canada is now a moderate multiparty system (at least after the 2004 elections).

PARTY SYSTEM INSTITUTIONALIZATION

All of the party systems listed above describe patterns that are both clear and durable, with, for example, the number of relevant parties in a country remaining more or less constant over several elections. In most cases, the patterns have also involved the *same* specific parties over several elections. However, such stability in parties is not a given in democracies. This leads us to our other contemporary aspect of party systems, that of party system institutionalization, a concept developed by Mainwaring and Scully in their 1995 edited book on Latin America.[21] An updated analysis of Latin America has been done for the Inter-American Development Bank.[22] With some modifications, the Mainwaring and Scully approach has also been applied to Africa by Kuenzi and Lambright.[23] However, no cross-continent global study of party system institutionalization has ever been done. The studies that do exist have used largely the same variables in assessing institutionalization in a given country: the inter-election volatility in parties' support, summed for all parties (the lower the better); the difference between presidential and legislative election support (the more people vote for the same party at both levels the better); the age of all parties with at least 10 per cent of the vote, or alternatively the top two parties (the older the better); the dominance of long-established parties; the general legitimacy of parties and elections, including seeing elections as the only legitimate way to gain and hold power; and the acceptance of electoral defeat by losing parties. To repeat, institutionalized party systems have low volatility over time, durable parties with clear roots in society (presumably based on relevant social cleavages such as ethnicity, language, religion, religiosity, class, or region), and broad support for parties and elections as legitimate political institutions. These studies rank the countries concerned on a continuum or at least suggest multiple broad categories of institutionalization, with the lowest category being called by Mainwaring and Scully "inchoate" party systems.[24]

Unfortunately, what works for one region becomes problematic when applied globally. Some countries lack credible—or any!—party vote statistics, which are needed to calculate volatility (and also disproportionality; see Table 7.3). Measuring variations in presidential and legislative voting does not require a full presidential system as defined in the previous chapter, but it does assume an elected president. Mainwaring and Scully define a long-established

TABLE 7.4 :: PARTY SYSTEM INSTITUTIONALIZATION

MORE INSTITUTIONALIZED PARTY SYSTEMS

Albania	Cyprus	Japan	Seychelles
Andorra	Czech Republic	Lesotho	Slovenia
Antigua and Barbuda	Denmark	Liechtenstein	South Africa
Argentina	Dominica	Luxembourg	Spain
Australia	El Salvador	Macedonia	Sri Lanka
Austria	Finland	Malta	Saint Kitts and Nevis
Bahamas	France	Mexico	Saint Lucia
Bangladesh	Germany	Mozambique	Saint Vincent and the Grenadines
Barbados	Greece	Namibia	
Belgium	Honduras	Netherlands	Sweden
Belize	Hungary	New Zealand	Switzerland
Botswana	Iceland	Norway	Taiwan
Canada	India	Paraguay	Trinidad and Tobago
Cape Verde	Ireland	Portugal	United Kingdom
Chile	Israel	Samoa	United States
Costa Rica	Italy	San Marino	Uruguay
Croatia	Jamaica	Senegal	

LESS INSTITUTIONALIZED PARTY SYSTEMS

Benin	Guatemala	Moldova	São Tomé and Príncipe
Bolivia	Guyana	Mongolia	Serbia and Montenegro
Brazil	Indonesia	Nicaragua	Sierra Leone
Bulgaria	Kenya	Niger	Slovakia
Colombia	Korea, South	Nigeria	Solomon Islands
Dominican Republic	Latvia	Panama	Suriname
Ecuador	Lithuania	Papua New Guinea	Thailand
Estonia	Madagascar	Peru	Timor-Leste (East Timor)
Georgia	Malawi	Philippines	Turkey
Ghana	Mali	Poland	Vanuatu
Grenada	Mauritius	Romania	Venezuela

SYSTEMS WITHOUT POLITICAL PARTIES

Kiribati	Micronesia	Palau
Marshall Islands	Nauru	Tuvalu

party as one founded by 1950; Kuenzi and Lambright note that, since most African countries did not become independent until around 1960, 1970 is the relevant cut-off date for that continent. They also add that, "[s]hould one want to conduct a study that includes countries from multiple world regions, this indicator may need to be adjusted accordingly."[25] However, adjusting this indicator back and forth may cause it to lose its comparative utility.

Consequently, rather than developing a full continuum of party system institutionalization, we shall settle for a basic dichotomy of more institutionalized party systems versus less institutionalized ones, as listed in Table 7.4. Latin American and African classifications come from the aforementioned analyses; others are more impressionistic. Hard numbers have been used where they exist, but so too has been a general sense of party's "rootedness" in society in various countries. Furthermore, caution is needed with a dichotomy, since the extent of a wrong classification is at a maximum. However, when all is said and done, there should not be many wrong classifications. Beyond less institutionalized party systems are those Pacific states with no parties at all. For the more institutionalized party systems, the various numerical features of fragmentation and specific types outlined earlier are quite likely to remain with only modest variations for a given country. However, for the less institutionalized party systems "all bets are off"; these may well look very different come their next election.

Beyond being relevant in and of itself, party system institutionalization has clear broader ramifications for comparative democratic performance and stability. The advantages of an institutionalized party system are multiple.[26] First, institutionalized parties are better able to not only articulate but also to aggregate, channel, and reach compromises among citizen's demands. Second and conversely, an institutionalized party system is obviously more accountable than one where parties come and go, or change themselves constantly. Third and consequently, in an institutionalized system where the parties have value in and of themselves, politicians are more likely to consider the long-term effects of their decisions. Fourth, an institutionalized party system will have greater party discipline, making it easier for the legislature to function (all other things being equal in terms of fragmentation). Fifth and related, an institutionalized party system is more likely to be able to deliver support to the political executive, producing less gridlock and immobility than in an inchoate system. Although this might seem a point applicable only to presidential systems, it in fact holds for parliamentary ones as well; for example, in the inchoate party system of Papua New Guinea, no prime minister has ever served a full parliamentary term. Sixth and finally, party system institutionalization reduces the corruption that occurs under traditional patterns of personal relationships and politicians who are patrons to local clients. Indeed, a comparison between the more and less institutionalized party systems in terms of the 2004 scores of Transparency International's Corruption Perceptions Index[27] where the data exist) yields an average score of 5.857 for the more institutionalized party systems and an average score of 3.150 for the less institutionalized party systems (with a higher score indicating less corruption). A t-test here, with equal variances not assumed, gives a value of 7.502, which is significant at the .000 level. Overall, then, party system institutionalization can certainly be seen to lead to more effective government.

NOTES

1 David M. Farrell, *Electoral Systems: A Comparative Introduction* (Basingstoke, UK: Palgrave, 2001) 4 (italics in original).

2 See Farrell 6 on these three central aspects.

3 The total number of districts is not in itself a relevant factor.

4 The United States electoral college (for almost all states) illustrates well this winner-take-all qualification.

5 See in particular Arend Lijphart, *Electoral Systems and Party Systems: A Study of Twenty-Seven Democracies, 1945–1990* (Oxford, UK: Oxford University Press, 1994) 12.

6 John Loosemore and Victor J. Hanby, "The Theoretical Limits of Maximum Distortion: Some Analytical Expressions for Electoral Systems," *British Journal of Political Science* 1:4 (October 1971): 467–77. In fact, Loosemore and Hanby's original index (469) ranged from 0 to 1; however, it is standard now to measure this from 0 to 100. For a comparison of the Loosemore-Hanby and other measures of disproportionality, see Lijphart, *Electoral Systems and Party Systems* 58–67.

7 Indeed, to be precise all votes beyond one more than the second-placed candidate are "surplus" and thus wasted.

8 Farrell 130.

9 See Dag Anckar and Carsten Anckar, "Democracies Without Parties," *Comparative Political Studies* 33:2 (March 2000): 225–47.

10 See Giovanni Sartori, *Parties and Party Systems: A Framework for Analysis* (New York, NY: Cambridge University Press, 1976).

11 On this point in Latin America, see J. Mark Payne *et al.*, *Democracies in Development: Politics and Reform in Latin America* (Washington, DC: Inter-American Development Bank, 2002) 148.

12 Scott Mainwaring and Timothy R. Scully, "Introduction: Party Systems in Latin America," *Building Democratic Institutions: Party Systems in Latin America*, ed. Scott Mainwaring and Timothy R. Scully (Stanford, CA: Stanford University Press, 1995) 5; Payne *et al.* 127.

13 On party institutionalization see, for example, Huntington's *Political Order in Changing Societies*.

14 For the calculation of an "effective number," see the end of Chapter 1.

15 Alan Ware, *Political Parties and Party Systems* (Oxford, UK: Oxford University Press, 1996) 158–59.

16 Belgium and Denmark have each had P3%S values of 10 in the past.

17 The United States has actually been most competitive between its two parties at the level of the presidency.

18 On this type of party system in longstanding democracies, and the varied role of the "half" party or parties therein, see Alan Siaroff, "Two-and-a-Half-Party Systems and the Comparative Role of the 'Half,'" *Party Politics* 9:3 (May 2003): 267–90.

19 Japan's last elections in 2003 yielded a much more concentrated party system; the issue is whether this will last. In any case, Table 7.3 also gives Japan's 2000 elections for an example of its traditional one-party predominance.

20 On these "classic cases," see T.J. Pempel, ed., *Uncommon Democracies? The One-Party Predominant Systems* (Ithaca, NY: Cornell University Press, 1990).

21 Mainwaring and Scully.

22 Payne *et al.* Chapter Six.

23 Michelle Kuenzi and Gina Lambright, "Party System Institutionalization in 30 African Countries," *Party Politics* 7:4 (July 2001): 437–68.

24 Mainwaring and Scully 19.

25 Kuenzi and Lambright 446.

26 Mainwaring and Scully 25–26; Payne *et al.* 127–28.

27 See <http://www.transparency.org.cpi/2004>.

CHAPTER EIGHT

Varieties of Autocracies: Totalitarianism, Sultanism, and Authoritarianism

IN THIS CHAPTER YOU WILL LEARN:

» *what is a totalitarian regime;*
» *how full totalitarianism differs from pre- (or incomplete) totalitarianism and from post-totalitarianism;*
» *what is a sultanistic regime;*
» *how authoritarianism is a residual category of autocracy and thus the importance of noting the specific subtype of authoritarianism;*
» *how monarchs range from being all powerful to being mere figureheads; and*
» *(once again) how semi-liberal autocracies may have a certain level of political pluralism, but not the free and fair elections of democracies.*

CONTEXT

Hitherto we have either treated all autocracies as a group (as opposed to democracies) or simply distinguished between semi-liberal and closed autocracies. Of course, just as democracies vary in their institutional features, so do autocracies. Beyond such institutional variations, autocracies also differ in the aspects of the importance of ideology, the extent of their legitimacy, and the durability of their specific autocratic leaders. In this chapter, we shall look at the three varieties of autocracy: totalitarianism, sultanism, and authoritarianism, the first and last of which can be further subdivided for a total of eight subtypes. These subtypes are outlined in Table 8.1, which follows the layout of Table 3.2. In the analysis we shall not cover every aspect given for each subtype but rather focus on the key features.

TOTALITARIANISM

Although some authors treat totalitarianism as a subtype of authoritarianism, it is in fact a distinctive variant of autocracy. Existing for more or less time in all communist regimes as well as in Nazi Germany, a **totalitarian regime** can be characterized by three key characteristics, as detailed by Linz:

» There is a monistic [unitary] but not monolithic center of power, and whatever pluralism of institutions or groups [that] exists derives its legitimacy from that center, is largely mediated by it, and is mostly a political creation rather than an outgrowth of the dynamics of the preexisting society.

» There is an exclusive, autonomous, and more or less intellectually elaborate ideology [involving an ultimate utopian goal] with which the ruling group or leader, and the party serving the leaders, identify and which they use as a basis for policies....[1]

» Citizen participation in and active mobilization for political and collective social tasks are encouraged, demanded, rewarded, and channelled through a single party and many monopolistic secondary groups. Passive obedience and apathy, ... characteristic of many authoritarian regimes, are considered undesirable by the rulers.[2]

In terms of the first point, power is monopolized by the totalitarian party and its leaders. All other parties are banned, forced to merge with the totalitarian party, or "at best" allowed to continue as puppet parties under the control of the totalitarian party. This point does not mean that the official party always has and speaks only with one voice; differences, especially within the leadership, may exist (subject to the constraints of the second point on ideology). However, these differences can never crystallize into political factions, and certainly and crucially there is no political pluralism in such a totalitarian system.

Equally, there is no, or at least no significant, social and economic pluralism under totalitarianism either. Autonomous organizations, and thus an independent civil society, are forbidden. (Pre-existing) organized religion is suppressed or heavily controlled, although many modern organizations do exist: trade unions, youth groups, sporting clubs, and so on. However, all of these are official groups with monopolies in their field (that is, just one trade union rather than a plurality). Usually, their name includes that of the totalitarian party or its leader. Moreover, and in terms of the third point, people are expected to join such groups as a sign of *active* support for the regime. Likewise, elections not only are normal under totalitarianism (albeit without partisan choice), but an intense effort is made to mobilize every possible voter so that a claim can be made of up to 99 per cent (or even 99.9 per cent) support for the regime. Totalitarian regimes are unique among autocracies in the extent of their mobilization efforts, because (at least according to the ideology) such regimes seek to *transform* fundamentally the existing society towards some ultimate utopia. Totalitarianism is thus, from this perspective, a modernizing type of autocracy.

In addition to these key features of party, ideology, and mobilization, many scholarly analyses, especially in the 1950s and 1960s when Stalinism was a vivid memory, added political terror. Political terror can be defined as "the arbitrary use, by organs of political authority, of severe coercion against individuals or groups, the credible threat of such use, or the arbitrary extermination of individuals or groups" as a means to achieve political control.[3] Linz argues that the extent of terror has varied under totalitarianism and that it can be found in non-totalitarian systems, such as the "sultanistic" ones described below or certain military regimes in Latin America.[4] Of course, as Dallin and Breslauer note, the extent of terror tends to be temporal: it is high in what they call the "mobilization phase" of totalitarianism, where society's resources are directed to achieving quickly a specific end or related ends, such as industrialization and/or the creation of a "new man." In contrast, in the "post-

TABLE 8.1 :: SUB-TYPES OF AUTOCRATIC REGIMES

	PRE-TOTALITARIANISM INCOMPLETE TOTALITARIANISM	FULL TOTALITARIANISM
POLITICAL PARTIES AND ELECTIONS AND OVERALL POLITICAL OPPOSITION	One official party with a monopoly of power and no political pluralism.	One official party with a monopoly of power and no political pluralism; political terror is often used initially to eliminate any (possibility of) organized opposition.
SOCIO-ECONOMIC PLURALISM	Some social and economic pluralism, perhaps predating the regime.	No significant social or economic pluralism; basically total regime control; strong hostility to pre-existing organized religion.
CIVIL LIBERTIES	Civil liberties are non-existent or at best limited.	No civil liberties.
IDEOLOGY	Elaborate and guiding ideology that includes a desired utopian vision.	Elaborate and guiding ideology that includes a desired utopian vision.
MOBILIZATION	Beginning of or partial mobilization into a wide range of regime-created obligatory organizations.	Extensive mobilization into a wide range of regime-created obligatory organizations; active participation and enthusiasm both encouraged and expected.
LEGITIMACY OF AUTHORITY	Legitimacy comes initially more from the method of coming to power (elections, independence struggle, etc.) than from the official ideology.	Legitimacy comes from some combination of official ideology (especially its utopian goals) and charisma of dictator.
CONSTRAINTS ON AUTHORITY	Constrained somewhat by any remaining separate political actors and broadly supported private actors.	Key totalitarian leader rules with undefined limits and great unpredictability; successors tend to be more predictable and bureaucratic.
POLITICAL ACCOUNTABILITY TO POPULATION	No political accountability.	No political accountability.
LEADERSHIP DURATION	For arrested totalitarianism, leadership is indefinite but effectively conditional on avoiding major policy failure.	Leadership effectively for life unless regime is defeated; usually a power struggle for new leader.
TRANSITION TO (LIBERAL) DEMOCRACY	For arrested totalitarianism, the ruling party must first accept giving up or be forced to give up its monopoly of power.	Needs to go first through a post-totalitarian phase with some pluralism unless defeat in war and occupation by foreign power(s) willing to democratize.

POST-TOTALITARIANISM	SULTANISM
Still one official party with monopoly of power and no political pluralism.	There may be an official party, but it is not well institutionalized; political terror is often used to eliminate any (possibility of) organized opposition.
Limited social and economic pluralism, involving dissidents and some market actors and forces.	Some economic and social pluralism, but this is subject to arbitrary despotic intervention.
Tentative but limited civil liberties.	No civil liberties.
Still a state-sanctioned elaborate and guiding ideology but weakened faith in this.	No ideology worth its name; instead, personal glorification of leader and family.
Still extensive mobilization into regime-sponsored organizations, but enthusiasm replaced by boredom and/or careerism; dissidents organize clandestinely.	Only occasional mobilization, such as of violent parastate groups.
Legitimacy weakened by de-ideologization; shift to (attempts at) performance legitimacy.	Regime lacks broad legitimacy; compliance is based largely on fear, rewards, and/or personal ties to leader.
Top leaders constrained by party bureaucracy and state technocrats, but not by broader civil society.	Highly personalistic and arbitrary rule which is highly unpredictable; no bureaucratic professionalism possible.
No political accountability (except to other party elites).	No political accountability.
Leadership effectively for life, subject to performance; successor picked peacefully by (and from) party oligarchy.	Leadership effectively for life unless overthrown.
Depending on the maturity of the post-totalitarianism, scenarios can range from regime collapse followed by an interim government to a negotiated transition.	Sultan highly unlikely to abdicate so must be overthrown; however, actors close to sultan may fill the resulting power vacuum and frustrate true democratization.

continues...

	TRADITIONAL AUTHORITARIANISM	MILITARY AUTHORITARIANISM
POLITICAL PARTIES AND ELECTIONS AND OVERALL POLITICAL OPPOSITION	Can range from all parties being forbidden and no elections held to a multi-party system with competitive elections and limited political opposition (but without elections actually determining the government).	Usually all parties are forbidden, but there could be one official party; limited political opposition may be tolerated.
SOCIO-ECONOMIC PLURALISM	Can range from no significant to quite extensive social pluralism; usually economic pluralism	Some social and economic pluralism, perhaps predating the military regime.
CIVIL LIBERTIES	Civil liberties can range from none at all to merely incomplete.	Civil liberties are non-existent or at best limited.
IDEOLOGY	Stress on deference to traditional authority.	Often very nationalistic; stress on economic (and occasionally social) development.
MOBILIZATION	Participation largely generated autonomously by civil society (where permitted).	Emphasis on demobilization, especially of pre-existing autonomous civil society.
LEGITIMACY OF AUTHORITY	Traditional legitimacy.	Legitimacy comes from claims of acting in the national interest.
CONSTRAINTS ON AUTHORITY	Constrained at most only somewhat by the bureaucracy, private economic actors, and general public opinion.	Constrained at most only somewhat by the bureaucracy and private economic actors and maybe by any private media.
POLITICAL ACCOUNTABILITY TO POPULATION	No political accountability of the monarch, but there may be some of officials.	No political accountability.
LEADERSHIP DURATION	Leadership is for life and then carries on within the royal family.	Leadership is indefinite unless the military rotates power.
TRANSITION TO (LIBERAL) DEMOCRACY	The monarch (or the royal family) must be willing to settle for a (largely) figurehead role.	Transition does not usually occur until the military loses legitimacy (for example by losing a war) or feels that it has sufficiently restructured the socio-political order.

Source: Based in part on Juan J. Linz and Alfred Stepan, *Problems of Democratic Transition and Consolidation: Southern Europe, South America, and Post-Communist Europe* (Baltimore, MD: The Johns Hopkins University Press, 1996) Table 3.1 and Table 4.2, with modifications.

THEOCRATIC AUTHORITARIANISM	ELECTORAL AUTHORITARIANISM
Either one official party or all parties are forbidden, although anti-regime independents may be elected.	More than one political party; limited political pluralism and consequent political opposition; however, national elections are not free and fair enough to actually change the government.
No significant social pluralism; usually some economic pluralism.	Many autonomous actors in economy and broader society.
Civil liberties are non-existent or at best limited.	Civil liberties are usually incomplete if not indeed limited.
Ideology derived from specific religious text and/or school.	Stress on economic growth and social peace.
Emphasis on religious mobilization.	Participation largely generated autonomously by civil society and by competing parties.
Legitimacy comes from religious position(s) and the authority to interpret relevant scripture.	Legitimacy comes from the illusion of legal-rational authority.
Constrained at most only somewhat by any private economic actors or private media.	Constrained only somewhat by the constitution, the courts and the rule of law, the bureaucracy, and socio-political pluralism.
No political accountability.	No true political accountability, although regime does prefer to be popular in actuality.
Leadership at the top is for life; a religious assembly chooses successors.	Leadership is indefinite unless the ruling party has internal limits (which have been as little as one term).
Transition has never occurred willingly.	The key step is having a truly free and fair election; then it becomes improving civil liberties and government fairness.

[intensive] mobilization phase," where the central goal is progressing "on track" without much resistance, and more generally where an established process of socialization has led to the general legitimacy of the regime, terror is no longer needed, and social compliance comes basically from "peer-group pressure."[5] That said, what is unique about totalitarian terror is its ideological justification and the organizational ability to use party cadres to carry it out.[6] Consequently, political terror per se does not seem so much a separate feature of totalitarianism as it is a reinforcement of the second and first characteristics given above.

Beyond these characteristics, we can note that totalitarianism has been around only since the interwar period. For some, totalitarianism—especially fascism—has been seen at least in part as a reaction to modernity. More convincingly, it has been noted that interwar fascism had little appeal in the older, long-established countries of Northern and Northwest Europe; its appeal was to be found in the newer countries of Central and Eastern Europe established in the 1860s and 1870s—Austria-Hungary, Italy, Germany, and Romania (see Table 1.1)—with their frustrations *vis-à-vis* the established powers and their desires for rapidly increased might and respect.[7] Most crucially, perhaps, it is better to stress that totalitarianism is in fact *conditional* on a certain level of modernity (and definitely on a functioning state) without which its penetrative and transformative capacities could not exist. As was noted by a leading political scientist, Gabriel A. Almond, back in the 1950s:

> This type of political system has become possible only in modern times, since it depends on the modern technology of communication, on modern types of organization, and on the modern technology of violence. Historic tyrannies have no doubt sought this kind of domination but were limited in the effectiveness of their means. Totalitarianism is tyranny with a rational bureaucracy, a monopoly of the modern technology of communication, and a monopoly of the modern technology of violence.[8]

PRE- AND POST-TOTALITARIANISM

What we have analyzed so far can perhaps be more rigorously defined as *full* totalitarianism (see Table 8.1). However, a totalitarian regime does not come into existence the day or even the year totalitarian forces take power; instead, at least in each of Nazi Germany and the Soviet Union, totalitarianism took some time to establish, especially in terms of establishing control over, or at least neutralizing, previously powerful independent actors. For example, the Soviet Union under Lenin had much weaker communist control than under Stalin (especially Stalin from 1929 onwards); indeed, Lenin had to switch back towards free market capitalism with his New Economic Policy of 1921. Linz has aptly called *pre-totalitarian* those situations in which

> there is a political group of sufficient importance pursuing a total-
> itarian utopia but that has not yet fully consolidated its power ...;
> a situation in which institutions like the armed forces, the churches,
> business organizations, interest groups, notables or tribal rulers,
> the courts, or even a monarch, not clearly committed to a system
> excluding all pluralisms even though largely favoring a limitation of
> pluralism, still retain considerable autonomy, legitimacy, and effec-
> tiveness....[9]

That said, if pre-totalitarianism inevitably led to totalitarianism, it would not be worth elaborating on here. However, in many real-world cases, this initial pre-totalitarian stage did *not* lead to full totalitarianism. Instead, the pre-totalitarian situation continued indefinitely. Linz refers to situations where "the development toward totalitarianism is arrested and stabilized," although with the totalitarian ideology continuing to affect "considerable spheres of social life" and participation in the totalitarian party and its other organizations remaining significant as "defective totalitarianism"; one could also call them situations of incomplete totalitarianism.[10]

The most important of these "incomplete totalitarian" cases was Fascist Italy, where Mussolini remained constrained by the army, the state bureaucracy, business interests, the Catholic Church, and the monarchy—and conversely where each of these actors retained some autonomy from him and the PNF (the

211

National Fascist Party). The autonomy of the state bureaucracy reflected the failure of establishing full totalitarianism, since "[o]nly when the party organization is superior or equal to the government can we speak of a totalitarian system."[11] As for the monarchy, King Victor Emmanuel III not only appointed Mussolini prime minister in 1922, but also formally removed him in 1943. (In contrast, in Germany after President von Hindenburg's death in 1934, there was no one authorized to "fire" Hitler.) The central communist example of "incomplete totalitarianism" was Poland, where the Catholic Church was always able to maintain "a sphere of relative autonomy which gave it organizational and ideological capacities to resist its and the Polish nation's full incorporation into totalitarian structures."[12] Furthermore, agriculture was never collectivized in Poland, since the Polish communist leaders did not see this as part of the "Polish road to socialism." The consequent social pluralism of an autonomous and powerful Church and autonomous farmers not only was the central aspect of the "incompleteness" of Polish totalitarianism, but it also spilled over into weaker communist ideology, less communist mobilization, and an unstable party leadership.[13] In the 1960s and 1970s, many one-party regimes were established in Africa that were either basically communist in ideology or which largely copied communist rule with a more indigenous ideology; they should be considered "incomplete totalitarianism" too.

If full totalitarianism is established, one may ask whether it remains for generations. Here we are limited empirically to the communist systems, since Nazi Germany lasted only 12 years, rather short of Hitler's "thousand year Reich." A critical juncture for all totalitarian communist systems has been the death of the key initial (and usually charismatic) leader—Stalin, Mao, Ho Chi Min. Their successors have tended to be less "revolutionary," in the sense of having transformative goals and being willing to use terror to this end, being more concerned with preserving the status quo; thus, they are more "conservative" and predictable. So, the totalitarian system shifts from a mobilization phase to a post-(intensive) mobilization, bureaucratic one. However, such a system—for example, the Soviet Union under Khrushchev and then Brezhnev—must still be considered fully totalitarian, since the regime still tolerates no real pluralism. (That said, Khrushchev's removal from power by the rest of the communist party leadership was incongruent with full totalitarianism.)

212

An actual *regime* change comes with a shift from totalitarianism to *post-totalitarianism*. Post-totalitarianism certainly does *not* mean political pluralism in the sense of, say, multiple and competing political parties. However, political dissidents begin to organize (or increase this) and become somewhat more open, and there is increased social and economic pluralism, in the latter case perhaps driven by necessity. Crucially, under post-totalitarianism, the official ideology becomes more and more of a facade with fewer and fewer true believers (including in the leadership). Likewise, social mobilization into state organizations becomes less passionate and more a matter of "going through the motions"; the people who join the official party are largely "careerists" or, more bluntly, opportunists. With ideology (and terror) no longer motivating the ossified bureaucracy, there is a parallel increase in corruption.[14] Such post-totalitarianism, for better or worse, is what occurred in the Soviet Union under Gorbachev in the late 1980s. However, such a regime arose earlier in parts of Eastern Europe—in Yugoslavia in the mid-1950s and in Hungary starting in 1962 and continuing through formal recognition in the economic sphere in 1982. On the other hand, Czechoslovakia and East Germany remained "hardline" and fully totalitarian until the collapse of communism, thus having only a brief post-totalitarian phase (and Albania had none at all). Only Bulgaria copied Gorbachev's reforms when they still seemed viable. China certainly has been post-totalitarian in economic matters since the late 1970s, but remains highly repressive otherwise. It has been argued that Cuba has become post-totalitarian, but Fidel Castro (who still speaks of the Cuban revolution in speeches that last for hours) would likely beg to differ.

Finally, it should be noted that, under an alternative definition of totalitarianism that requires a charismatic leader, political terror, and purges within the ruling party, then totalitarianism is seen as ending with the death of Stalin in Europe and of Mao in China. What follows—and what we have called the "bureaucratic" phase of totalitarianism—is deemed to be "post-totalitarianism," which goes through "early" and "frozen" phases.[15]

SULTANISTIC REGIMES

One communist regime that we did not mention above was Romania; another was—and still is—North Korea. In fact, although these regimes have/had certain totalitarian features—above all, a communist party and related organizations—they can be better seen as examples of *sultanism*. A **sultanistic regime** is the term applied to regimes which are built around an individual and her/his family, who to a greater or lesser extent plunder the country; which glorify this leader; which exercise control by fear, terror, and spreading paranoia; and which lack any effective legitimacy. Chehabi and Linz offer a more thorough definition:

> a contemporary sultanistic regime ... is based on personal rulership, but loyalty to the ruler is motivated not by his embodying or articulating an ideology, nor by a unique personal mission, nor by any charismatic qualities, but by a mixture of fear and rewards to his collaborators. The ruler exercises power without restraint, at his own discretion and above all unencumbered by rules or by any commitment to an ideology or value system. The binding norms and relations of bureaucratic administration are constantly subverted by arbitrary personal decisions of the ruler, which he does not feel constrained to justify in ideological terms. As a result corruption reigns supreme at all levels of society. The staff [and cabinet] of such a ruler is constituted not by an establishment with distinctive career lines, like a bureaucratic army or a civil service, recruited based on more or less universal criteria, but largely by people chosen directly by the ruler. Among them we very often find members of his family, friends, business associates, or individuals directly involved in using violence to sustain the regime. Their position derives from their purely personal submission to the ruler, and their position of authority in society derives merely from this relation[ship]. The ruler and his associates do not represent any class or corporate [group] interests. Although such regimes can in many ways be modern, what characterizes them is the weakness of traditional and legal-rational legitimation and the lack of ideological justification.[16]

In many ways sultanistic regimes are the least "defendable" type of regime, since they cannot claim any ultimate utopian goal as totalitarianism does. Today, the main examples of sultanism are the regimes of Mu'ammar al-Qadhafi in Libya, Kim Jong-il in North Korea, and Saparmurad Niyazov in Turkmenistan. However, there have been several important historical examples of sultanism in recent decades, these being the regimes of Fulgencio Batista in Cuba, Rafael Trujillo in the Dominican Republic, Jean-Claude Duvalier in Haiti, the Somoza family in Nicaragua, Ferdinand Marcos in the Philippines, Jean-Bédel Bokassa in the Central African Republic, Francisco Macías Nguema in Equatorial Guinea, Idi Amin in Uganda, Mobutu Sese Seko in Zaire, the Pahlavi dynasty in Iran (especially the later stages of each Shah), Saddam Hussein in Iraq, Hafez al-Assad in Syria, Kim Il-sung (the father of Kim Jong-il) in North Korea, and Nicole Ceausescu in Romania. For obvious reasons, the recently deposed regime of Saddam Hussein in Iraq is probably the best known to the reader.

Sultanistic regimes generally begin as some form of authoritarianism. For example, the regimes in Iraq and Syria were initially military, in the sense of rule by the military-backed *Ba'ath* party in each country. Likewise, the sultanistic rulers of the Central African Republic, Libya, and Uganda led military coups. For their part, Marcos and Nguema initially came to power via democratic elections.[17] In any case, the checks and balances of democracy or the collective rule (where this exists) of authoritarianism give way to personal rule by an individual which winds up destroying any functioning autonomous state (assuming there was one).

Among the various bizarre features of a sultanistic regime, it is those of personalism which stand out. The first element is the ruler's personality cult, which probably compensates for their general or total lack of charisma. This is probably most evident to the outside observer in the many statues that are erected and portraits that are hung of them. Yet, beyond such omnipresence, sultanistic rulers love to give themselves titles, not only politically formal ones like emperor, field marshal, or *generalísimo* (supreme commander), but more general ones like "hero," "saviour," "Great Leader" (Kim Il-sung), or "Dear Leader" (Kim Jong-il). Sometimes they change their names to this end. For example, since 1991 President Niyazov of Turkmenistan has been known as "Turkmenbashi" ("Head of the Turkmen"). If not renaming themselves, sultanistic rulers (while still alive, of course) rename cities, islands, and lakes after themselves. Finally, sultanistic rulers often proclaim their own ideology, since they conceive of themselves as great thinkers, and/or publish volumes of their thoughts and speeches.

The second element of personalism in a sultanistic regime is the central role played by the ruler's immediate family members, who are given formal positions. For example, Imelda Marcos (Ferdinand's wife) was a cabinet minister and mayor of Manila. Elena Ceausescu became the second-in-command of the Romanian Communist Party. Saddam Hussein's sons became as infamous as their father: Uday for a time oversaw the state media and national sports; his (relatively) more stable younger brother Qusay, the presumed heir-apparent, controlled the security and intelligence services and the armed forces. Indeed, one of the ultimate elements of "success" of sultanistic rulers appears to be achieving enough personal and family control that a son will (be able to) take over after their death; very few sultanistic rulers have been so "successful."[18]

The "cult of personality" around certain totalitarian leaders such as Stalin and Mao can be considered a sultanistic feature. However, the cult of personality did not carry on to their successors. More generally, Chehabi and Linz have summarized the various differences between sultanism and totalitarianism as follows: first, sultanistic regimes (Romania, North Korea, and the Dominican Republic excepted) have lacked any ideology worthy of the term and any pro-regime intellectuals who support it. Second, sultanistic rulers are "in it" for personal enrichment and power for its own sake, whereas totalitarian rulers are exponents of a cause and often live modestly—or at least cultivate an ascetic image. Third, sultanistic regimes lack the dominant and well-organized single party and the related organizations that are central to totalitarianism. Fourth and related, sultanism—like authoritarianism (below)—lacks the political mobilization which is central to totalitarianism. Fifth and finally, whereas totalitarianism penetrates all aspects of society and all areas of the country, sultanism varies in the extent of its penetration, with groups and/or areas that are neither a source of enrichment nor a threat to the ruler likely to be left more or less alone.[19] To these differences we can add the empirical fact that no sultanistic regime has ever lasted as long as the six decades of full totalitarianism in the Soviet Union.

AUTHORITARIAN REGIMES

The last, and probably vaguest, subtype of autocracy is *authoritarianism*. The classic definition of **authoritarian regimes** is that of Linz, as follows:

> political systems with limited, not responsible, political pluralism, without elaborate and guiding ideology, but with distinctive mentalities, without extensive nor intensive political mobilization, except at some points in their development, and in which a leader or occasionally a small group exercises power within formally ill-defined limits but actually quite predictable ones.[20]

Thus, authoritarian regimes are defined largely in a negative way: they lack the roles of ideology and mobilization found in totalitarianism, and they also lack the broad arbitrariness of sultanism. Authoritarian regimes are to some extent a *residual category* of autocracies, which makes them somewhat vaguer than totalitarian or sultanistic regimes. Furthermore, the four subtypes of authoritarianism vary in certain key ways, above all with respect to their political legitimacy.

The first subtype is **traditional authoritarianism**, based on an hereditary monarchy. We find such a regime today not only in many Middle Eastern and North African countries—Bahrain, Jordan, Kuwait, Morocco, Oman, Qatar, Saudi Arabia, and the United Arab Emirates—but also in Swaziland in Africa, Brunei in Asia, and Tonga in the Pacific. As autocracies go, traditional monarchies have the advantage of having normally a clear pattern of succession, which confirms legitimacy on the new monarch. Moreover, there is hopefully (for the regime) still a broad legitimacy of traditional authoritarianism as a form of government, something which certainly lost its legitimacy in Europe over time.

The notion of a ruling or non-ruling monarch is a clear dichotomy, but the reality has been, and is, more nuanced than this. Indeed, assuming a monarch as head of state, one can outline the following continuum of monarchs and increasing democracy (in terms of increasing responsible government):

» At one extreme, the monarch holds all executive powers and rules by decree. There is no elected legislature. This is the pattern in Oman and Saudi Arabia, although they both have appointed assemblies. This was also the pattern in Imperial Russia until 1905.

» The monarch appoints a cabinet and perhaps a separate prime minister, but they are totally responsible to the monarch. The monarch chairs cabinet meetings and rules through the cabinet. There is no elected legislature. This is the pattern in Brunei.

» The monarch appoints a separate prime minister and cabinet, as in the previous scenario, but the monarch (or perhaps the constitution) also "permits" the existence of a legislature that can comment on legislation or possibly even is empowered to give or refuse necessary assent to legislation, but which has little or no say over government formation. This is the pattern in Bahrain, Kuwait, Monaco, Qatar, and the United Arab Emirates, with the Kuwait assembly having little, and the other four assemblies no, say over government formation. This was also the pattern in Imperial Germany and briefly the pattern in Imperial Russia.[21]

» There is a prime minister and cabinet separate from the monarch and a legislature that must approve legislation and can remove the prime minister and cabinet through a motion of non-confidence, which may be unlikely if the legislature lacks discipline and organized parties. However, the monarch (still) picks the prime minister and cabinet, dismisses them freely, and indeed either directly or indirectly still rules the country through them. The monarch also has many direct supporters (in a partisan sense) in the parliament, perhaps elected with the monarch's help. This is the pattern in Jordan and Morocco. This was also the historic pattern in seventeenth- and eighteenth-century Britain (in fact, up to the 1830s).

» There is a prime minister and cabinet separate from the monarch and account-able to the legislature, which can remove the prime minister and cabinet through a motion of non-confidence. Conversely, support in the legislature is not only needed for a prime minister and cabinet to get and keep power, it is also the only means to this end. In other words, the monarch does not deter-mine the cabinet (at least the civilian ministers), nor does the monarch run the cabinet. However, the monarch still has a say—if not indeed the say—in for-eign policy or other policy areas and can veto legislation. This is the pattern in Liechtenstein today and was the pattern in Japan in the 1920s.

» At the other extreme, the monarch plays no role in determining the cabinet, as in the previous scenario. Nor does the monarch attend cabinet meetings, have any powers over policy, or any legislative vetoes. In other words, this is a parliamentary system (Chapter 6) with a figurehead monarch. This is the pattern in the United Kingdom, the Benelux countries, and Scandinavia.

Of these six categories, the first four would be considered autocratic and the last two democratic (granted, the second-last one is borderline). Focussing on the first four categories, we can see that there is a clear range within traditional authoritarian regimes in the extent to which the monarch is all-powerful or not. Suffice it to say that countries do not suddenly switch from, say, the first cat-egory to the last one. Thus, if a traditional monarchy is going to become a democratic figurehead (constitutional) monarchy, it invariably will go through some if not most of the intermediate categories. Of course, in many places democratization, or at least political change, has involved removing the monarchy altogether, especially where the monarch of the day has not wanted to "evolve."

The second subtype of authoritarianism is **military authoritarianism**. In Chapter 4 we outlined a continuum of civil-military relations. As we noted there—and paralleling the situation of traditional authoritarianism—there is a range of categories of military authoritarianism: military rule, military con-trol, and military tutelage, which vary both in the nature of the head of gov-ernment (military, civilian figurehead, and civilian respectively) and in the number of military ministers in the cabinet (from a majority to a few). Yet all of these categories involve an autonomous military either running the country outright or at least exercising so much control and oversight that the regime cannot be called democratic.

At the end of 2004 military authoritarianism may seem to be a "dying" regime type compared with the 1960s and 1970s, but military authoritarianism in its various forms does exist in about a dozen countries (see Chapter 4), most crucially Algeria (military tutelage), Burma/Myanmar (military rule), Egypt (military tutelage), and Pakistan (military control). The region where there has been a clear swing away from military authoritarianism is Latin America, where as recently as the late 1970s no less than 11 countries (that is, over half in the region) were under military rule broadly defined.[22] Of course, one of the realities of military authoritarianism is that it does not last forever, inasmuch as whatever initial legitimacy there is—arising from the corruption and incompetence of the previous government and the military's pledge to act in the national interest—will dissipate over time. Thus, it is rare for a single military regime to last more than a couple of decades (Burma since 1962 is the main exception here).

The third subtype of authoritarianism is **theocratic authoritarianism**, which involves religious-based rule. So far, all the modern examples of this have been cases of Islamic rule—Afghanistan under the Taliban, Iran since the 1979 Islamic Revolution, North Yemen for centuries until 1962, and Sudan (where Islamicists are a central component and support base of the regime). Of these few cases, it is Iran which has developed the most elaborate institutionalized form of a theocratic regime. Figure 8.1 outlines the formal structure of power in Iran since 1989, when the separate post of prime minister was abolished. As can be seen, Iranians elect both a president and a parliament, which are the semi-liberal aspects of the regime. However, the Iranian president is a relatively weak head of state and government. As Buchta stresses:

> Because of constitutional shackles, the power of the presidential office is not as great as is often assumed in the West. Moreover, the high public profile of the president ... in the media and at international conferences encourages the false belief that the executive plays a dominant role in setting the domestic and foreign policy of Iran.[23]

FIGURE 8.1 :: THE FORMAL STRUCTURE OF POWER IN IRAN SINCE 1989

		Council of Guardians (six-year terms)		serves	as the *de facto* upper house
				functions	as a religious supreme court
		approves all candidates for			
	elects	President (four-year term)		appoints	cabinet ministers (subject to parliamentary confirmation)
				controls	Planning and Budget Organization
				chairs	National Security Council
		and			
ELECTORATE	elects	Parliament (four-year term)		recommends	half of the Council of Guardians (six lay members) (to be appointed by the Head of the Judiciary)
		and			
	elects	Assembly of Experts (eight-year term)	elects Supreme Leader (life term)	serves as	Commander-in-Chief
				appoints	half of the Council of Guardians (six clerical members)
				appoints	Head of the Judiciary (who in turn appoints the lay jurists of the Council of Guardians, the Head of the Supreme Court, and the Chief Public Prosecutor)
				appoints	Expediency Council (which arbitrates between Parliament and the Council of Guardians)
				appoints	Chief of the General Staff of the Armed Forces
				appoints	president of state radio and television

Source: Buchta 8, with additions.

In fact, the Iranian president is clearly second in terms of the overall power structure. The most powerful political position—and the first of three key religious-based political institutions—is the *vali-ye faqih* or "ruling jurisprudent," also referred to as the Supreme Leader. The first such "supreme jurisprudent" was Grand Ayatollah Khomeini, the leader of Iran's Islamic Revolution; after Khomeini's death, he was replaced by Ayatollah Khamene'i.

221

The *faqih* not only formally confirms the president, but is the effective head of government in terms of major policy decisions and changes, and is the actor who makes many other key appointments (see Figure 8.1). This ruling jurisprudent was initially required to be a "source of emulation" and one of the highest-ranking Shi'i clerics. However, in 1989 Grand Ayatollah Khomeini—after a conflict with Grand Ayatollah Montazeri, Khomeini's likely successor—amended the constitution to lower the requirement to being a religious leader, but not necessarily a leading authority.[24] This change opened up the position of *faqih* from the 20 or so Grand Ayatollahs (worldwide) to the 5000 or so Ayatollahs in Iran.[25]

The *faqih* is chosen for life, making this position unaccountable—and meaning that Iran does not have responsible government. The choice of the supreme jurisprudent is done by the Assembly of Experts, the second religious-based political institution in Iran. The Assembly is composed of 86 clerics deemed knowledgeable in Islamic jurisprudence and who are elected for an eight-year term. With the supreme jurisprudent serving for life, it is quite possible that a given Assembly of Experts may never be called on to make a selection. The Assembly of Experts itself is elected by universal suffrage, with the various regions of Iran each electing a set number based on population. In theory, the Assembly of Experts can also *remove* a supreme jurisprudent who is deemed unfit to serve, but this has never happened and seems highly unlikely.

The third religious-based political institution in Iran is the Council of Guardians, which in various ways ensures that Iran is ruled according to shari'a law. The Council has 12 members: six religious clerics appointed by the supreme jurisprudent, and six lay scholars recommended by parliament and formally appointed by the Head of the Judiciary (see Figure 8.1). The Council of Guardians functions as a religious supreme court. Yet, it is much more than this. Since all legislation passed in parliament must be approved by the Council of Guardians, it effectively serves as Iran's upper house. (As Figure 8.1 shows, a separate Expediency Council appointed by the supreme jurisprudent is used to mediate between the two "chambers.") Finally, the Council of Guardians also oversees all national elections and referenda, not merely in the sense of organizing them but most crucially having the task of approving on religious grounds *all* candidates for elections to the presidency, the parliament, and the

Assembly of Experts. Since the Council of Guardians is free to, and indeed does, reject candidates if they are too liberal or radical, this greatly limits the range of choices given to the voters. (It is still a broader range than a voter would have under totalitarianism, though.) For the candidates who clear this central hurdle, competition is basically free—and indeed the 1997 and 2001 presidential elections, as well as the 2000 parliamentary elections, were all won by reformist candidates in opposition to Ayatollah Khamene'i, the supreme jurisprudent. Overall, then, we can characterize elections in Iran as being "unfree but fair."

The last subtype of authoritarianism is one that has been around for decades but has only recently been conceptualized by scholars: **electoral authoritarianism**. In this situation, multiple political parties compete, with the winning party claiming a right to govern. Political legitimacy is based on election outcomes, which certainly sounds democratic. However, the elections are rarely free and are never fair, so the same party stays in power indefinitely. From the 1930s through the 1990s, Mexico under its Institutional Revolutionary Party (PRI) was the classic case of such electoral authoritarianism. The main longstanding contemporary examples of this type of regime are the parliamentary systems of Malaysia and Singapore, and various presidential systems such as Azerbaijan and Tunisia. Moreover, the recent breakdown of democracy in Russia has given way to electoral authoritarianism.

Singapore is a good contemporary example of electoral authoritarianism; data on its post-independence elections are given in Table 8.2. The People's Action Party (PAP) has governed Singapore continuously since independence, not only winning each election but winning every, or almost every, *seat* in each election. The PAP itself attributes this to its highly competent and basically corruption-free governments, which have presided over Singapore's economic transformation into one of the world's most wealthy and developed countries. Certainly these facts, and the PAP's consequent genuine popularity with many voters, cannot be denied. However, it is not as if the electorate is given a free choice of alternatives. The PAP has controlled the domestic media for some time and censors the foreign media. Singapore had a diverse print media before independence and for some years thereafter, but over time, through both direct attacks on the press and the broader Internal Security Act, the media has

TABLE 8.2 :: ELECTIONS IN SINGAPORE SINCE INDEPENDENCE

| YEAR | TOTAL SEATS | PEOPLE'S ACTION PARTY | | | OPPOSITION | OPPOSITION |
		SEATS WON	SEAT PERCENTAGE	VOTE PERCENTAGE	SEATS CONTESTED	SEATS WON
1968	58	58	100.0	86.7	7	0
1972	65	65	100.0	70.4	57	0
1976	69	69	100.0	74.1	53	0
1980	75	75	100.0	77.7	38	0
1984	79	77	97.5	64.8	47	2
1988	81	80	98.8	63.2	69	1
1991	81	77	95.1	61.0	36	4
1997	83	81	97.6	65.0	34	2
2001	84	82	97.6	73.7	29	2

been made to toe the party line.[26] Opposition parties do exist—without them there could be no claim of competitive elections—but they are constantly harassed by the government, and opposition candidates are now required to put up a substantial deposit (about $10,000 Canadian) just to compete. Perhaps the most nefarious means of attacking the political opposition has been the launching of civil defamation lawsuits against individual opposition politicians when they criticize government leaders. These are invariably successful, not surprisingly given the PAP-biased judiciary, and have at times resulted in said opposition politicians being penalized by large sums. In part as a consequence of these monetary factors, and as a general admission that the PAP will continue to govern, in the last three elections the opposition parties have consciously contested only a minority of the seats (see Table 8.2).

Interestingly, as an admission that its victories have been somewhat excessive, starting in 1984 the PAP began to offer opposition parties up to three Non-Constituency Members of Parliament (NCMPs), to be awarded to the defeated opposition candidates who nevertheless got the highest share of the votes. The point here was and is to ensure that the opposition has a minimum of three seats in parliament, which presumably makes it look more "balanced." Of course, in the one election, 1991, where the opposition parties won more than this target, no NCMPs were offered. Although the NCMPs were initially disparaged and refused by the opposition when they were introduced, nowadays they are generally accepted as a sign of support to the voters who want an opposition.

Additionally, starting in 1990 an increasing number of Nominated Members of Parliament (NMPs) have also been appointed. These NMPs are supposed to be outstanding citizens and independent voices. In any case, they are nominated by the public and chosen by a parliamentary committee. Both the NCMPs and the NMPs can speak in parliament, take part in debates, raise questions, etc, but the NCMPs can only vote on limited measures—nothing involving the constitution, budgets, or other (non-) confidence matters—and the NMPs cannot actually vote on anything.[27] Thus, neither of these innovations is ever going to threaten the PAP's control of parliament.

NOTES

1 This ideology is central to the overall legitimacy of the totalitarian regime. Consequently, clear violations of it—that is, advocating distinctly alternative ideologies—are grounds for punishment.

2 Juan J. Linz, *Totalitarian and Authoritarian Regimes* (Boulder, CO: Lynne Rienner, 2000) 70.

3 Alexander Dallin and George W. Breslauer, *Political Terror in Communist Systems* (Stanford, CA: Stanford University Press, 1970) 1.

4 Linz, *Totalitarian and Authoritarian Regimes* 24–26 and 100ff.

5 Dallin and Breslauer 84–85.

6 Linz, *Totalitarian and Authoritarian Regimes* 105, 108.

7 Stanley G. Payne, *A History of Fascism, 1914–1945* (Madison, WI: The University of Wisconsin Press, 1995) 486, 490. More generally, see his Chapter 14, "Fascism and Modernization."

8 Gabriel A. Almond, "Comparative Political Systems," *The Journal of Politics* 18:3 (August 1956): 403–04.

9 Linz, *Totalitarian and Authoritarian Regimes* 241.

10 Linz, *Totalitarian and Authoritarian Regimes* 244. Finally, Linz notes that "[s]ituations in which the strength of prototalitarian forces is reversed might be labelled 'arrested totalitarianism.'" Romania in 1941 is an example.

11 Linz, *Totalitarian and Authoritarian Regimes* 94.

12 Linz and Stepan, *Problems of Democratic Transition and Consolidation* 256.

13 Linz and Stepan, *Problems of Democratic Transition and Consolidation* 256–58.

14 Keith Crawford, *East Central European Politics Today* (Manchester, UK: Manchester University Press, 1996) 51.

15 See, for example, Mark R. Thompson, "Totalitarian and Post-Totalitarian Regimes in Transitions and Non-Transitions from Communism," *Totalitarian Movements and Political Religions* 3:1 (Summer 2002): 86–90.

16 H.E. Chehabi and Juan J. Linz, "A Theory of Sultanism 1: A Type of Nondemocratic Rule," *Sultanistic Regimes*, ed. H.E. Chehabi and Juan J. Linz (Baltimore, MD and London, UK: The Johns Hopkins University Press, 1998) 7.

17 Chehabi and Linz 9.

18 Chehabi and Linz 13–16.

19 Chehabi and Linz 3–24.

20 Juan J. Linz, "An Authoritarian Regime: The Case of Spain," *Mass Politics: Studies in Political Sociology*, ed. Erik Allard and Stein Rokkan (New York, NY: Free Press, 1970), as cited in Linz, *Totalitarian and Authoritarian Regimes* 159.

21 Given this lack of responsible government, it is unclear why Freedom House considers Monaco to be an electoral democracy. It is not treated as such in this analysis (cf. Table 3.3).

22 These 11 were Argentina, Brazil, Bolivia, Ecuador, El Salvador, Guatemala, Honduras, Panama, Paraguay, Peru, and Uruguay.

23 Wilfried Buchta, *Who Rules Iran? The Structure of Power in the Islamic Republic* (Washington, DC: The Washington Institute for Near East Policy and the Konrad Adenauer Stiftung, 2000) 23.

24 Buchta 52–53.

25 Interestingly, none of the other Grand Ayatollahs actually support the principle of *velayat-e faqih* or "rule by the jurisprudent." Buchta 54 (his Diagram 10).

26 On this history, see Francis T. Seow, *The Media Enthralled: Singapore Revisited* (Boulder, CO: Lynne Rienner, 1998).

27 Diane K. Mauzy, "Electoral Innovation and One-Party Dominance in Singapore," *How Asia Votes*, ed. John Fuh-Sheng Hsieh and David Newman (New York, NY: Chatham House Publishers of Seven Bridges Press, 2002) 243.

CHAPTER NINE

Democratic Transitions, Consolidations, and Breakdowns

IN THIS CHAPTER YOU WILL LEARN:

» *how democratic transition and democratic breakdown are opposite phenomena;*
» *what is a wave of democratization;*
» *where and why such waves have occurred;*
» *how and why there is some scholarly debate as to when the waves of democratization have actually occurred;*
» *what are the four different processes of democratization;*
» *which ones of these are superior, and why;*
» *what are the three components of democratic consolidation;*
» *what are the three main challenges of democratic consolidation; that is, what is needed to achieve this;*
» *how and why democracies break down; and*
» *how in very exceptional circumstances a (brief) democratic breakdown may be followed by democratic re-equilibration.*

DEMOCRATIZATION AND RELATED CONCEPTS

Simplifying somewhat our four categories in Table 3.3, all regimes are either autocratic or democratic. Viewed in this dichotomous sense, **democratization** is the process of changing from an autocracy to a democracy or, more precisely with regards to our four categories, changing from an autocracy to at least an electoral democracy. The key step is the holding of free and fair elections to select the government, under the qualification that this government actually governs and is not just a front for a tutelary military or monarch wielding the actual power behind the scenes. If the political changes in an autocracy do not involve (culminate) in having free and fair elections for the key position(s) of power, then one should not speak of democratization. Instead, if a country makes varying reforms that result in electing lesser offices, increasing press freedoms, releasing political prisoners and/or generally enlarging the scope of public debate, then one can refer to the political *liberalization* of an autocracy.[1] Such liberalization and increased openness could well involve the change from a closed autocracy to a semi-liberal one. (Remember that we use the term *semi*-liberal autocracy to distinguish its civil liberties from the full range of freedoms and their guarantees in a liberal democracy.) However, further steps— which may or may not happen—are needed to produce democratization. Finally, the change from an electoral democracy to a liberal one can be called the *deepening* of democracy.[2]

In this chapter, we shall be concerned mainly with democratization as opposed to mere liberalization. An alternative term for the process of democratization—and the one we shall more often use—is that of **democratic transition**. The opposite of a democratic transition, that is, the change from a democracy to an autocracy, is known as a **democratic breakdown**. A democratic breakdown occurs in the context of a lack of **democratic consolidation**, or broad support for a democratic regime. (This last concept is multifaceted and will be outlined later.) As we shall see, democratic transitions and democratic breakdowns occur in individual countries at identifiable times. Interestingly, though, countries—especially neighbouring countries—often have transitions, or breakdowns, fairly close in time to each other. This observation has led to the notion of "waves" of democratization, which we shall first analyze before getting to the specifics of transition, consolidation, breakdown, and related matters.

WAVES OF DEMOCRATIZATION

As originally conceived by Huntington,

> A **wave of democratization** is a group of transitions from nonde-
> mocratic [autocratic] to democratic regimes that occur within a
> specified period of time and that significantly outnumber transi-
> tions in the opposite direction during that period of time. A wave
> also usually involves liberalization or partial democratization in
> political systems that do not become fully democratic. Three waves
> of democratization have occurred in the modern world. ... During
> each wave some regime transitions occurred in a nondemocratic
> direction. In addition, not all transitions to democracy occurred
> during democratic waves.[3]

Thus, a wave of democratization is a clear pattern leading to an overall increase
in the number of democracies, but it is also a pattern with some exceptions.

Huntington's first, long wave of democratization begins in 1828 (with the
United States presidential election of that year) and lasts until 1926. Its roots
were in the democratic ideals of the American and French revolutions of the
late 1700s and it occurred initially in Western and Northern Europe and the
British settler countries of the United States, Canada, Australia, and New
Zealand. All these societies were experiencing social and economic development with industrialization, urbanization, the formation of middle and working classes, growing national income, and also, eventually, somewhat of a
decrease in economic inequality. Their intellectuals and many political leaders also had a strong belief in classical liberal thought. Moreover, most of these
countries were either overwhelmingly or largely Protestant in religion. After
World War I, this wave spread into Central and Eastern Europe due to the
break-up of the empires there.

Huntington's second wave of democratization lasted from 1943 to 1962 and
was broadly based geographically. Two factors were central in this second
wave. The first was the Allied victory in World War II, their direct imposition
of democracy on the defeated Axis powers, and their support, or more specifically United States support (especially in the late 1940s), for democracy else-

229

where, particularly in Latin America and the Mediterranean. The second factor was the decolonization occurring in Africa and Asia, which produced a huge number of new states (see Chapter 1), many of which were at least initially democratic.

Huntington's third—and ongoing—wave of democratization begins in 1974 with the collapse of autocracy in Portugal (although Portugal did not instantly become democratic) and spreads out from Southern Europe to Latin America, Asia, and then ex-communist Europe. In the 1990s (subsequent to Huntington's book), this wave spread into Africa. Huntington argues that the third wave was multi-causal, involving global economic growth in the 1960s, the economic failures of various autocracies, a new pro-democratic attitude of the Catholic Church, (renewed) support for democracy by the United States and the then-European Community, and Gorbachev's abandonment of Soviet control over Central and Eastern Europe—all reinforced in a "snowballing" way by modern communications that let people quickly know what was happening elsewhere in the world.[4] This notion of "the third wave of democratization" has become a frequent point of context in the social science literature, so students need to be familiar with it.

Huntington also argues that there have been two reverse waves of democratization, a **reverse wave** being a significant group of transitions in a non-democratic (autocratic) direction. His first reverse wave lasted from 1922 to 1942, beginning with Mussolini's March on Rome (although it would be a couple more years before Italian democracy could be deemed definitely to be over), and then spreading throughout Southern and Eastern Europe, Latin America, and on to Japan. The turmoil of the post-World War I environment, the rise of both totalitarian and militaristic ideologies, and finally the Great Depression were central to this non-democratic wave. Of course, not all countries experienced breakdowns of democracy during this period; the breakdowns occurred mainly in places where democracy was newer and essentially where it was weaker. Yet even in the countries where democracy survived, there was generally a rise in anti-democratic movements during this period. For Huntington, a second reverse wave of democratization occurred from 1958 to 1975, most dramatically in Latin America, but also in the Mediterranean, Asia, and Africa; in Africa, this involved the failure in many countries of new democracies to get off the ground in the first place. During this second reverse wave, the most common pattern of overthrowing democracy was a military coup and subsequent military rule (the patterns were more varied during the first reverse wave). Fear of communism, especially after Castro's successful revolution in Cuba and his subsequent shift to a socialist economy, was often a central factor for autocrats and their supporters in the second reverse wave, regardless of how "serious" the communist threat really was. Certainly during this period the United States was relatively tolerant towards the new autocracies, especially if and when they pledged to be pro-Western.[5]

METHODOLOGICAL CRITIQUES AND REVISIONS OF HUNTINGTON'S WAVES

Huntington's analysis and classifications are commonly used, and his concept of democratic "waves" was certainly groundbreaking. That said, various criticisms can be made of his methodology. We shall accept some but not all of these criticisms and come up with our own time periods of global regime change.

The first of these criticisms concerns Huntington's criteria for democracy: (1) the suffrage being held by at least 50 per cent of adult males (at least for the nineteenth century) and (2) responsible government.[6] Both Doorenspleet and Paxton have criticized the first criterion for allowing a country to be called democratic when it excludes women; for her part, Doorenspleet argues for a suffrage criterion of at least 80 per cent of the adult population.[7] On the other hand Rueschemeyer, Stephens, and Stephens use a suffrage criterion of at least 60 per cent of adult males—quite close to Huntington's—or literate adult male suffrage, since either of these is sufficient to establish multi-class suffrage rights, which is their focus.[8]

This issue could be solved by using a continuous measure of democracy: obviously, a system with both genders voting is more democratic than one with only (partial) male suffrage; likewise, a system with universal suffrage is more democratic than one with only 80 per cent or so of adults having the right to vote—for the latter, think of the United States prior to the Voting Rights Act of 1965. Furthermore, as was noted in Chapter 3 (but what is not mentioned

231

TABLE 9.1 :: TRANSITIONS TO AND BREAKDOWNS OF DEMOCRATIC REGIMES (MIEDS)

COUNTRY	TRANSITION	BREAKDOWN	NOTES
ALBANIA	1992	1995	
	1997		
ANDORRA	1993		
ANTIGUA AND BARBUDA	2004		
ARGENTINA	1916	1930	
	1946	1948–49	
	1958	1966	
	1973	1976	
	1983		
AUSTRALIA	1901		
AUSTRIA	1919	1934	
	1945		
BAHAMAS	1967		
BANGLADESH	1980	1982	
	1991		
BARBADOS	1961		
BELGIUM	1919		occupation 1940–1945
BELIZE	1981		
BENIN	1991		
BOLIVIA	1952	1964	
	1982		
BOTSWANA	1966		
BRAZIL	1945	1964	re-equilibration 1954–1955
	1985		
BULGARIA	1919	1923	
	1990		
BURMA	1956	1962	
CANADA	1867		
CAPE VERDE	1991		
CHILE	1952	1973	
	1989		
COLOMBIA	1922	1949	
	1974		
CONGO	1992	1996	
COSTA RICA	1928		re-equilibration 1948
CROATIA	1992	1993–94	
	2000		
CUBA	1944	1952	
CYPRUS	1960		re-equilibration 1974
CZECHOSLOVAKIA	1919		conquest 1938
	1946	1948	

COUNTRY	TRANSITION	BREAKDOWN	NOTES
CZECHOSLOVAKIA/ CZECH REPUBLIC	1990 1992		
DENMARK	1915		occupation 1940-1945
DOMINICA	1978		
DOMINICAN REPUBLIC	1962 1978	1963	
ECUADOR	1948 1978	1963	
EL SALVADOR	1967 1984	1979	
ESTONIA	1920 1992	1934	
FIJI	1970 1999	1987 2000	
FINLAND	1919		re-equilibration 1930–1932
FRANCE	1848 1875	1850	occupation 1940–1945
GAMBIA	1965	1994	
GEORGIA	1992		failed *autogolpe* attempt in 2003
GERMANY / WEST GERMANY	1919 1949	1933	
GHANA	1957 1969 1979 2000	1960 1972 1981	
GREECE	1875 1910 1927 1950 1974	1909 1915 1935 1967	
GRENADA	1984		
GUATEMALA	1966 1985	1982	failed *autogolpe* attempt in 1993
GUINEA-BISSAU	1994	2003	
GUYANA	1966 1992	1970	
HONDURAS	1982		
HUNGARY	1945 1990		conquest 1947
ICELAND	1918		
INDIA	1952 1977	1975	

continues...

233

COUNTRY	TRANSITION	BREAKDOWN	NOTES
INDONESIA	1950	1957	
	1999		
IRELAND	1922		
ISRAEL	1948		
ITALY	1918	1925	
	1948		
JAMAICA	1962		
JAPAN	1928	1932	
	1947		
KENYA	2002		
KIRIBATI	1979		
KOREA, SOUTH	1960	1961	
	1987		
LATVIA	1922	1934	
	1993		
LEBANON	1946	1972	
LESOTHO	2002		
LIECHTENSTEIN	1921		
LITHUANIA	1922	1926	
	1992		
LUXEMBOURG	1919		occupation 1940–1945
MACEDONIA	1991		
MADAGASCAR	1993		
MALAWI	1994		
MALAYSIA	1957	1969	
MALI	1992		
MALTA	1964		
MARSHALL ISLANDS	1986		
MAURITIUS	1968		
MEXICO	2000		
MICRONESIA	1986		
MOLDOVA	1994		
MONGOLIA	1990		
MOZAMBIQUE	1994		
NAMIBIA	1990		
NAURU	1968		
NEPAL	1959	1960	
	1991	2002	
NETHERLANDS	1917		occupation 1940–1945
NEW ZEALAND	1890		
NICARAGUA	1990		
NIGER	1993	1996	
	1999		

COUNTRY	TRANSITION	BREAKDOWN	NOTES
NIGERIA	1960	1966	
	1979	1983	
	1999		
NORWAY	1905		occupation 1940–1945
PAKISTAN	1947	1958	
	1970	1977	
	1988/1990	1999	
PALAU	1994		
PANAMA	1952	1968	
	1989		
PAPUA NEW GUINEA	1975		
PARAGUAY	1993		failed coup attempt in 1996
PERU	1956	1962	
	1963	1968	
	1979	1992	
	2001		
PHILIPPINES	1946	1972	
	1986		
POLAND	1922	1926	
	1990		
PORTUGAL	1910	1926	
	1975		
ROMANIA	1992		
RUSSIA	1993	2003	
ST. KITTS AND NEVIS	1983		
ST. LUCIA	1979		
ST. VINCENT AND THE GRENADINES	1979		
SAMOA	1991		
SAN MARINO	1906	1923	
	1945		
SÃO TOMÉ AND PRÍNCIPE	1991		failed coup attempts in 1995 and 2003
SERBIA	1880	1883	
SERBIA / YUGOSLAVIA	1903	1929	
SERBIA AND MONTENEGRO	2000		
SENEGAL	2000		
SEYCHELLES	1993		
SIERRA LEONE	1998		
SLOVAKIA	1992		
SLOVENIA	1991		
SOLOMON ISLANDS	1978		
SOMALIA	1960		
SOUTH AFRICA	1994		

continues...

COUNTRY	TRANSITION	BREAKDOWN	NOTES
SPAIN	1931	1936	
	1977		
SRI LANKA	1947		
SURINAME	1975	1980	
	1987	1990	
	1991		
SWEDEN	1921		
SWITZERLAND	1848		
TAIWAN	1987		
THAILAND	1945	1947	
	1949	1951	
	1974	1976	
	1992		
TIMOR-LESTE (East Timor)	2003		
TRINIDAD AND TOBAGO	1962		
TURKEY	1950	1960	
	1961	1970	
	1973	1980	
	1983		
TUVALU	1978		
UKRAINE	1991	1999	
	2005		
UNITED KINGDOM	1885		
UNITED STATES	1829		
URUGUAY	1918	1973	re-equilibration 1933–1942
	1984		
VANUATU	1980		
VENEZUELA	1959		failed coup attempts in 1992 (twice) and 2002
ZAMBIA	1991	1996	

by any of the authors mentioned above), is that a system with a voting age of 18 is more democratic than one with a voting age of 23 or 25. What we are talking about here is the establishment of a basic level of electoral democracy, and the notion and dating of democratic transitions are much more manageable when democracy is treated as a dichotomy. The relevant question here is: at what level of suffrage does the political system function in response to the needs (and potential votes) of more than just the elites? For our purposes, we shall use a suffrage criterion of more than 20 per cent of the 18-and-above population (even when the voting age was well above this); anything below that with competitive elections and responsible government can be deemed to be (only) a **competitive oligarchy**. (In pre-1994 South Africa, such an oligarchy was racial in nature.)

Our cut-off cannot claim to be that of an unqualified electoral democracy in the sense of universal suffrage, but certainly one where the suffrage has become broad enough that politics is more than an elite game. Consequently, such a system can and will be called a **moderately inclusive electoral democracy** or **MIED**. Table 9.1 presents a reference list, by country, of the dates of transition to such a MIED when and where these have occurred.[9] It also gives the dates of democratic breakdowns. (To this end, it should be noted that every breakdown listed involved the ending of responsible government and never the reducing of suffrage rights while responsible government was maintained.)

A second problem with Huntington's calculations is that he includes as countries with a transition away from democracy all those (European) countries conquered by Nazi Germany, thus amplifying his first reverse wave. Yet, as Doorenspleet points out, these were interruptions rather than breakdowns of democracy.[10] Consequently, such cases will be treated as ones of occupation rather than regime change. A third problem, also noted by Doorenspleet, is that the vast increase in the number of countries in the world means a very different denominator if one is measuring the *percentage* of democracies (or autocracies).[11] Consequently, we shall avoid percentages and focus on total changes, but also weight these by the number of countries. A fourth, and presumably obvious, problem with Huntington's categories is some temporal overlap, especially between the first wave of democratization and the first reverse wave. Presumably both cannot occur at the same time, and one must note which wave is the more numerous one for any and all years. Fifth and related, it may not actually be the case that a wave is occurring at all in a given period. Doorenspleet uses the term "trendless fluctuation" to describe a pattern where there are (opposing) waves of both democratization and democratic breakdown.[12] Finally, although a wave reflects an overall pattern, this pattern may be more intense for a sub-period of time; consequently, where appropriate, a distinction will be made between phases of "normal" and concentrated intensity of a wave.

Using the data from Table 9.1 and the aforementioned qualifications, what historical patterns do we find? As shown in Table 9.2, there is indeed a long wave of democratization—in the sense of countries becoming MIEDs—from 1829 to 1922. Within this long wave is a particularly intense phase during and after World War I, reflecting both the "trade-off" of the mass mobilization during the war and the creation of new states as a consequence of it. Then there is a reverse wave from 1923 through 1936. From 1937 to 1943 "nothing happens"—even if there was World War II and the occupation of various democracies (starting with Czechoslovakia in 1938–39). That is, no country made a transition to democracy or suffered an internal breakdown of democracy during these years. A second wave of democratization occurred from 1944 through 1957, followed not by a global reverse wave, but by a period of trendless fluctuation from 1958 through 1973. This finding confirms that of Doorenspleet, although with slight differences from her start and especially end year of this trendless period.[13] That said, however, there was certainly a *regional* reverse wave in Latin America in this period, with about half of the countries in that region undergoing a democratic breakdown during this time. Finally, a third wave of democratization began in 1974 (as Huntington argued) and is still ongoing. This third wave was particularly intense from 1990 through 1994, when it reached Central and Eastern Europe and Africa.

THE PROCESSES OF DEMOCRATIC TRANSITION

A transition to democracy can occur in one of four ways, as is shown in Table 9.3, which gives various illustrative postwar examples as opposed to a complete list. First, the process of democratization may be *dictated* by those in power, such as the Brazilian military or the Hungarian communists; this is a top-down process. Second, formal *negotiations* between the regime and the (leaders of the) pro-democratic opposition may take place, such as between the Polish communists and the Solidarity movement or between the whites-only government of South Africa and the African National Congress.[14] Third, the autocratic regime may collapse, in which case the leaders *abdicate* power and simply walk away. Such a regime collapse can occur because of a military defeat of a mil-

TABLE 9.2 :: **WAVES OF DEMOCRATIZATION** (Year-End Totals)

	NUMBER OF TRANSITIONS	NUMBER OF BREAKDOWNS	DIFFERENCE	TOTAL N	DIFFERENCE WEIGHTED BY TOTAL STATES AT THE END OF THE PERIOD (absolute values)
FIRST WAVE, 1829–1922	36	4	+32	64	50%
of which:					
MODERATE PHASE, 1829–1914	15	3	+12	56	21%
INTENSE PHASE, 1915–1922	21	1	+20	64	31%
REVERSE WAVE, 1923–1936	4	15	−11	66	17%
STABILITY, 1937–1943	0	0	0		
SECOND WAVE, 1944–1957	28	8	+20	88	23%
FLUCTUATION, 1958–1973	27	24	+3	144	2%
THIRD WAVE, 1974–PRESENT (2004)	96	24	+72	192	38%
of which:					
MODERATE PHASE, 1974–1989	40	12	+28	167	17%
INTENSE PHASE, 1990–1994	41	3	+38	191	20%
MODERATE PHASE, 1995–PRESENT	15	9	+6	192	3%

itary regime, such as of Greece in Cyprus or of Argentina in the Falkland Islands; alternatively, autocracies have collapsed due to the combination of the withdrawal of external support and massive public demonstrations (the communist regimes of Czechoslovakia and East Germany). All of these are internal processes. Fourth and finally, after military defeat and foreign occupation, the occupying power(s) may choose to *impose* democracy on the occupied country, as was done in Germany and Japan after World War II.[15] Overall, in terms of the internal processes, the *dictated* process occurs when the ruling autocrats are stronger than any opposition, the *negotiated* process occurs when the ruling autocrats and the opposition are roughly equal in power (at least to the extent that neither can impose their wishes), and the *abdicated* process occurs when the ruling autocrats (often quite quickly) become weaker than the political opposition.

Of these four processes, the negotiated and dictated ones (in that order) are seen to be "superior" in the sense of being more likely to produce a durable democracy. This is because elements of the old regime help to produce the new

COMPARING POLITICAL REGIMES

TABLE 9.3 :: PROCESSES OF TRANSITION TO DEMOCRACY

NON-DEMOCRATIC REGIME TYPE

PROCESS	RACIAL OLIGARCHY	ELECTORAL AUTHORITARIAN	MILITARY AUTHORITARIAN	THEOCRATIC AUTHORITARIAN	INCOMPLETE TOTALITARIAN OR POST-TOTALITARIAN	FULL TOTALITARIAN	SULTANISTIC
DICTATED		Mexico Taiwan	Brazil Chile (Spain) Turkey		Bulgaria Hungary		
NEGOTIATED	South Africa		South Korea Uruguay		Mongolia Poland		
ABDICATED			Argentina Greece Portugal			Czechoslovakia East Germany	Philippines under Marcos Romania under Ceausescu
IMPOSED BY OUTSIDE POWER(S)		Grenada	Japan Panama	Afghanistan?		Nazi Germany	Iraq?

Note: European traditional authoritarian regimes tended to become competitive oligarchies.
Source: Adapted from Huntington, *The Third Wave* 113, Table 3.1, with additions.

democratic regime, thus lending it "forward legitimacy," especially among the supporters of the old regime who presumably were not in favour of such a change. The negotiated scenario adds to this "forward legitimacy" a separate legitimacy among the supporters of the political opposition, whose leaders have agreed to the specifics of the regime change. In contrast, when an autocratic regime abdicates or is conquered, elements of the old regime, not to mention its supporters, remain who not only oppose the new democratic regime but who may well actively try to undermine it. For example, this was the pattern of Weimar Germany after the military defeat of World War I.[16] In the imposed democracy scenario, a major and long-term military occupation is likely necessary to root out the elements of the old regime, as happened, for example, in the "denazification" of Germany after 1945.

Yet, for either a dictated or negotiated process to occur, the ruling autocrats have to be less than fully autocratic, in the sense of being willing to open up the political process. As noted, this initially may involve a desire for liberalization but not full democratization, with the former change then snowballing into the latter. In any case, the leadership of the ruling autocracy has to be in the hands of a reformer rather than a hard-line "standpatter"—a King Juan Carlos and not a *Generalísimo* Franco, or a Gorbachev and not a Brezhnev. Indeed, a country may go through more than one reform leader, possibly interrupted by another "standpatter," as part of a process of democratization or even liberalization.[17] Moreover, in either a dictated or a negotiated process, such a leader has to have the foresight to want to change things before change is forced on the leadership; although it may seem obvious that it is better to be in control of the process (or to be able to negotiate from a position of strength), if the ruling autocracy is strong, then there is usually a great temptation to do nothing in the way of reforms. Equally, for a negotiated transition to occur there has to be an *organized* political opposition with recognized leaders, not only massive spontaneous protests. The reality is that an organized political opposition is, by definition, not something that does or can occur under full totalitarianism or sultanism. Thus, as Table 9.3 implies, if and when these regime types ever do make a transition to democracy, it is under less favourable processes (cf. Table 8.1 on subtypes of autocracies).

DEMOCRATIC TRANSITIONS AND CONSOLIDATION

The transition to democracy needs to be kept separate from what follows the transition, which is ideally the **consolidation** of democracy. Gunther, Puhle, and Diamandouros are clear and useful in this regard:

> Transition and consolidation are conceptually distinct aspects of [democratic development], although in practice they may temporally overlap or sometimes even coincide. Transition begins with the breakdown of the former [autocratic] regime and ends with the establishment of a relatively stable configuration of political institutions within a democratic regime. Consolidation ... refers to the achievement of substantial attitudinal support for and behavioral

compliance with the new democratic institutions and the rules of the game which they establish. In most cases, the consolidation of democracy requires more time than the transition process …; consolidation is much more complex and it involves a much larger number of actors in a wider array of political arenas. The outcomes of these processes are also distinct: transition results in the creation of a new regime; consolidation results in the stability and persistence of that regime, even in the face of severe challenges.[18]

Consequently, then, there can be no democratic consolidation without a democratic transition; however, a democratic transition will not necessarily be followed by democratic consolidation.

We can see a "successful" pattern of democratic transition and consolidation in Figure 9.1.1. The sequence goes as follows: at some instant there is an autocracy, or perhaps an oligarchy (such as South Africa); this is period A. This regime could hold elections (certainly the case in a competitive oligarchy), but these elections do not produce responsible government (and/or do not involve even a moderately inclusive franchise). Pressures build up for regime change, perhaps from within, perhaps from international opinion. A reformist leader or leadership decides to open up the system; this decision is point *b*. This may involve agreeing to negotiate with pro-democracy leaders. Alternatively, the autocracy collapses or is conquered, and the new authorities seek to make the system more open and democratic; this is another version of point *b*. A transition begins. However, for this to be a transition *to democracy*, indicated as period C, various events must occur. First, as we have noted, there has to be agreement, especially by the ruling autocracy (if they have not abdicated or been conquered), that democracy is the actual goal, not just some limited liberalization. The mechanics of the new democratic regime—that is, its main institutional features (parliamentary or presidential democracy, etc.—have to be agreed to. This may involve agreement on a new constitution. Any direct control or tutelary power by a monarch or national military (or regional warlords) must be given up. Such a requirement may not be as "obvious" if this power was exercised behind the scenes in the outgoing autocracy, but it is necessary nevertheless. The central element in a transition for oligarchies, and pos-

FIGURE 9.1.1 :: STAGES OF DEMOCRATIC TRANSITION AND CONSOLIDATION

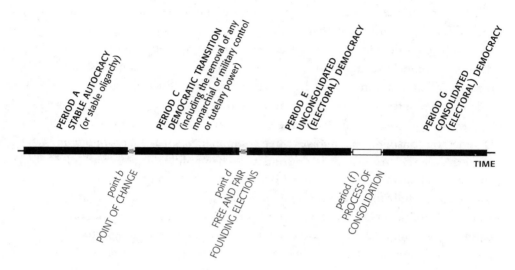

sibly a required step for some autocracies, is the extension of the franchise to make this sufficiently broad; in the contemporary context, the presumption is universal adult suffrage. Finally, a date is set for the founding elections of the new democracy; these elections are point *d*. (If prior to these elections there were separate elections for a constitutional assembly to produce a new constitution, those elections remain part of the transition stage.)

Still, things can go "wrong" at the transition stage. In particular, transitions (or liberalizations that might become transitions to democracy) could fail before getting to the founding elections, if the ruling autocrats, or key elements within, "change their minds" and restore autocracy, including replacing the reformist leader with a hardliner. Such reactions happened, for example, in Greece in 1973 and in Burma in 1988 (although Greece had a successful democratic transition the following year, in 1974). The crackdown in China in 1989, including the crushing of the student demonstrations in Tiananmen Square, should also be seen in this light.[19] Yet, even if elections are not only agreed to but are held, there may still be no responsible government since, say, the military remains in effective control. This is the current situation in Pakistan, whose 2002 elections *cannot* be seen as the founding elections of a

243

new democracy. On the other hand, to look at the bright side, if all of the necessary events of the transition (period C) occur, and if the founding elections (point *d*) are free and fair with everyone accepting the results, then the country can be considered a democracy, at least an electoral one. Getting to and then past point *d* is certainly reason to cheer, but it is not reason to be complacent. What guarantee do we have that the country concerned will still be a democracy in five or ten years, or even the next year?

Such a question returns us to the concept of democratic consolidation. Democratic consolidation involves three components.[20] The first is *law-abidingness*; a democratic regime is consolidated when political leaders and other elites, as well as most of the population, obey the laws and the constitution, compete peacefully for power through the specified procedures and institutions, and avoid political violence. The second is *partisan behaviour*; a democratic regime is consolidated when political elites respect each other's right to compete, are tolerant of opposing views, hand over power unconditionally when defeated in elections, recognize as legitimate duly elected governments of other parties, do not sympathize with or apologize for any extremists on their side of the political spectrum, and do not attempt to use the military or foreign agents for partisan advantage. In this sense we can speak of political parties in opposition being a *loyal opposition* as opposed to a disloyal or semi-loyal one.[21] Third and finally, in terms of *political attitudes* or *beliefs*, a democratic regime is consolidated when the leaders of all significant political parties, most other elites and opinion-makers, and an overwhelming majority of public opinion consistently believe that democracy is the best form of government both theoretically and specifically for their country. Diamond argues that the threshold of "overwhelming public majority" is having at least 70 to 75 per cent of the mass public holding such pro-democratic beliefs and conversely no more than 15 per cent of the mass public definitively preferring some form of non-democratic government. (The remainder of the population would not have any clear or strong opinion one way or another.) Consequently, no anti-democratic movement or party, existing or hypothetical, would have a significant mass following.[22]

These three components of democratic consolidation reinforce each other; however, they do not necessarily develop in perfect parallel patterns. For example, the elites of a country may be strongly committed to democracy, but the masses are rather indifferent; one suspects that this was the case in early post-independence India. On the other hand, certain political leaders may trail their population in terms of commitment to democracy; for example, in Argentina in the 1990s, President Carlos Menem used undemocratic means (especially stacking the judiciary) to expand and maintain his power and interests as well as those of his cronies when mass support for democracy was at the 70 per cent and above level.[23] Thus in Figure 9.1.1 we refer to a multi-faceted *process* of consolidation, (*f*), at the end of which one has a consolidated democracy, period G. In contrast to point *b* and point *d*, there is no specific "point *f*," as this is more of a conceptual than an actual point in time. In other words, we can certainly identify consolidated democracies, but we cannot easily refer to a precise date at which they become fully consolidated.[24] In terms of scholarly analysis and, where possible, survey data, most any democracy that has been around continuously since before the "third wave" (that is, before 1974; see Table 9.2) as well as those of Southern Europe and several new democracies in Central and Eastern Europe are generally considered to be consolidated. In contrast, most of the other "third wave" democracies, especially in Africa, are considered to be unconsolidated, especially at the mass level.[25]

Following Diamond, we can note that the main challenges of democratic consolidation are three-fold.[26] The first of these tasks is the need to "deepen" and thus improve democracy so that it becomes more comprehensive, accountable, and fair. In the typology of our analysis, this involves going from an electoral democracy to a liberal one. Indeed, very few electoral (but not liberal) democracies can be considered to be consolidated; India remains the main one here, but we can also add Jamaica and the idiosyncratic case of Liechtenstein. Democratic "deepening" and improvement are central for democratic consolidation inasmuch as the latter involves both elites acting fully democratically and the mass public strongly supporting democracy. Consequently, as Diamond notes:

> The less respectful of political rights, civil liberties, and constitutional
> constraints on state power are the behaviors of key political actors,
> the weaker is the procedural consensus underpinning democracy.

245

Consolidation is, by definition, obstructed. Furthermore, the more shallow, exclusive, unaccountable, and abusive of individual and groups rights is the electoral regime, the more difficult it is for that regime to become legitimated at the mass level (or to retain such legitimacy) [since its citizens, with reason, tend to have a low opinion of democracy as they experience and see it], and thus the lower are the perceived costs for the elected president or the military to overthrow the system ... .[27]

A second task of democratic consolidation is to achieve successful regime performance in terms of public policy outcomes. This not only produces legitimacy but is easier to achieve when there is legitimacy and consolidation: regimes with high(er) levels of legitimacy can solve problems more easily than those with low(er) levels, since in the former case politicians are more likely to co-operate and the public is more likely to be patient while necessary reforms are undertaken. The final task of democratic consolidation is that of political institutionalization, so that political institutions (including, as was discussed in Chapter 7, political parties) function with greater coherence, effectiveness, adaptability, and autonomy from each other. This task is in a sense antecedent to the other two. Political institutionalization, especially of the judiciary and the legislature, means there are better "checks and balances" on the executive so that power is not abused. Political institutionalization also facilitates the ability of the regime to aggregate the desires of the citizenry and to produce effective responses to these, as well as solving crises and adapting to (global) change(s).

Of course, all of these facets of consolidation can be reversed. That is, a democratic regime which is consolidated (and perhaps has been for decades) could experience an outburst of political violence, as did Uruguay in the 1960s. Its political incumbents could make elections less competitive (although still democratic). Such a regime could weaken its commitment to civil liberties and/or civilian control over the military, perhaps because of regional insurgencies, as happened in Colombia, India, and Sri Lanka. It could slide into economic stagnation for decades, as in postwar Uruguay, or become less adept at solving problems and/or simply become more corrupt, as in Venezuela in the

FIGURE 9.1.2 :: STAGES OF DEMOCRATIC TRANSITION, CONSOLIDATION, AND DECONSOLIDATION

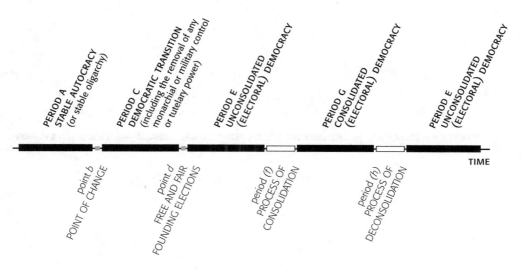

1980s. Finally, such a regime could see political de-institutionalization if, for example, judicial independence is eroded (Argentina under Menem, as noted) or the established political parties become less responsive to voters (Venezuela again, also Italy in the 1980s). These negative developments, especially if there is more than one of them, will produce **democratic deconsolidation**, as is illustrated in Figure 9.1.2. With deconsolidation, a consolidated democracy (period G) experiences a process (not a point) of deconsolidation, (*h*), thus reverting back to an unconsolidated stage (period E). (Of course, there could be differences compared to the earlier unconsolidated period as to the crucial categories where consolidation is lacking, but let us still term the later stage "period E" as well.)

THE HOWS AND WHYS OF DEMOCRATIC BREAKDOWN

Is it important that a given democracy be unconsolidated (or deconsolidated)? The answer is a definite yes, and, as for why, one only has to think of Weimar Germany historically or Pakistan in the contemporary era. Democracies that

FIGURE 9.1.3 :: STAGES OF DEMOCRATIC TRANSITION, CRISIS, AND BREAKDOWN

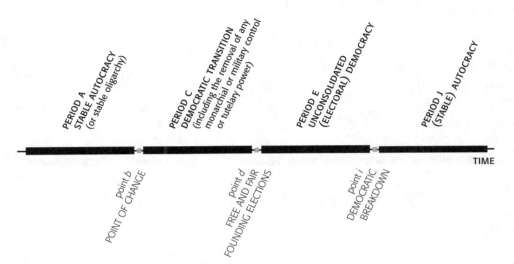

are unconsolidated and that are faced with serious crises will tend to break down and be replaced by an autocracy, perhaps for a couple of years, perhaps for a couple of decades or more. Figure 9.1.3 outlines this sequence under which, instead of consolidating, a democracy suffers a breakdown (at point *i*) and the country reverts to an autocracy lasting for period J. Note that this may not be the same type of autocracy as existed in period A (for example, the first could be traditional authoritarian, the second military), hence the different label.

Democratic breakdowns have occurred in various ways (the "hows"), specifically:

» A military coup d'état, of which there have been many as noted earlier.

» A "self-coup" (*autogolpe* in Spanish), where the democratically elected leader suspends or violates the constitution (or replaces it undemocratically) and proceeds to rule indefinitely as an autocrat. This happened in parts of Eastern Europe in the 1920s and 1930s, with Perón in Argentina in the late 1940s, and with Fujimori in Peru in 1992. An alternate version of this scenario occurs where the (initially) democratically elected leader rigs their re-election (or that of their party) to usher in electoral authoritarianism. For example, such "electoral self-coups" were carried out by President Kuchma of Ukraine in 1999 (regarding his presidential re-election) and President Putin of Russia in 2003 (regarding the Duma elections) and 2004 (regarding his presidential re-election).

» A "royal coup," where a monarch who had not been directly running the country (in the sense that there was a prime minister and responsible government, at least in terms of the last two categories of the "continuum of monarchs" in Chapter 8) decides to assume all power. Yugoslavia in 1929 was an example of this.

» An anti-democratic mass party "winning" an election (in the sense of coming first) and then being handed power, such as the Nazi Party in Germany in 1933 or the communists in Czechoslovakia in 1948. One may argue that the largest party in parliament should have the right to govern, or at least be part of the government, but what if its intent is to end democracy? In Algeria in 1992, the military intervened to prevent such an outcome. Of course, Algeria is still under military tutelage today.

» A civil war, such as in Spain 1936–39. Of course, this would be a breakdown only if the governing democratic side lost, as it did in Spain.

What is important to note by its *absence* from the above list is revolution: no democracy has ever been overthrown by revolution. Conversely, all successful revolutions have been against some form of autocracy. Note also that we are not considering as democratic breakdowns the conquest of democracies by hostile foreign powers, such as the conquests of Czechoslovakia and Western Europe by Nazi Germany.

A specific event can be seen as being the "trigger" that leads to a breakdown. However, what is more important is the larger context in which breakdowns occur (the "whys"). Five broad factors can be noted: (1) external "shocks" like the Great Depression; (2) more generally, a high "load" on the system—in other words, many (difficult) problems to solve; (3) political polarization and wide social and political divisions, including the strength of radical leftists, which frightens conservatives into supporting or even calling for a military coup and "excessive nationalism" on the part of the political right; (4) negative external pressures, or at least the lack of positive external support for democracy; and in the more contemporary period (5) economic mismanagement and corruption. Each of these factors feeds into the key contextual point here, which is the *loss of legitimacy* (or its absence in the first place) of the democratic system. By definition, as Linz notes,

> At the very least, legitimacy is the belief that in spite of shortcomings and failures, the existing political institutions are better than any others that might be established, and that they therefore can demand obedience. Ultimately it means that when the rulers who hold power constitutionally demand obedience, and another group questions that demand in the name of alternative [non-democratic] political arrangements, citizens will voluntarily opt for compliance with the demands of those in authority. ... Ultimately, democratic legitimacy is based on the belief that for that particular country at that particular historical juncture, no other type of regime could assure a more successful pursuit of collective goals.[28]

Democratic legitimacy is thus a relative concept (compared to other regime types), and one based very much on outputs or "ends."

Consequently, democratic legitimacy itself is produced, maintained, ideally increased, but potentially decreased (even to the point of "deconsolidation") by the *system performance* of the democratic regime, which we can more precisely define as not only its general ability to achieve broadly desired goals such as economic and social development, but also its ability to find acceptable solutions (and actually to implement these effectively) for any problems that might arise. Following Linz, we can make a distinction between the efficacy (producing solutions) and the effectiveness (implementing these) of the regime.[29] Ultimately, if the democratic system is seen as dysfunctional *and* if key elites (presumably with a certain level of public support or at least indifference) consider some type of autocracy more likely to deliver the desired "ends," then a successful breakdown may well occur. Of course, an actor or a group may try to seize power for its own sake without any intention of improving the public interest, but such an actor or group invariably claims to be acting in the national interest even if this is a lie. The issue, again, is whether the level of dissatisfaction with the democratic regime is sufficient for the lie to be widely believed. If not, and if (because) there is a reasonably high level of democratic political culture, then such a seizure of power will ultimately fail.

Not all governments are equally competent, of course, but successful democracies generally have competent (or at least not totally incompetent) governments most of the time. All other things being equal, democratic legitimacy will increase over time in a generally successful democracy as more and more people see the positive outputs of the democratic regime, until such legitimacy reaches a high level (as noted, 70 to 75 per cent or more). Such an increase will not necessarily be linear; there could be a "two steps forward, one step back" pattern. That said, however, new democracies face two particular challenges with regards to democratic legitimacy. The first is that they may well lack a "reserve" of legitimacy. In older democracies, democratic legitimacy is broadly based and more or less taken for granted, so a badly performing regime can "coast" for a while if need be. In contrast, a new democratic regime tends to be under greater pressure to prove itself continually since people may not necessarily support broadly the notion of democracy. Of course, this "pressure" will vary depending on the performance of the previous autocratic regime; where this was incompetent and/or corrupt, the bar will not be that high for the new democratic regime, inasmuch as legitimacy is a relative concept. Second and related is the issue of distinguishing the regime as a political system from the government of the day. In older democracies, an incompetent (or corrupt) government is likely to lead to said government being unpopular but not to any delegitimation or deconsolidation of democracy per se, as people can remember previous competent governments and assume (or hope) that future ones will be better than the current one. In other words, people may wait impatiently for the next election so that they can throw out an incompetent and unpopular government, but they do not wish to throw out democracy—at least, not after just one bad government. In contrast, however, in a new democracy, especially during its first government (which could be multi-term), people may find it hard to distinguish the government of the day from the democratic political system in which it operates since there is no previous competent democratic government (perhaps of another party) to serve as a reference point. Dissatisfaction with the government of the day, then, can easily become dissatisfaction with democracy as a political regime.

DEMOCRATIC RE-EQUILIBRATION

Finally, in exceptional circumstances, a political crisis in an unconsolidated democracy may not lead to a political breakdown but rather to what Linz has called a **re-equilibration of democracy**. This he defines as follows:

> Reequilibration of a democracy is a political process that, after a crisis that has seriously threatened the continuity and stability of the basic democratic political mechanisms, results in their continued existence at the same or higher levels of democratic legitimacy, efficacy, and effectiveness. It assumes a severe jolting of these institutions, a loss of either effectiveness or efficacy, and probably legitimacy, that produces a temporary breakdown of the authority of the regime. ... Breakdown followed by reequilibration of democracy can be effected by anti- or aconstitutional means, by the interference in the normal democratic processes of a political actor (like a charismatic leader) whose initial legitimation is ademocratic, or by the use of force, as in a military putsch. ... The new regime might be established illegally, but it must be legitimated by the democratic process afterward, and above all, it must operate thereafter according to the democratic rules.[30]

Assuming that the new (or modified) regime does have higher levels of legitimacy, we can suggest that re-equilibration will produce consolidation, as suggested in Figure 9.1.4. The issue here is whether re-equilibration occurs at a specific point or is an ongoing process. It does seem to be the latter, albeit

252

FIGURE 9.1.4 :: STAGES OF DEMOCRATIC TRANSITION, CRISIS, AND RE-EQUILIBRATION

with key events as part of the process. This process, (*k*), leads to a consolidated democracy, period L, where there was not one before, but it does so in a very different way than under process (*f*) of Figure 9.1.1.

The classic example of democratic re-equilibration is France in 1958, with its change from the Fourth to the Fifth Republic. The Fourth Republic was an unconsolidated democracy with little love for its political institutions, extreme political polarization, highly unstable governments, and by the mid-to-late 1950s an unsolvable crisis in the Algerian War. With divisions over Algeria threatening to produce a military coup and possibly a civil war, Charles de Gaulle (who by 1958 had been retired as a former political leader for a decade) offered to come back to "save France"—on his own terms, of course. The traditional political leaders acquiesced to this and made de Gaulle what amounted to a temporary dictator for several months. During this time, he produced a new constitution with a powerful president (although not technically a presidential system; see Chapter 6), submitted this successfully to a national referendum, and then got himself elected as the first president of the new Fifth Republic. We thus see the after-the-fact confirmation and legitimation of de Gaulle's "seizure of power." De Gaulle's charisma, prestige, and legit-

253

imacy beyond that of his direct supporters were crucial in this process, just as they and his World War II military leadership were in bringing the French Army back under control. It took a few years for de Gaulle to "solve" the Algerian crisis (ultimately by granting that country its independence), but overall the Fifth Republic, with de Gaulle at its head for the first decade, proved to be more efficacious at solving problems than the Fourth Republic ever was (except in economic matters, where the Fourth Republic was successful).

Besides France in 1958, Finland in 1930–32 (with Pehr Evind Svinhufvud playing the "de Gaulle" role), Costa Rica in 1948–49, and to some extent Uruguay in 1933–42 can be seen as cases of re-equilibration. Overall, though, there have been few such cases since re-equilibration requires (1) political leadership which has been hitherto untainted by the major crisis and the resulting loss of legitimacy of the regime, (2) the ability of this leadership to be acceptable to both supporters and opponents of the old regime, and (3) that the leadership of the old regime willingly transfers power to what is formally an anti-regime actor who has no constitutional claim to (increased) power, but who can be assumed to be the only saviour of democracy.[31] Needless to say, very few unconsolidated democracies have a de Gaulle of their own waiting around in the wings and traditional parties willing to grant "him" power when push comes to shove, so this should not be seen as a likely option. The reality is that the vast majority of unconsolidated democracies must slowly consolidate, by the various means noted above, if they are to be truly durable.

NOTES

1 Huntington, *The Third Wave* 9.

2 For example, see Diamond, *Developing Democracy* 74.

3 Huntington, *The Third Wave* 15. Bold added to stress key concept.

4 Huntington, *The Third Wave* 16–46 *passim*.

5 Huntington, *The Third Wave* 16–21.

6 Huntington, *The Third Wave* 16.

7 Renske Doorenspleet, "Reassessing the Three Waves of Democratization," *World Politics* 52 (April 2000): 384–406, suffrage criterion on 391; Pamela Paxton, "Women's Suffrage in the Measurement of Democracy: Problems of Operationalization," *Studies in Comparative International Development* 35:3 (Fall 2000): 92–111.

8 Dietrich Rueschemeyer, Evelyne Huber Stephens, and John D. Stephens, *Capitalist Development and Democracy* (Chicago, IL: University of Chicago Press, 1992), suffrage and other minimum criteria of democracy on 303.

9 The dates given are of a government coming into office based on the first election with moderately inclusive suffrage, not the election year per se (thus 1829 not 1828 for the United States), nor the (earlier) year when the suffrage law was changed; cf. Doorenspleet 391, fn 26.

10 Doorenspleet 394–95.

11 Doorenspleet 395.

12 Doorenspleet 386, 398–99.

13 Doorenspleet 399, Table 1.

14 This second process could also involve a political pact or settlement among various party leaders who are equally democratic but sharply divided on partisan, ideological, and sociological grounds, such as with the Dutch "Pacification Settlement" of 1913–17 or the Venezuelan Pact of Punto Fijo and related Declaration of Principles and Minimal Program for Government of 1958. Thus, this second process is sometimes called a "pacted transition."

15 Huntington, *The Third Wave* 113. Note that we are using what are hopefully clearer terms for the different processes and that some changes have been made to Huntington's classifications.

16 In terms of the schema in Table 9.3, Germany in 1918 should be placed with Argentina, Greece, and Portugal as a case of *military abdication*. Although pre-1914 Imperial Germany was certainly an example of traditional authoritarianism, this was changed by the world war. As Smith remarks, "As the 1914–18 war progressed, the country slithered towards military dictatorship. Nominally responsible to the Emperor, the German High Command became increasingly contemptuous of any restrictions on its power." Once they realized that the war was lost, the High Command found it expedient to hand power over to a civilian government, which would reach an armistice and thus take the blame. See Gordon Smith, *Democracy in Western Germany: Parties and Politics in the Federal Republic*, 3rd ed. (New York, NY: Holmes and Meier, 1986) 16.

17 Huntington, *The Third Wave* 130–33.

18 Richard Gunther, Hans-Jürgen Puhle, and P. Nikiforos Diamandouros, "Introduction," *The Politics of Democratic Consolidation: Southern Europe in Comparative Perspective*, ed. Richard Gunther, Hans-Jürgen Puhle, and P. Nikiforos Diamandouros (Baltimore, MD and London, UK: The Johns Hopkins University Press, 1995) 3.

19 Huntington, *The Third Wave* 135.

20 Linz and Stepan, *Problems of Democratic Transition and Consolidation* 6; and Diamond, *Developing Democracy* 69. Their various categories have been modified somewhat here.

21 On this component, see also Juan J. Linz, *The Breakdown of Democratic Regimes: Crisis, Breakdown, and Reequilibration* (Baltimore, MD and London, UK: The Johns Hopkins University Press, 1978) 16 and 27–37.

22 Diamond, *Developing Democracy* 68–69.

23 Diamond, *Developing Democracy* 70.

24 One may be tempted here to use a specific crisis point which was successfully overcome, such as the failed coup in Spain in 1981; however, such a democratic success is more a demonstration of (being on the road to) democratic consolidation. Indeed, Spanish democracy was probably not fully consolidated until the change in government from the centre to the socialists after the elections of 1982.

25 For an alternative definition of consolidation with respect to post-communist Europe that focusses solely on elites (including the bureaucracy) but has no "requirements" in terms of mass attitudes, see Stephen E. Hanson, "Defining Democratic Consolidation," *Postcommunism and the Theory of Democracy*, ed. Richard D. Anderson, Jr., M. Steven Fish, Stephen E. Hanson, and Philip G. Roeder (Princeton, NJ: Princeton University Press, 2001) 141–42.

26 Diamond, *Developing Democracy* 73ff.

27 Diamond, *Developing Democracy* 74–75.

28 Linz, *The Breakdown of Democratic Regimes* 16–17 and 18.

29 Linz, *The Breakdown of Democratic Regimes* 18–23.

30 Linz, *The Breakdown of Democratic Regimes* 87.

31 Linz, *The Breakdown of Democratic Regimes* 87–88.

CHAPTER TEN

Postscript: Democracies and Autocracies in the Future

IN THIS CHAPTER YOU WILL LEARN:

» *what are the prospects for viable democratic transitions in the not-too-distant future, and which autocracies might this involve; and conversely*

» *what are the prospects for democratic breakdowns; specifically, what factors threaten the world's democracies, and how many of these factors do different democracies currently have.*

It was some 20 years ago when Samuel Huntington wrote an article entitled "Will More Countries Become Democratic?"[1] Overall, outside of South America, he concluded that the prospects for the (further) spread of democracy were "not great." This conclusion, however, was wisely qualified by noting that it assumed no major changes in world developments.[2] The collapse of the Soviet Union (and the ending of its empire) a few short years later led to the democratization of most of Central and Eastern Europe. The 1990s also saw a peaceful transition to democracy in what had been the racial oligarchy of South Africa. More surprising has been the spread of democracy to many other countries in Africa which have quite low levels of development.

All this goes to show that political science cannot predict precisely the future of democracy any more than it can other political events. Moreover, democracy is, in fact, definitely something that can be established by national political elites (or occasionally imposed from outside) as a clear political deci-

257

sion regardless of the level of development of the country.[3] It is possible that any of the world's autocracies of today could be a democracy (at least an electoral one) 10 or 20 years from now. Possible, yes, but how probable? Or, to phrase the question differently, if democracy were introduced into a current autocracy, would it survive and ultimately consolidate? This question is obviously central for both Afghanistan and Iraq, but it applies to all autocracies today and, indeed, to various new democracies. Echoing Huntington's scepticism of two decades ago, the probably of *both* democratization and democratic survival does not seem "great" for the world's remaining autocracies as a group. As has been noted, most of these suffer from low levels of development, very unequal distributions of what wealth there is, a lack of democratic political culture or any democratic history, and/or a high degree of militarization.

The best prospects for democratic survival should democracy be established would be in the more developed autocracies, such as Malaysia and especially Singapore. More generally, since average years of schooling is such an important factor for explaining regime types, we might well want to note all of the autocracies (as of the end of 2004) where this value is 6.0 or more. Besides Malaysia and Singapore, this list (in alphabetical order) comprises Belarus, Bosnia-Herzegovina, Brunei, Jordan, Monaco (presumably), Qatar, Russia, Ukraine, and the United Arab Emirates. Falling close to this cut-off are Fiji, Iraq, Lebanon, and, as a best guess, Tonga. This gives us around 15 countries that are consequently more likely to survive as (potential) democracies than the rest of the world's autocracies, but almost every one of these countries is ruled by an anti-democratic elite (monarch, party, president, or clique) that either would have to have a change of heart or be removed from power for democratization to occur. In 2004–2005, such a process was indeed successful in Ukraine, bolstered by massive demonstrations in the capital. However, next door in Russia the inverse, a breakdown of democracy, occurred not that long ago and Russia has remained autocratic despite a well-educated population.

Of course, inasmuch as the world today contains relatively few autocracies, it is not a stretch to argue that (most of) those that are left are the least viable ones for democracy. On the other hand, if one flips this point around, one can note that never have there been so many democracies as in the world today.

How confident should we be that all of these will remain democracies? An answer to this question is a two-step process. The first consideration is to note the global trends in democratization. As pointed out in Chapter 9 (Table 9.2) we appear to be in a third wave of democratization, albeit a modest phase of this. That is, since 1995 the world has seen a net gain of six democracies. However, there is nothing "stopping" world or least regional circumstances from leading to a reverse wave at some point. Obviously, we cannot predict if and when this will (would) occur, but history dictates that we stress that both previous waves of democratization were followed by setbacks.

The second consideration, or question, is the following: if democracy does in fact break down in a reasonable number of countries at some point in the next generation, in which countries might this occur? To speculate on this, we shall pull together various points from this text into a list of "threatening factors" in the world's current democracies, as shown in Table 10.1 below. Fifteen potential threatening factors are so listed, all of which are dichotomous (yes or no for each factor). It is important to raise two cautions here. First, for every factor there is a cut-off point or assessment, and a couple of these involve values that are admittedly arbitrary (even if hopefully reasonable). Second and more crucially, every factor is weighted the same to get a total score. One may consider certain factors to be much more important than others; to this end, the reader is free to recalculate the totals. With these two caveats in mind, the 15 "threatening factors" are as follows:

» The country is only an electoral democracy. Liberal democracies are more democratic than electoral democracies (that is, they are democratic in more areas), and thus they have "further to fall" to be reversed to an autocracy. Electoral democracies, conversely, have "less far to fall."

» The country is a new democracy, defined as having democratized (most recently) in the third wave of democratization. All other things being equal, a very-long established democracy is quite likely to remain democratic, at least with greater likelihood than a rather new democracy. This speaks to issues of established elite behaviour and democratic consolidation.

» There is a lack of mass support for democracy. If (certain) elites in a country try to overthrow democracy, how would the public react? Where there is broad public support for democracy as the only legitimate regime type, then such anti-democratic behaviour would be resisted (or probably not even attempted). However, where such mass support does not exist, a successful overthrow is much more likely. In other words, we are talking here about the level of mass democratic culture.

» There is a weak state. This is perhaps a more specific aspect of the first point. Where the central state is weak, with problems of penetration and legitimacy, *any* political regime is less institutionalized and secure than it otherwise would be.

» GDP per capita is less than "high income," in the categorization of the World Bank. Very wealthy countries are extremely unlikely to suffer a democratic breakdown; certainly, they are less likely than poorer countries where the "power resources" of individuals are fewer and where socio-economic pluralism is likely to be less developed. Thus, we are noting here the countries at greater economic risk of democratic breakdown.

» Adult literacy is below 70 per cent. As stressed in Chapter 5, education even more than wealth per se is central to democracy. If a country's majority or even a large minority of its population is illiterate, the ability of the population as a whole to participate effectively in the polity is limited.

» Average years of schooling are below 7.0. Basic literacy, although necessary, may not be enough to understand fully and insist on one's civil and political rights. Phrased differently, democratic procedures and values are more likely to occur and endure where there is a well-educated population (as opposed to a barely literate one).

» There is a medium-to-high concentration of income. Regardless of the level of income (or education) of a country, if its wealth is concentrated in relatively few hands, there is likely to be strong polarization, social hierarchies, and non-egalitarian values. All of these consequences are problematic for democracy. For this purpose, following Muller, a medium-to-high concentration of income is deemed to be where the wealthiest 20 per cent of the population has 45 per cent or more of the national income or consumption.[4]

» The population is 40 million or more. We have seen that small(er) countries—in terms of population—are more likely to be democratic, even allowing for other factors. Conversely, then, large (larger) countries are less likely to be democratic. The issue here is the appropriate definition of a large country; 40 million is suggested as a tentative cut-off point.

» The effective number of ethnic groups is 1.50 or more. We can speak of an ethnically heterogeneous society, which is harder to unify and govern (democratically) than a homogeneous one, or at least requires more formal solutions to its heterogeneity combined with very high levels of national perspectives and resulting cooperation in terms of its political elites.

» The military participation ratio is 8.00 or above per 1000 people. The extent of militarization relates very strongly to regime type. Globally, highly militarized countries are far less likely to be democratic. Various countries today do combine democracy with high militarization, but this is a potentially threatening combination. Looking at the global distribution of military participation ratios, a (rounded) cut-off of 8.00 seems reasonable in terms of indicating high militarization.

» The military is only conditionally subordinate. In Chapter 4, we noted that civilian supremacy, civilian control, and conditional subordination were all compatible with the definition of a democracy. However, inasmuch as the military is only conditionally subordinate in certain democracies, in these it poses a much greater potential threat of intervention than in situations of civilian supremacy or civilian control.

» The party system is fragmented. Where this is the case, effective governance is likely to be harder. A fragmented party system by definition also implies great diversity in the society (not necessarily just ethnic diversity).

» The party system is not institutionalized. Chapter 7 outlined the various advantages of an institutionalized system in terms of accountability, effectiveness, and so on. Where the party system lacks institutionalization, these advantages are also lacking.

» The country is in Asia or the Middle East. In most of the world's regions, democracy is broadly (even if shallowly) established, and the current democracies support each other as democracies, looking unfavourably on attempts to subvert a neighbour's democracy. Often such support occurs through regional organizations. These patterns, however, do not occur in either Asia or the Middle East.

Adding together all of these (potentially) threatening factors give us the total values in Table 10.1. Countries are ranked by these total values, with half a dozen countries having the highest score of 11. Of these half-dozen countries, three—Bolivia, Brazil, and Ecuador—are in South (Latin) America. At the other extreme, Australia and several small Western European countries have no threatening factors. Canada has a score of 1, reflecting our ethnic fragmentation. However, rather than the specific score out of 15, what seems more useful as a classification (especially given our earlier caveats) is to group the countries into four consequent categories. These are: countries at high risk of democratic breakdown (totals of 9 or more out of 15); countries at medium risk of democratic breakdown (totals of 6 through 8); countries at low risk of democratic breakdown (totals of 3 through 5); and countries at essentially no risk of democratic breakdown (totals of 0 through 2). It is worth noting that two major countries recently experiencing breakdowns—Ukraine in 1999 and Russia in 2003—had each been high risk in terms of this measurement.

Interestingly, of the (still) democratic countries that are at high risk, *every single one* has the following three traits: being only an electoral democracy, being a "third wave" democracy in terms of its current democratic regime

TABLE 10.1 :: THREATENING FACTORS IN CURRENT DEMOCRACIES (End of 2004)

FACTOR	1 — only an electoral democracy	2 — a "third wave" democracy	3 — lack of mass support for democracy	4 — a weak state	5 — GDP per capita less than "high income"	6 — adult literacy rate below 70 percent	7 — average years of schooling below 7.0	8 — high concentration of income	9 — population 40 million or more	10 — effective number of ethnic groups 1.50 or more	11 — military participation ratio 8.00 or above	12 — military only conditionally subordinate	13 — a fragmented party system	14 — party system not institutionalized	15 — in Asia or the Middle East	TOTAL
COUNTRIES AT HIGH RISK:																
BOLIVIA	1	1	1	1	1			1	1	1	1	1		1		11
BRAZIL	1	1	1		1			1	1	1		1	1	1	1	11
ECUADOR	1	1	1	1	1			1	1	1			1	1	1	11
INDIA	1	1	1		1	1	1	1	1	1				1	1	11
SIERRA LEONE	1	1	1	1	1	1	1	1		1			1	1		11
TURKEY	1	1	1		1			1	1	1	1	1		1	1	11
BANGLADESH	1	1	1	1	1	1		1	1					1	1	10
COLOMBIA	1	1	1	1				1	1	1		1	1	1		10
GUATEMALA	1	1	1	1	1	1	1	1		1				1		10
MADAGASCAR	1	1	1		1	1	1	1		1			1	1		10
MALI	1	1	1	1	1	1	1	1		1				1		10
NICARAGUA	1	1	1	1	1	1	1	1		1				1		10
NIGER	1	1	1	1	1	1	1	1		1				1		10
NIGERIA	1	1		1	1	1	1	1	1	1				1		10
PAPUA NEW GUINEA	1	1	1	1	1	1	1					1	1	1		10
THAILAND	1	1	1		1		1	1	1	1				1	1	10
GEORGIA	1	1	1	1	1		1	1		1				1		9
GHANA	1	1		1	1		1	1		1		1		1		9
COUNTRIES AT MEDIUM RISK:																
BENIN		1		1	1	1	1	1*				1		1		8
DOMINICAN REPUBLIC	1	1	1		1		1	1			1			1		8
INDONESIA	1	1	1		1		1		1	1				1		8
KENYA	1	1	1		1		1	1		1				1		8
MALAWI	1	1		1	1	1	1	1			1					8
MEXICO	1	1	1		1		1	1	1	1						8
MOLDOVA	1	1	1	1	1		1			1				1		8
MOZAMBIQUE	1	1	1	1	1	1	1	1								8
PERU	1	1	1	1	1			1		1				1		8
PHILIPPINES	1	1	1	1	1			1	1					1		8

continues…

FACTOR	only an electoral democracy (1)	a "third wave" democracy (2)	lack of mass support for democracy (3)	a weak state (4)	GDP per capita less than "high income" (5)	adult literacy rate below 70 percent (6)	average years of schooling below 7.0 (7)	high concentration of income (8)	population 40 million or more (9)	effective number of ethnic groups 1.50 or more (10)	military participation ratio 8.00 or above (11)	military only conditionally subordinate (12)	a fragmented party system (13)	party system not institutionalized (14)	in Asia or the Middle East (15)	TOTAL
SENEGAL	1	1		1	1	1	1	1		1						8
SERBIA AND MONTENEGRO	1	1	1	1	1					1	1			1		8
SURINAME		1	1		1		1	1*		1		1		1		8
VENEZUELA	1		1	1	1			1		1		1		1		8
ALBANIA	1	1	1	1	1		1				1					7
EL SALVADOR	1	1	1	1	1		1	1								7
GUYANA		1	1		1		1	1		1				1		7
MACEDONIA	1	1	1	1	1					1	1					7
MONGOLIA	1	1	1		1			1						1	1	7
NAMIBIA	1	1	1		1		1*	1		1						7
PANAMA	1	1			1			1		1		1		1		7
SÃO TOMÉ AND PRÍNCIPE	1	1	1		1		1	1*						1		7
SOLOMON ISLANDS	1	1	1	1	1		1							1		7
SOUTH AFRICA		1	1		1		1	1	1	1						7
VANUATU		1	1		1	1	1						1	1		7
BULGARIA	1	1	1		1						1			1		6
CAPE VERDE		1	1		1		1	1*		1						6
GRENADA		1	1		1		1	1*						1		6
HONDURAS	1	1	1		1		1	1								6
LESOTHO	1	1	1		1		1	1								6
PARAGUAY	1	1	1		1		1	1								6
ROMANIA	1	1	1		1							1		1		6
SRI LANKA	1			1	1					1	1				1	6
TIMOR-LESTE (East Timor)	1	1	1		1		1*							1		6

COUNTRIES AT LOW RISK:

FACTOR	1	2	3	4	5	6	7	8	9	10	11	12	13	14	15	TOTAL
ANTIGUA AND BARBUDA	1	1			1		1	1*								5
BELIZE		1			1		1	1*		1						5
CROATIA	1	1	1		1					1						5
DOMINICA		1	1		1		1	1*								5
ESTONIA		1			1			1		1				1		5
LATVIA		1			1					1			1	1		5

FACTOR	only an electoral democracy	a "third wave" democracy	lack of mass support for democracy	a weak state	GDP per capita less than "high income"	adult literacy rate below 70 percent	average years of schooling below 7.0	high concentration of income	population 40 million or more	effective number of ethnic groups 1.50 or more	military participation ratio 8.00 or above	military only conditionally subordinate	a fragmented party system	party system not institutionalized	in Asia or the Middle East	TOTAL
	1	2	3	4	5	6	7	8	9	10	11	12	13	14	15	
SEYCHELLES	1	1	1		1		1									5
ST. VINCENT AND THE GRENADINES		1			1		1	1*		1						5
ARGENTINA	1	1		1	1											4
BOTSWANA					1		1	1		1						4
CHILE	1	1			1			1								4
ISRAEL									1	1		1	1			4
JAMAICA	1				1		1	1								4
KIRIBATI		1	1		1		1*						?			4
KOREA, SOUTH		1								1		1			1	4
LITHUANIA		1	1		1									1		4
MAURITIUS					1		1			1				1		4
MICRONESIA		1			1		1*			1			?	?		4
PALAU		1			1		1*			1			?	?		4
PORTUGAL		1					1	1			1					4
SAMOA		1	1		1		1									4
SLOVAKIA		1			1								1	1		4
ST. KITTS AND NEVIS		1			1		1	1*								4
ST. LUCIA		1			1		1	1								4
TRINIDAD AND TOBAGO	1				1			1		1						4
COSTA RICA					1		1	1								3
MARSHALL ISLANDS		1			1		1*						?	?		3
POLAND		1			1									1		3
SPAIN		1							1	1						3
TAIWAN		1										1			1	3
TUVALU		1	1		?		1*						?	?		3
UNITED STATES								1	1	1						3
URUGUAY		1			1			1								3

COUNTRIES AT ESSENTIALLY NO RISK:

	1	2	3	4	5	6	7	8	9	10	11	12	13	14	15	TOTAL
ANDORRA		1								1						2
BARBADOS					1		1*									2

continues...

	only an electoral democracy	a "third wave" democracy	lack of mass support for democracy	a weak state	GDP per capita less than "high income"	adult literacy rate below 70 percent	average years of schooling below 7.0	high concentration of income	population 40 million or more	effective number of ethnic groups 1.50 or more	military participation ratio 8.00 or above	military only conditionally subordinate	a fragmented party system	party system not institutionalized	in Asia or the Middle East	
FACTOR	1	2	3	4	5	6	7	8	9	10	11	12	13	14	15	TOTAL
BELGIUM										1			1			2
CZECH REP.	1				1											2
GREECE	1										1					2
HUNGARY	1				1											2
ITALY									1		1					2
JAPAN									1						1	2
NAURU					?		1*			1			?	?		2
SAN MARINO										1	1					2
SWITZERLAND										1		1				2
BAHAMAS								1*								1
CANADA										1						1
CYPRUS											1					1
FRANCE									1							1
GERMANY									1							1
LIECHTENSTEIN	1															1
LUXEMBOURG										1						1
MALTA						1										1
NEW ZEALAND										1						1
NORWAY														1		1
SLOVENIA	1															1
UNITED KINGDOM									1							1
AUSTRALIA																0
AUSTRIA																0
DENMARK																0
FINLAND																0
ICELAND																0
IRELAND																0
NETHERLANDS																0
SWEDEN																0

* estimate

(although several countries had earlier democratic periods), and not being a wealthy country (that is, being less than a "high income" country). Moreover, *none* of the countries at medium risk is a wealthy country either. That said, one should note that relatively few countries are deemed "high income." More generally, although economic development (especially where it is broadly based) is certainly important, what we argue to be really crucial for democratic survival in the world's democracies is the deepening of democracy—that is, making electoral democracies liberal ones—and the related consolidation of democracy at both the elite and mass level. Unfortunately, both of these developments have been rare in the "third wave" of democratization, and both require more domestic changes in the countries concerned than any magic international solution.

NOTES

1 Samuel P. Huntington, "Will More Countries Become Democratic?," *Political Science Quarterly* 99:2 (Summer 1984): 193–218.

2 Huntington, "Will More Countries Become Democratic?" 218.

3 Przeworski and Limongi 177.

4 Muller 63. One can note here that Muller stresses more the effects of having a high level of income inequality, with this being defined as where the wealthiest 20 per cent of the population has more than 55 per cent of the national income (cf. Chapter 5, note 28 in this book). We are thus defining the threatening factor of income inequality somewhat more broadly.

Glossary of Selected Key Terms

Authoritarian Regime: In effect, this is a residual category of **autocracy** defined largely in a negative way: an authoritarian regime is an autocratic regime that lacks the roles of ideology and mass mobilization found in a **totalitarian regime** and that also lacks the broad arbitrariness of a **sultanistic regime**.

Autocracy: Literally, (absolute) rule by one individual (the autocrat), but more generally rule by an individual or group who/which is effectively unaccountable to the population. Autocracy is thus the opposite of a **democracy**.

Bureaucracy: In the Weberian sense, a system of government administration based on a rational hierarchy of authority and which employs full-time civil servants who are hired and promoted based on training and experience and by formal contracts. These bureaucrats have defined rights and duties and fixed salaries, and are expected to serve the public neutrally and without (using their position for) direct personal gain.

Civilian Supremacy: The ability of a civilian government to conduct general policy without interference from the military; to define the goals, size, resources, and general organization of the military; to formulate and conduct defence policy knowledgeably; and to monitor effectively the implementation of said defence policy. This is the most civilian, and thus most democratic, category of civil-military relations.

Clientelism: An informal power relationship between unequals, in which a higher status "patron" provides benefits to (a) client(s); these clients in turn reciprocate by providing the patron with support, including voting for the patron or for a third party of the patron's wish.

Collapsed State: One where the state authority has totally disintegrated, to be replaced by anarchy or civil war.

Competitive Oligarchy: A **political regime** with responsible government and competitive elections but with 20 per cent

269

or less of the 18-and-above population eligible to vote.

Confederation: Where a group of sovereign entities form a common government for specific and limited purposes. **Sovereignty** remains with the constituent governments, who take all key decisions (and who normally work by unanimity). The common government does not directly act upon the population and leaves matters of implementation to the constituent governments.

Consociational Democracy: A political system found in certain heterogeneous democracies which is based around power-sharing—especially in terms of broad coalition cabinets that include most if not all of the key groups—as opposed to pure majoritarianism.

Critical Mass: A sufficiently large minority group. Critical mass theory suggests that there will be a qualitative change in the nature of collective group behaviour and within-group interactions only when the minority group reaches such a critical mass, perceived to be around 30 per cent of the whole.

De facto State: A **state** with effective internal control, control over its borders, and domestic legitimacy, but lacking international recognition.

De jure State: A **state** which is recognized as a state by the international community but which is so weak and/or

illegitimate that it cannot actually control most of its own people or its borders.

Democracy: A **political regime** which involves at a minimum the competition of political elites for public support and the accountability of elected politicians to the voters. Within these broad parameters there are key differences between **liberal democracy** and **electoral democracy**.

Democratic Breakdown: The collapse of a **democracy**. More formally, the change from a democracy to an **autocracy**; thus, the opposite of a **democratic transition**.

Democratic Consolidation: Broad support for a democratic regime, involving law-abidingness, partisan behaviour consistent with **democracy**, and broadly held democratic values and beliefs.

Democratic Deconsolidation: The loss of support for a democratic regime and the general legitimacy of **democracy**, involving increased lawlessness, undemocratic partisan behaviour, and an increase in anti-democratic values and beliefs.

Democratic Re-equilibration: A political process that, after a crisis that involves the paralysis and de-legitimation of national democratic institutions and a temporary breakdown of the authority of the regime, results in their continued existence or speedy re-creation at the same or higher levels of democratic legitimacy, efficacy, and effectiveness. A central role here is normally played by a (charismatic) national leader, who may come to power through undemocratic means but thereafter governs democratically.

Democratic Transition/Democratization: The process of changing from an **autocracy** to a **democracy**, or more precisely changing from an autocracy to at least an **electoral democracy**. The key step here is the holding of free and fair elections to select the government, under the qualification that there is actually (also) **responsible government**—in other words, that the elected national politicians are the ones in control.

District Magnitude: The number of seats to be filled in (members to be elected from) an electoral district (constituency). For example, for the Canadian House of Commons the district magnitude has been one everywhere for some decades now.

Earned Majority: Where a party wins a majority of seats based on a majority of the popular vote (even if its vote percentage is still less than its seat percentage). This is contrasted with a **manufactured majority**.

Effective State: Where the **state** controls the national territory and the borders, and where it has sufficient capacity, bureaucratic autonomy and competence, domestic penetration, and legitimacy to ensure that national laws and policies are actually in effect throughout the country.

Electoral Authoritarianism: Authoritarianism based on a ruling party or president which (who) does not allow free and fair elections but which (who) derives authority from their election victories (indeed claiming that these are free and fair). Elections are held regularly and with some opposition parties or candidates allowed on the ballot so as to maintain a pretence of competition. Where this regime is based around a president, sometimes referenda (again, not free and fair) are used to extend the president's term or at least the term limits.

Electoral College: A group of people (chosen by elections or by virtue of their office) whose task is to select a president. This group performs no other (subsequent) function, unlike a legislature (there being various parliamentary systems where the parliament selects the president, that is, the country's head of state).

Electoral Democracy: A **political regime** which contains the following three elements (sufficiently although perhaps not perfectly): **responsible government**, free and fair political competition, and full and equal rights of political participation, but which is deficient in terms of civil liberties and/or a legally based, limited, but well-functioning state.

Electoral System: The process used for voting (ballot structure) and then for translating votes into seats in the context of an election, thereby determining the partisan composition of the legislature (but not specifically the government).

COMPARING POLITICAL REGIMES

Federalism: A political system with a central government and constitutionally entrenched regional governments with similarly entrenched powers, as well as some role in national politics. Domestic sovereignty is thus shared between the two levels, but only the central government exercises international sovereignty.

Human Development Index (HDI): A measure of the UN which combines three factors: (1) per capita income, which is corrected for variations in purchasing power and is adjusted by being logged; (2) life expectancy; and (3) a combination of literacy rates and school enrollments. These combined factors lead to a standardized score in which a higher value indicates a higher level of development.

Hung Parliament: Where no one party has a majority of the seats. The lack of decisiveness in the term (and the result) parallels that of a "hung jury." Often this situation is called a minority government, but a minority government is only one possible outcome of a hung parliament—even if is the "normal" one in Canada. Alternatively, for example, two or more parties may get together in a hung parliament to form a majority coalition government.

Index of Disproportionality: As used in this analysis, a mathematical index which sums the absolute value of each party's vote share (percentage) to seat share difference, and then divides this total by two to get a value between zero and 100. The higher the number the greater is the disproportionality.

Liberal Democracy: A **political regime** which combines the following five elements: **responsible government**, free and fair political competition, full and equal rights of political participation, civil liberties, and a legally based, limited, but well-functioning state.

Manufactured Majority: Where a party wins a majority of seats despite winning a minority of the popular vote, the majority of seats thus being "manufactured" by the **electoral system**. This is contrasted with an **earned majority**.

Military Authoritarianism: Authoritarianism based on an autonomous military running the country either outright or indirectly.

Moderately Inclusive Electoral Democracy (MIED): A **political regime** with **responsible government**, competitive elections, and more than 20 per cent of the 18-and-above population eligible to vote—but not the universal suffrage of an unqualified **electoral democracy**.

Parliamentary System: A political system with a dual executive, with the head of government (and the government generally) accountable to the legislature, not least through the possibility of a motion of non-confidence.

Party System: The relationship among the various political parties (there must be at least two) in a territory, that is, their total number, relative size, competitiveness, and so on.

Political Culture: The attitudes, values, and beliefs that individuals have with respect to their **political regime**/system and the way(s) it allocates power and resolves political conflicts.

Political Development: The achievement, where this does not exist, of national autonomy, political order, **political institutionalization** and possibly also **democracy**.

Political Institutionalization: The process by which political organizations (for example, executives, legislatures, and judiciaries, but also political parties) and political procedures become complex (with formal internal structures and hierarchies), adaptable, coherent, stable, and autonomous from other institutions.

Political Regime: Broader than the government of the day, this is the method or system of government, including both formal and informal structures of the state, governmental roles and processes, and the method of selection of these.

Power Resources: A term developed by Tatu Vanhanen referring to the economic, intellectual, and organizational resources that an individual or group can bring to bear in the struggle for political power. The deconcentration (wide diffusion) of these resources facilitates **democracy**; the concentration of these resources works against democracy.

Presidential System: A political system with a single executive, chosen by the voters (perhaps indirectly via an **electoral college**) and not accountable to the legislature.

Rechtsstaat: A "state subject to law." The law thus protects the citizens against the power of the **state**, specifically the abuse (arbitrary use) of this power by the police or other state actors.

Responsible Government: Where the government is responsible to the people, in the sense of accountability "downwards" (at least by way of elections), but also where the government is *only* responsible to the people and not to a monarch or military who may be "pulling the strings" either openly or secretly.

Reverse Wave (of democratization): Within a specified period of time, a significant group of transitions in an autocratic (non-democratic) direction that outnumbers **democratic transitions** during that period of time. One could call this a "wave of autocratization" if that were a word.

Sovereignty: The sense of a **state** being the highest authority in a territory and exercising this authority with respect to its domestic population, its borders, and its interactions with other states. Sovereignty also has the connotation of enjoying a monopoly on the legitimate use of force within a territory.

State: There are two different concepts of a state. In the first usage, wherein one refers to "a state," this involves a sover-

273

COMPARING POLITICAL REGIMES

eign power effectively ruling over the population within a fixed territory. In the second usage, wherein one refers to "the state," this is the organizationally differentiated political, bureaucratic, legal, and usually military system of a country.

Strong Bicameralism: Where the upper house truly matters, since: (1) both houses are equal or relatively equal in terms of legislative powers; (2) the upper house has the legitimacy to use its powers; and (3) the upper house is composed, or (s)elected, in a different way from the lower house.

Sultanistic Regime: An autocratic regime which is built around an individual and her/his family who to a greater or lesser extent plunder the country; which glorifies this leader; which exercises control by fear, terror, and spreading paranoia; and which lacks any effective legitimacy. An alternative term here is "personalistic regime."

Theocratic Authoritarianism: Authoritarianism based on religious-based rule.

Totalitarian Regime: An autocratic regime based around: (1) a ruling party; (2) an official and genuine ideology; and (3) the active mobilization of the population into supporting the regime, including membership in various regime-sponsored organizations.

Traditional Authoritarianism: Authoritarianism based on a ruling monarch.

Vote of Investiture: A formal vote by the parliament on a would-be government/prime minister, which/who must then win this vote to take office (or remain in office after an election). Such a procedure makes the system one of positive parliamentarianism, since there must be a positive parliamentary endorsement of the government (as opposed to negative parliamentarianism where there is no such formal vote).

Wave of Democratization: Within a specified period of time, a significant group of transitions from autocratic to democratic regimes that significantly outnumbers transitions in the opposite direction (**democratic breakdowns**) during that period of time. A wave of democratization also usually involves political liberalization in some autocratic political systems that nevertheless remain autocratic.

Weak State: Where the state lacks some combination of control over the national territory and/or the borders, capacity, bureaucratic autonomy and competence, domestic penetration, and/or legitimacy, thus rendering it generally ineffective and usually unable to impose national policies evenly throughout the country.

Recommended Sources for Further Research

WEB REFERENCES

The United Nations annual *Human Development Report* is available on-line: <http://www.undp.org>.

New York-based Freedom House's annual *Freedom in the World* is the most-cited international survey of political rights and civil liberties: <http://www.freedomhouse.org>. They also publish a separate, more detailed yearly analysis of post-communist countries called *Nations in Transit* and an annual survey of media independence, *Freedom of the Press*.

The Organization for Security and Co-operation in Europe has an Office for Democratic Institutions and Human Rights (OSCE/ODIHR) which contains documents on international standards of elections as well as field reports on elections observed by said office in Europe, Central Asia, and the United States: <http://www.osce.org/ohihr>.

The Berlin-based Transparency International publishes annually its *Corruption Perceptions Index*: <http://www.transparency.org>, as well as a *Global Corruption Report*.

Chronological lists of national and sub-national leaders can be found in "Rulers": <http://www.rulers.org>.

For election results, the traditional reference site is "Elections around the World," edited by Wilfried Derksen of the Netherlands: <http://www.electionworld.org>.

A popular newer election site is from Australia, namely Adam Carr's Election Archive: <http://psephos.adam-carr.net>.

The Geneva-based Inter-Parliamentary Union also provides the most recent national election results for almost every country and with (usually) a couple of paragraphs of commentary: <http://www.ipu.org>; go to their "Parline" database.

Finally, the International Foundation for Election Systems in Washington, DC has a very thorough "Election Guide" with useful links: <http://www.ifes.org>.

ACADEMIC JOURNALS

The *Journal of Democracy* publishes short, highly informative articles which are very up-to-date as these things go.

Electoral Studies includes detailed analyses of elections in most major and many other countries (but certainly not all countries).

CHRONOLOGICAL REFERENCES

By far the most thorough chronology is the ongoing monthly *Keesing's Record of World Events*, which has been published since 1931.

Also useful is the six-volume, regionally based *Political Chronologies of the World*, published in 2001 by Europa Publications. They also publish the very comprehensive *Europa World Year Book* (previously the *Europa Year Book*), which goes back to 1959.

Bibliography

Agüero, Felipe. "Institutions, Transitions, and Bargaining: Civilians and the Military in Shaping Postauthoritarian Regimes." *Civil-Military Relations in Latin America: New Analytical Perspectives.* Ed. David Pion-Berlin. Chapel Hill, NC: The University of North Carolina Press, 2001. 194–222.

——. *Soldiers, Civilians, and Democracy: Post-Franco Spain in Comparative Perspective.* Baltimore, MD: The Johns Hopkins University Press, 1995.

Alagappa, Muthiah. "Asian Civil-Military Relations: Key Developments, Explanations, and Trajectories." *Coercion and Governance: The Declining Political Role of the Military in Asia.* Ed. Muthiah Alagappa. Stanford, CA: Stanford University Press, 2001. 433–98.

——. "Investigating and Explaining Change: An Analytical Framework." *Coercion and Governance: The Declining Political Role of the Military in Asia.* Ed. Muthiah Alagappa. Stanford, CA: Stanford University Press, 2001. 29–66.

Almond, Gabriel A. "Comparative Political Systems." *The Journal of Politics* 18:3 (August 1956): 391–409.

Anckar, Dag. "Democratic Standard and Performance in Twelve Pacific Micro-states." *Pacific Affairs* 75:2 (Summer 2002): 207–25.

Anckar, Dag, and Carsten Anckar. "Democracies Without Parties." *Comparative Political Studies* 33:2 (March 2000): 225–47.

Auma-Osolo, Agola. "Objective African Military Control: A New Paradigm in Civil-Military Relations." *Journal of Peace Research* 17:1 (1980): 29–46.

Barro, Robert J., and Jong-Wha Lee. "International Data on Educational Attainment: Updates and Implications." Working Paper No. 42. Cambridge, MA: Harvard University, Center for International Development, April 2000.

Bergman, Torbjörn. "Constitutional Design and Government Formation: The Expected Consequences of Negative Parliamentarianism." *Scandinavian Political Studies* 16 (1993): 285–304.

Binder, Leonard, James S. Coleman, Joseph LaPalombara, Lucian W. Pye, Sidney Verba, and Myron Weiner. *Crises and Sequences in Political Development.* Princeton, NJ: Princeton University Press, 1971.

Blais, André, Louis Massicotte, and Antoine Yoshinaka. "Deciding Who has the Right to Vote: A Comparative Analysis of Election Laws." *Electoral Studies* 20:1 (2001): 41–62.

Buchta, Wilfred. *Who Rules Iran? The Structure of Power in the Islamic Republic.* Washington, DC: The Washington Institute for Near East Policy and the Konrad Adenauer Stiftung, 2000.

Butler, David, and Austin Ranney. *Referendums around the World: The Growing Use of Direct Democracy.* Washington, DC: American Enterprise Institute, 1994.

Centeno, Miguel Angel. "Blood and Debt: War and Taxation in Nineteenth-Century Latin America. *American Journal of Sociology* 102:6 (May 1997): 1565–1605.

Chehabi, H.E. "Small Island States." *The Encyclopedia of Democracy.* Ed. Seymour Martin Lipset. Washington, DC: Congressional Quarterly, 1995. 1134-37.

Chehabi, H.E., and Juan J. Linz. "A Theory of Sultanism 1: A Type of Nondemocratic Rule." *Sultanistic Regimes.* Ed. H.E. Chehabi and Juan J. Linz. Baltimore, MD and London, UK: The Johns Hopkins University Press, 1998. 3–25.

Child, Jack. "The Military and Democracy in Argentina." *Assessing Democracy in Latin America: A Tribute to Russell H. Fitzgibbon.* Ed. Philip Kelly. Boulder, CO: Westview Press, 1998. 273–92

Collier, David, and Steven Levitsky. "Democracy With Adjectives: Conceptual Innovation in Comparative Research." *World Politics* 49:3 (April 1997): 430–51.

Collier, Ruth, and David Collier. *Shaping the Political Arena: Critical Junctures, the Labor Movement, and Regime Dynamics in Latin America.* Princeton, NJ: Princeton University Press, 1991.

Crawford, Keith. *East Central European Politics Today.* Manchester, UK: Manchester University Press, 1996.

Dahl, Robert A. *Democracy and its Critics.* New Haven, CT: Yale University Press, 1989.

——. *Polyarchy: Participation and Opposition.* New Haven, CT: Yale University Press, 1971.

Dallin, Alexander, and George W. Breslauer. *Political Terror in Communist Systems.* Stanford, CA: Stanford University Press, 1970.

Desch, Michael C. "Threat Environments and Military Missions." *Civil-Military Relations and Democracy.* Ed. Larry Diamond and Marc F. Plattner. Baltimore, MD: The Johns Hopkins University Press, 1996. 12–29.

Diamond, Larry. *Developing Democracy: Toward Consolidation.* Baltimore, MD: The Johns Hopkins University Press, 1999.

——. "Economic Development and Democracy Reconsidered." *American Behavioral Scientist* 35:4–5 (March/June 1992): 457–60.

Diamond, Larry, Jonathan Hartlyn, and Juan J. Linz. "Introduction: Politics, Society, and Democracy in Latin America. *Democracy in Developing Countries: Latin America.* 2nd ed. Ed. Larry Diamond *et al.* Boulder, CO: Lynne Rienner, 1999. 1–70.

Diamond, Larry, Juan J. Linz, and Seymour Martin Lipset. "Introduction: What Makes for Democracy?" *Politics in Developing Countries: Comparing Experiences with Democracy*, 2nd ed. Ed. Larry Diamond *et al*. Boulder, CO: Lynne Rienner, 1995. 1–66.

Dix, Robert H. "History and Democracy Revisited." *Comparative Politics* 27:1 (October 1994): 91–105.

Doorenspleet, Renske. "Reassessing the Three Waves of Democratization." *World Politics* 52 (April 2000): 384–406.

Eckstein, Harry. *Division and Cohesion in Democracy: A Study of Norway*. Princeton, NJ: Princeton University Press, 1966.

Elklit, Jørgen, and Palle Svensson. "What Makes Elections Free and Fair?" *Journal of Democracy* 8:3 (July 1997): 32–46.

Euromonitor International. *European Marketing Data and Statistics 2003*. London, UK: Euromonitor Publications.

——. *International Marketing Data and Statistics 2003*. London, UK: Euromonitor Publications.

Evans, Peter. *Embedded Autonomy: States and Industrial Transformation*. Princeton, NJ: Princeton University Press, 1995.

Farrell, David M. *Electoral Systems: A Comparative Introduction*. Basingstoke, UK: Palgrave, 2001.

Finer, Samuel E. *The Man on Horseback: The Role of the Military in Politics*. 2nd rev. ed. Boulder, CO: Westview Press, 1962.

Fitch, J. Samuel. *The Armed Forces and Democracy in Latin America*. Baltimore, MD: The Johns Hopkins University Press, 1998.

Geddes, Barbara. *Politician's Dilemma: Building State Capacity in Latin America*. Berkeley and Los Angeles, CA: University of California Press, 1994.

Gunther, Richard, Hans-Jürgen Puhle, and P. Nikiforos Diamandouros. "Introduction." *The Politics of Democratic Consolidation: Southern Europe in Comparative Perspective*. Ed. Richard Gunther, Hans-Jürgen Puhle, and P. Nikiforos Diamandouros. Baltimore, MD and London, UK: The Johns Hopkins University Press, 1995. 1–32.

Hadenius, Axel. *Democracy and Development*. Cambridge, UK: Cambridge University Press, 1992.

Halperin, Morton H., and Kristen Lomasney. "Guaranteeing Democracy: A Review of the Record." *Journal of Democracy* 9:2 (April 1998): 134–47.

Handelman, Howard. *The Challenge of Third World Development*. 3rd ed. Upper Saddle River, NJ: Prentice Hall, 2003.

Hanson, Stephen E. "Defining Democratic Consolidation." *Postcommunism and the Theory of Democracy*. Ed. Richard D. Anderson, Jr., M. Steven Fish, Stephen E. Hanson, and Philip G. Roeder. Princeton, NJ: Princeton University Press, 2001. 126–51.

Herbst, Jeffrey. *States and Power in Africa: Comparative Lessons in Authority and Control*. Princeton, NJ: Princeton University Press, 2000.

Howard, Michael. *War and the Nation State*. Oxford, UK: Clarendon Press, 1978.

Howe, Herbert M. *Ambiguous Order: Military Forces in African States*. Boulder, CO: Lynne Rienner, 2001.

279

Huber, Evelyne, Dietrich Rueschemeyer, and John D. Stephens. "The Paradoxes of Contemporary Democracy: Formal, Participatory, and Social Dimensions." *Comparative Politics* 29:3 (April 1997): 323–42.

Hunter, Wendy. "Civil-Military Relations in Argentina, Brazil, and Chile: Present Trends, Future Prospects." *Fault Lines of Democracy in Post-Transition Latin America*. Ed. Felipe Agüero and Jeffrey Stark. Miami, FL: North-South Center Press, 1998. 299–322.

Huntington, Samuel P. "Armed Forces and Democracy: Reforming Civil-Military Relations." *Journal of Democracy* 6:4 (1995): 9–34.

——. *Political Order in Changing Societies*. New Haven, CT: Yale University Press, 1968.

——. *The Soldier and the State: The Theory and Politics of Civil-Military Relations*. Cambridge, MA: Harvard University Press, 1957.

——. "The Goals of Development." *Understanding Political Development*. Ed. Myron Weiner and Samuel P. Huntington. Glenview, IL: Scott, Foresman/Little, Brown, 1987. 3–32.

——. *The Third Wave: Democratization in the Late Twentieth Century*. Norman, OK: University of Oklahoma Press, 1991.

——. "Will More Countries Become Democratic?" *Political Science Quarterly* 99:2 (Summer 1984): 193–218.

Jackson, Robert H. *Quasi-States: Sovereignty, International Relations and the Third World*. Cambridge, UK: Cambridge University Press, 1990.

Johnson, Chalmers. *MITI and the Japanese Miracle: The Growth of Industrial Policy, 1925–1975*. Stanford, CA: Stanford University Press, 1982.

Karatnycky, Adrian. "The 2001 Freedom House Survey: Muslim Countries and the Democracy Gap." *Journal of Democracy* 13:1 (January 2002): 99–112.

Karl, Terry Lynn. "Electoralism." *International Encyclopedia of Elections*. Ed. Richard Rose. Washington, DC: CQ Press, 2000.

——. "The Hybrid Regimes of Central America." *Journal of Democracy* 6:3 (1995): 72–86.

Katz, Richard S. *Democracy and Elections*. New York, NY: Oxford University Press, 1997.

Kohn, Richard H. "How Democracies Control the Military." *Journal of Democracy* 8:4 (1997): 140–53.

Krasner, Stephen D. "Abiding Sovereignty." *International Political Science Review* 22:3 (2001): 229–51.

Kuenzi, Michelle, and Gina Lambright. "Party System Institutionalization in 30 African Countries." *Party Politics* 7:4 (July 2001): 437–68.

Liebenow, J. Gus. *African Politics: Crises and Challenges*. Bloomington and Indianapolis, IN: Indiana University Press, 1986.

Lijphart, Arend. *Democracy in Plural Societies: A Comparative Exploration*. New Haven, CT: Yale University Press, 1977.

——. *Electoral Systems and Party Systems: A Study of Twenty-Seven Democracies, 1945–1990*. Oxford, UK: Oxford University Press, 1994.

——. *Patterns of Democracy: Government Forms and Performance in Thirty-Six Countries*. New Haven, CT: Yale University Press, 1999.

———. "The Puzzle of Indian Democracy: A Consociational Reinterpretation." *American Political Science Review* 90:2 (1996): 258–68.

Lindblom, Charles E. *Politics and Markets: The World's Political-Economic Systems*. New York, NY: Basic Books, 1977.

Linder, Wolf. *Swiss Democracy: Possible Solutions to Conflict in Multicultural Societies*. 2nd ed. Basingstoke, UK: Macmillan, 1998.

Linz, Juan J. "An Authoritarian Regime: The Case of Spain." *Mass Politics: Studies in Political Sociology*. Ed. Erik Allard and Stein Rokkan. New York, NY: Free Press, 1970.

———. *The Breakdown of Democratic Regimes: Crisis, Breakdown, and Reequilibration*. Baltimore, MD and London, UK: The Johns Hopkins University Press, 1978.

———. *Totalitarian and Authoritarian Regimes*. Boulder, CO: Lynne Rienner, 2000.

Linz, Juan J., and Alfred Stepan. *Problems of Democratic Transition and Consolidation: Southern Europe, South America, and Post-Communist Europe*. Baltimore, MD: The Johns Hopkins University Press, 1996.

———. "Toward Consolidated Democracies." *Journal of Democracy* 7:2 (April 1996): 14–33.

Lipset, Seymour Martin. *Political Man: The Social Bases of Politics*. Expanded ed. Baltimore, MD: Johns Hopkins University Press, 1981.

———. "Some Social Requisites of Democracy: Economic Development and Political Legitimacy." *American Political Science Review* 53 (1959): 69–105.

———. "The Social Requisites of Democracy Revisited," *American Sociological Review* 59 (1994): 1–22.

Loosemore, John, and Victor J. Hanby. "The Theoretical Limits of Maximum Distortion: Some Analytical Expressions for Electoral Systems." *British Journal of Political Science* 1:4 (October 1971): 467–77.

López-Pintor, Rafael. *Electoral Management Bodies as Institutions of Governance*. New York, NY Bureau for Development Policy, United Nations Development Program, 2000.

Loveman, Brian. *The Constitution of Tyranny*. Pittsburgh, PA: University of Pittsburgh Press, 1993.

———. "Historical Foundations of Civil-Military Relations in Spanish America." *Civil-Military Relations in Latin America: New Analytical Perspectives*. Ed. David Pion-Berlin. Chapel Hill, NC: The University of North Carolina Press, 2001. 246–90.

Maddison, Angus. *The World Economy: A Millennial Perspective*. Paris, FR: OECD, 2001.

Mainwaring, Scott, and Timothy R. Scully. "Introduction: Party Systems in Latin America." *Building Democratic Institutions: Party Systems in Latin America*. Ed. Scott Mainwaring and Timothy R. Scully. Stanford, CA: Stanford University Press, 1995. 1–34.

Mann, Michael. "The Autonomous Power of the State: Its Origins, Mechanisms and Results." *States in History*. Ed. John A. Hall. Oxford, UK: Basil Blackwell, 1986. 109–36.

Mauzy, Diane K. "Electoral Innovation and One-Party Dominance in Singapore." *How Asia Votes*. Ed. John Fuh-Sheng Hsieh and David Newman. New York, NY: Chatham House Publishers of Seven Bridges Press, 2002. 234–54.

McAlister, Lyle N. "The Military." *Continuity and Change in Latin America*. Ed. John J. Johnson. Stanford, CA: Stanford University Press, 1964. 136–60.

Merquior, J.G. "Patterns of State-Building in Argentina and Brazil." *States in History*. Ed. John A. Hall. Oxford, UK: Basil Blackwell, 1986. 264–88.

Migdal, Joel S. *Strong Societies and Weak States: State-Society Relations and State Capabilities in the Third World*. Princeton, NJ: Princeton University Press, 1988.

Moore, Barrington. *Social Origins of Dictatorship and Democracy: Lord and Peasant in the Making of the Modern World*. Boston, MA: Beacon Press, 1966.

Muller, Edward N. "Democracy, Economic Development, and Income Inequality." *American Sociological Review* 53:1 (February 1988): 50–68.

Munck, Gerardo L. *Authoritarianism and Democratization: Soldiers and Workers in Argentina, 1976–1983*. University Park, PA: Pennsylvania State University Press, 1998.

Nordlinger, Eric A. "Political Development: Time Sequences and Rates of Change." *World Politics* 20:3 (April 1968): 494–520.

——. *Soldiers in Politics: Military Coups and Governments*. Englewood Cliffs, NJ: Prentice-Hall, 1977.

Ockey, James. "Thailand: The Struggle to Redefine Civil-Military Relations." *Coercion and Governance: The Declining Political Role of the Military in Asia*. Ed. Muthiah Alagappa. Stanford, CA: Stanford University Press, 2001. 187–208.

Onyszkiewicz, Janusz. "Poland's Road to Civilian Control." *Civil-Military Relations and Democracy*. Ed. Larry Diamond and Marc F. Plattner. Baltimore, MD: The Johns Hopkins University Press, 1996. 99–109.

Ott, Dana. *Small is Democratic: An Examination of State Size and Democratic Development*. New York, NY and London, UK: Garland Publishing, 2000.

Ottaway, Marina. *Democracy Challenged: The Rise of Semi-Authoritarianism*. Washington, DC: Carnegie Endowment for International Peace, 2003.

Paxton, Pamela. "Women's Suffrage in the Measurement of Democracy: Problems of Operationalization." *Studies in Comparative International Development* 35:3 (Fall 2000): 92–111.

Payne, J. Mark, Daniel Zovatto G., Fernando Carrillo Flórez, and Andrés Allamand Zavala. *Democracies in Development: Politics and Reform in Latin America*. Washington, DC: Inter-American Development Bank, 2002.

Payne, Stanley G. *A History of Fascism, 1914–1945*. Madison, WI: The University of Wisconsin Press, 1995.

Pempel, T.J., ed. *Uncommon Democracies? The One-Party Predominant Systems*. Ithaca, NY: Cornell University Press, 1990.

Pion-Berlin, David. "Introduction," *Civil-Military Relations in Latin America: New Analytical Perspectives*. Ed. David Pion-Berlin. Chapel Hill, NC: The University of North Carolina Press, 2001.

——. "Military Autonomy and Emerging Democracies in South America." *Comparative Politics* 25:1 (1992): 83–102.

Przeworski, Adam. *Democracy and the Market: Political and Economic Reforms in Eastern Europe and Latin America*. New York, NY Cambridge University Press, 1991.

Przeworski, Adam, and Fernando Limongi. "Modernization: Theories and Facts," *World Politics* 49 (1997): 155–83.

Remmer, Karen L. *Military Rule in Latin America*. Boulder, CO: Westview Press, 1991.

Riggs, Fred. *Thailand: The Modernization of a Bureaucratic Policy*. Honolulu, HI: East-West Center Press, 1964.

Rokkan, Stein. *Citizens, Elections, Parties: Approaches to the Comparative Study of the Processes of Development*. New York, NY: David McKay and Oslo: Universitetsforlaget, 1970.

Rose, Richard, and Doh Chull Shin. "Democratization Backwards: The Problem of Third-Wave Democracies." *British Journal of Political Science* 31 (2001): 331–54.

Rostow, W.W. *The Stages of Economic Growth: A Non-Communist Manifesto*. 3rd ed. New York, NY: Cambridge University Press, 1990.

Rotberg, Robert I. "The New Nature of Nation-State Failure." *The Washington Quarterly* 25:3 (Summer 2002): 85–96.

Rowen, Henry S. "The Tide Underneath the 'Third Wave.'" *Journal of Democracy* 6:1 (January 1995): 52–64.

Rueschemeyer, Dietrich, Evelyne Huber Stephens, and John D. Stephens. *Capitalist Development and Democracy*. Chicago, IL: University of Chicago Press, 1992.

Rustow, Dankwart A. "Transitions to Democracy: Toward a Dynamic Model," *Comparative Politics* 3 (April 1970): 337–64.

Rustow, Dankwart A., and Robert E. Ward. *Political Modernization in Japan and Turkey*. Princeton, NJ: Princeton University Press, 1964.

Sartori, Giovanni. *Parties and Party Systems: A Framework for Analysis*. New York, NY: Cambridge University Press, 1976.

Sattar, Babar. "Pakistan: Return to Praetorianism." *Coercion and Governance: The Declining Political Role of the Military in Asia*. Ed. Muthiah Alagappa. Stanford, CA: Stanford University Press, 2001. 385–412.

Schmitt, Carl. *Verfassungslehre* (1928; Berlin: Duncker and Humblot, 1970). Trans. by and quoted in Rune Slagstad, "Liberal Constitutionalism and its Critics: Carl Schmitt and Max Weber." *Constitutionalism and Democracy*. Ed. Jon Elster and Rune Slagstad. Cambridge, UK: Cambridge University Press and Oslo: Norwegian University Press, 1988. 103–29.

Schmitter, Philippe C., and Terry Lynn Karl. "What Democracy Is ... and Is Not." *Journal of Democracy* 2:3 (1991).

Schumpeter, Joseph A. *Capitalism, Socialism, and Democracy*, 3rd ed. New York, NY: Harper and Brothers, 1950.

Seow, Francis T. *The Media Enthralled: Singapore Revisited*. Boulder, CO: Lynne Rienner, 1998.

Siaroff, Alan. "Comparative Presidencies: The Inadequacy of the Presidential, Semi-Presidential, and Parliamentary Distinction." *European Journal of Political Research* 42:3 (May 2003): 287–312.

———. "Two-and-a-Half-Party Systems and the Comparative Role of the 'Half.'" *Party Politics* 9:3 (May 2003): 267–90.

Smith, Anthony D. "State-Making and Nation-Building." *States in History*. Ed. John A. Hall. Oxford, UK: Basil Blackwell, 1986. 228–63.

Smith, Gordon. *Democracy in Western Germany: Parties and Politics in the Federal Republic*, 3rd ed. New York, NY: Holmes and Meier, 1986.

Spero, Joan Edelman. *The Politics of International Economic Relations*. 4th ed. New York, NY: St. Martin's Press, 1990.

Spruyt, Hendrik. *The Sovereign State and Its Competitors: An Analysis of Systems Change*. Princeton, NJ: Princeton University Press, 1994.

Stepan, Alfred. *Arguing Comparative Politics*. New York, NY: Oxford University Press, 2001.

Sutton, Paul. "Democracy in the Commonwealth Caribbean." *Democratization* 6:1 (Spring 1999): 67–86.

Thompson, Mark R. "Totalitarian and Post-Totalitarian Regimes in Transitions and Non-Transitions from Communism." *Totalitarian Movements and Political Religions* 3:1 (Summer 2002): 79–106.

Tilly, Charles. "Reflections on the History of European State-Making." *The Formation of Nation-States in Western Europe*. Ed. Charles Tilly. Princeton, NJ: Princeton University Press, 1975.

Trinkunas, Harold A. "Crafting Civilian Control in Argentina and Venezuela." *Civil-Military Relations in Latin America: New Analytical Perspectives*. Ed. David Pion-Berlin. Chapel Hill, NC: The University of North Carolina Press, 2001. 161–93.

Trudeau, Pierre Elliott. "Some Obstacles to Democracy in Quebec." *The Canadian Journal of Economics and Political Science* 24:3 (August 1958): 297–311.

United Nations. *Human Development Report 2003*. New York, NY: Oxford University Press for the United Nations Development Programme (UNDP).

Valenzuela, Arturo. "Chile: Origins and Consolidation of a Latin American Democracy." *Democracy in Developing Countries: Latin America*, 2nd ed. Ed. Larry Diamond *et al.* Boulder, CO: Lynne Reinner, 1999. 191–247.

Valenzuela, J. Samuel. "Democratic Consolidation in Post-Transitional Settings: Notion, Process, and Facilitating Conditions." *Issues in Democratic Consolidation: The New South American Democracies in Comparative Perspective*. Ed. Scott Mainwaring, Guillermo O'Donnell, and J. Samuel Valenzuela. Notre Dame, IN: University of Notre Dame Press, 1992. 57–104.

Vanhanen, Tatu. *The Process of Democratization: A Comparative Study of 147 States, 1980–88*. New York, NY: Crane Russak, 1990.

Wade, Robert. *Governing the Market: Economic Theory and the Role of Government in East Asian Industrialization*. Princeton, NJ: Princeton University Press, 1990.

Ware, Alan. *Political Parties and Party Systems*. Oxford, UK: Oxford University Press, 1996.

Watts, Ronald L. *Comparing Federal Systems*. 2nd ed. Montreal, QC and Kingston, ON: McGill-Queen's University Press, 1999.

Weber, Max. *Economy and Society*. Vol. 2. Ed. Günther Roth and Claus Wittich. New York, NY: Bedminster Press, 1968.

——. *Max Weber: The Theory of Social and Economic Organization*. Trans. A.M. Henderson and Talcott Parsons. Ed. Talcott Parsons. New York, NY: The Free Press, 1964.

——. "The Theory of Social and Economic Organization." *From Max Weber: Essays in Sociology*. Ed. H.G. Gerth and C.W. Mills. New York, NY: Oxford University Press, 1946. 342–45.

Webster, Andrew. *Introduction to the Sociology of Development*. 2nd ed. Basingstoke, UK: Macmillan, 1990.

Welch, Claude E. Jr., and Arthur K. Smith. *Military Role and Rule: Perspectives on Civil-Military Relations*. North Scituate, MA: Duxbury Press, 1974.

Whittlesey, Derwent. *The Earth and the State: A Study of Political Geography*. New York, NY: Henry Holt and Company, 1944.

Woo-Cumings, Meredith. Ed. *The Developmental State*. Ithaca, NY: Cornell University Press, 1999.

World Bank. *World Development Report 2003*. Washington, DC: The World Bank and New York: Oxford University Press.

Zagorski, Paul W. *Democracy vs. National Security: Civil-Military Relations in Latin America*. Boulder, CO: Lynne Rienner, 1992.

Zartman, I. William, ed. *Collapsed States: The Disintegration and Restoration of Legitimate Authority*. Boulder, CO: Lynne Rienner, 1995.

Index